THE ADVERSARIES

The Adversaries
Politics and the Press

William L. Rivers

Beacon Press
Boston

The author gratefully acknowledges permission to reprint the
material by Martin F. Nolan, James McCartney, Laurence Stern,
David M. Rubin and Stephen Landers, and Geoffrey Wolff and
Book World.

For all my students who have taught me

Preface

This book has a peculiar history. It grew in part out of an earlier book published for me by Beacon Press, *The Opinion-makers* (1965), which sketched the relationships of journalists and officials in Washington. Writing that book gave me the idea for this one—the notion that there is an ideal relationship for government officials and journalists everywhere, and that the relationship should be that of adversaries. Briefly, this springs from the roots of the democratic idea that the people must be informed if democratic government is to work—and the corollary idea that public officials should not be alone in providing the information. Abraham Lincoln said that "in this and like communities, public sentiment is everything." Without a challenging journalism, officialdom is quite likely to win public sentiment for its own goals.

I attempted to define adversarity for my students, then suggested that they look into the real world of journalism and politics for examples—and perhaps for evidence that it did not exist. Thirteen of their investigations seemed to fit into the scheme of the book (together with a few published writings of professional journalists), and they are included here. The names of the contributors are included in the table of contents, and biographical notes on each of them appear with their contributions.

When the manuscript was completed, I sent it to Beacon Press. In due time, the manuscript was returned with suggestions for revision. This is a customary procedure in publishing, but in this case it is worth remarking. All the suggestions pointed to need for revision in *my* research and writing; except for a few items that needed updating, the contributions of my students were deemed ready for publication. Another important fact is that the students took my original idea, embellished it, and taught me that it was oversimplified. Their case studies (and some of the challenging little newspapers published by students and recent graduates) helped me to understand how limited my original thoughts had been. In the era of the military-industrial-education complex, the need for adversarity does not end with government. Most of the institutions of modern society are inextricably involved in governmental action. These, too, must be questioned and their actions probed—all must be subjected to one of the sharpest weapons of democratic life, pitiless publicity.

Almost instinctively, it seems, students today are alert to the need for an adversary stance. Perhaps it is because they look at modern society with fresh eyes. They see the comfortable moralities with which my generation rationalizes its failings, and they are aghast. Properly.

It is difficult, perhaps impossible, for those of us who were reared in an atmosphere of respect for property, and for civility in all things, to understand the corrective actions the modern college generation sometimes pursues. Certainly, we are alarmed by the excesses of some of the freelance wild men. But we can learn from the many other young activists the meaning and the value of being an adversary of a sick society.

Perhaps we can learn to appreciate them by altering slightly a familiar saying: He is a barbarian who thinks that the customs of his generation are the laws of the universe.

The fact that I had help in writing this book is implicit in the names of the contributors who are cited, and in the names of those who are quoted at shorter length. Several others whose names do not appear in this volume deserve special gratitude.

I am especially indebted to Pat Thomas, who helped with the typing in the last frenzied stages of putting all this together. Judy Mayo and Charlene Brown deserve special tribute not only for typing and similar chores, but also for some of the most acute editing I have experienced. Both have a sharp eye for inflated sentences, for wandering verbiage, and for nonsense. If I were running a publishing house, I would hire both of them instantly.

Finally, I am indebted to most of the students in my classes, especially David W. Jones, Jr., for talking about some of my ideas more explicitly and more imaginatively than I can, and for adding their own ideas in a way that makes this the most distinctively collaborative book I know.

William L. Rivers
December 1969
Stanford, California

Contents

THE ADVERSARIES

Prologue

> *Asked what he would do first if it were left to him to administer a country, Confucius replied: "It would certainly be to correct language."*
>
> *"Why?"*
>
> *"If language is not correct, then what is said is not what is meant; if what is said is not meant, then what ought to be done remains undone; if this remains undone, then morals and arts deteriorate; if morals and arts deteriorate, justice will go astray; if justice goes astray, the people will stand about in helpless confusion. Hence there must be no arbitrariness in what is said. This matters above everything."*

As Lyndon Johnson was preparing to leave the White House in 1968, he wrote for the *Encyclopaedia Britannica* a thirty-thousand–word article on his Presidency. One puzzled section he termed "the musings of a man who has seen the press in recent years only from the open end of the gun barrel—an angle from which the press rarely has occasion to see itself.... Frankly, I believe one of the shortcomings of my five years in the Presidency was my inability to establish better rapport with the communication media. If I had it to do over again, I would try harder."

Then Johnson made it clear that he did not consider himself to be primarily at fault: "My only stipulation would be an appeal to the news media to try harder also." The American people could have developed a better understanding of his "national goals," Johnson said, if the press did not operate on the theory that "good news is no news, bad news is news."

If these words did not echo the bitter judgments of so many public officials, one might wonder how a man who had been

1

through thirty-eight years in Washington as Congressional assistant, Congressman, Senator, Vice President, and President could at the end of his career be puzzled by the attitudes of the news media. But other public officials have been as genuinely puzzled and have wondered aloud why the stance of so many reporters is so pugnacious and their reports so abrasive. This is not recent. General Washington fumed over newspaper stories about the drunkenness of his troops. His successor as President, John Adams, became so embittered at press treatment of his public service that he wrote: "If there is ever to be an amelioration of the condition of mankind, philosophers, theologians, legislators, politicians, and moralists will find that the regulation of the press is the most difficult, dangerous, and important problem they have to resolve. Mankind cannot now be governed without it, nor at present with it." The list of public officials who have agreed with Washington and Adams is surely not much shorter than the list of public officials who have served since them.

Thus, it is one of the central ironies of democratic life that the politician and the political journalist have so much in common. They are generalists who must comprehend the over-arching issues in an age of specialization. They are committed to serving the people—who regard both politics and journalism with an edge of mistrust. (Not long after he had left the White House staff to become publisher of *Newsday,* Bill Moyers was questioned by a group of students. One of them asked why, since Moyers had been in government and was now in journalism, the students should believe anything he said.) They make their mistakes in public. Above all, politician and journalist depend upon each other. For, as Woodrow Wilson said, "In a democracy, public opinion is everything."

Why, then, are the politician and the political journalist so often at swords' points? Former Secretary of Labor Willard Wirtz offers an answer that will please many another public official:

> A considerable part of what the public reads and sees and hears about the conduct of its public affairs is such a diluted and artificially colored version of fact and truth that if it were mouthwash the Federal Trade Commission

would divide three-to-two on whether to let it on the market. Perhaps that is the answer: A Pure Speech and Press Law recognizing the consumer's equal need for protection against what gets into his stomach through his mouth and what gets into his head through his eyes and ears:

—So that speeches would include a note at the beginning: "Not written by the speaker. Prepared for another occasion, and altered to fit this audience. All classical references taken from Bartlett's *Familiar Quotations* or Elbert Hubbard's *Scrap Book*. All statistics conveniently adjusted. Cholesterol content 82 per cent. Low calories. No proteins. Sweetening added. Paragraph 23: Poison. Shake head well after hearing."

—And there would be a box at the head of the next day's story of the speech: "Written by Jones, who wasn't present, from ticker item filed by Smith, who wasn't there either. All quotes from speech taken out of context. Reported crowd reactions, including pickets, dubbed in. Headline written by Shrudlu, who can count but cannot read English. Dangerous if taken seriously or without a large grain of salt."

. . . It isn't a matter of truth and lies. There are, to be sure, always a handful of correspondents, columnists—and politicians—hungry enough to eat on their own knowingly false words, cold enough to use whole cloth, shameless enough to say or print what they know isn't true. They don't last long and rarely do lasting damage.

The problem is rather with the truth that lies—when it is turned against itself by someone's passing off part of it as the whole; by putting in words that deliberately mislead the reader but leave the writer ample alibi; by adding an adverb; by some trick juxtaposition of words and facts; by leading a story with some little sick fact that infects everything that follows.

I press the point, however, only in terms of the broader question of whether it is right that the Nation be given a selective coverage of what is happening to it and where it is going.

It could be no more than a matter of amusement that the press conferences for the AFL-CIO Executive Council meetings at Bal Harbour, Florida, had to be moved to a larger room this year [1967] because the open tensions within organized labor attracted so many more than the usual number of correspondents.

And if it is a matter of routine reporting to describe any expressed difference of point of view between members of the Administration in Washington as "discord" or "dissension" or "a controversy" or a "feud"—but to imply that any unanimity which emerges is the accord of parrots or puppets—surely no foul would be claimed.

But when the coverage of a major address by some public official seeking earnestly to find the common wisdom about how to achieve peace for the world is led by an account of fifty student hecklers, with pictures of the pickets in an adjoining front-page column, and the speaker's point appearing on the carry-over page—it becomes fair to ask whether the news editor and the makeup man are putting circulation and civilization in the proper balance.

When, among a generation of youth working harder at its books than any before it and announcing its ideals of service by over-subscribing the Peace Corps, only its maverick draft card burners, drug addicts, and lovers of four-letter words are publicized in the press—it is a fair question whether that press is more interested in its own future or that of the human race.

When there is reported diligently (as there should be) every incident of isolated indecency or immorality at a Job Corps camp, without putting it in the context of tens of thousands of inherently decent but previously deadend kids being pulled back at those camps from what would otherwise have been lifetime commitments to indecency and immorality—it seems not impertinent to ask whether it is truth or Mammon that is being served.

Whose side is the press on in the civil rights revolution? Any self-righteous answer about neutrality on the side of truth leaves the question of what ethic there is—except selling more papers—for giving daily front-page advertising to any white supremacist or non-white racist who coins an ugly phrase or whose dementia drives him to murder—while there is only occasional notice on the inside pages of the rest of the Nation's throwing off the shackles of centuries' bondage of bigotry.

This overstates it. But not much.

Nobody wants the press to play Pollyanna. But why shouldn't the causes of riots be covered as fully as their consequences? I wish there were front-page pictures every day in every New York paper of the alleys and the hallways and the schools in Harlem and Bedford-Stuyvesant —instead of stories about breaking the faith in Bimini.

When the worsening of any condition (a strike, for example; or an increase in the cost of living) is almost automatically front-page news, but its significant improvement gets little or no attention—it is a fair question why the press takes trouble as its special client, except that it pays so well.

Few public officials are so eloquent in their denunciations, but surely many of them share Wirtz's suspicion that the news media take trouble as a special client simply because it pays so well. And certainly the best of the officials are frustrated because modern mass communication is overwhelming. Justice Robert Jackson defined the ultimate authority of the Supreme Court with: "It is not that we are final because we are infallible. We are infallible because we are final." Even the most powerful of officials have often felt that however fallible the mass media may be, they are usually quite final.

One may grant the frustration of dedicated public servants, and sympathize with them, and yet hold that the question of the abrasive stance of journalists toward public officials is not really answered by stating that the news media are subverted by the dollar. It does not take account of the journalists and publications and broadcast programs that are quite obviously devoted more to the central public affairs of the time than they are to commerce.

Moreover, it does not take account of the fact that officialdom must be challenged by outside agencies. Wirtz himself is a case in point. Immediately before the 1962 Congressional elections, when it was to the advantage of the Kennedy Administration to make it appear that all was well with the economy, Labor Secretary Wirtz announced that unemployment had reached a three-year low and that the number of unemployed had declined by two million since Kennedy took over. Only after the election returns were in did Secretary Wirtz admit that his statement was marred by certain "invalid" statistical comparisons because the figures had not been adjusted for seasonal variations. Wirtz had also claimed before the election that "4,500,000 more Americans have jobs than when this Administration took office in January of 1961." But when the seasonal adjustments were made after the election, the figure became 1,224,000.

Most important, to dismiss the whole of journalism as a crass business poses a more perplexing question than it answers: If the press is only sordid, why did the framers of the United States Constitution give it—alone among business institutions—Constitutional protection?

CHAPTER ONE

The Delicate Balance

> *Do you gentlemen who control so largely public opin-*
> *ion, do you ever think how you might lighten the bur-*
> *dens of men in power—those poor unfortunates weighed*
> *down by care, anxieties and responsibilities?*
>
> —LINCOLN
> *to a correspondent*

> *No experiment can be more interesting than that we*
> *are now trying, and which we trust will end in establish-*
> *ing the fact, that man may be governed by reason and*
> *truth. Our first objective should therefore be, to leave*
> *open to him all avenues of truth. The most effectual hith-*
> *erto found, is the freedom of the press. It is therefore the*
> *first shut up by those who fear the investigation of their*
> *actions.*
>
> —THOMAS JEFFERSON

> *There are really only three ways to deal with the press:*
> *The best way is to tell them everything: this keeps them*
> *busy and eventually exhausts and bores them. The next*
> *best way is to tell them nothing, which at least excites the*
> *cop in them and gives them the excitement of a mystery.*
> *The worst way, which is Mr. Nixon's way and also Mr.*
> *Johnson's way, is to try to manipulate them, to pretend to*
> *be candid in private conversation, but to use every trick in*
> *the book to get them to fill the headlines and front pages*
> *with calculated trash.*
>
> —JAMES RESTON

The role the framers of American democracy foresaw for
the press bears some resemblance to how the system has actually

7

worked. But that may be less a tribute to the vision of the founding fathers than it is a commentary on their attempts to subvert it. For if anything is clear about press-government relationships throughout our history, it is this: in theory, America's leaders have wanted a free and independent press as a check upon government; in practice, they wanted no such thing.

The theory is quite clear. By carefully refraining from setting up an official information system within the government, and especially by granting freedom to the press in the First Amendment, the founders asserted their belief that an independent information system is central to democracy.

How strongly the founding fathers valued the theory of a free press is suggested by George Washington's ringing, "Sir, *concealment* is a species of misinformation." So convinced was General Washington of the value of the press that he issued a plea to patriot women asking that they save all available material for conversion into paper for printing.

James Madison was as emphatic, and a good bit more philosophical in viewing the role of the press: "Knowledge will forever govern ignorance. And a people who mean to be their own governors must arm themselves with the power knowledge gives. A popular government without popular information or the means of acquiring it, is but a prologue to a farce, or a tragedy, or perhaps both."

Thomas Jefferson made much the same point in a different way. Referring to Shays' Rebellion, which seemed to him to be a consequence of ignorance, he wrote:

> The way to prevent these irregular interpositions of the people, is to give them full information of their affairs through the channels of the public papers, and to contrive that these papers penetrate the whole mass of the people. The basis of our government being the opinion of the people, the very first object should be to keep that right; and were it left to me to decide whether we should have a government without newspapers or newspapers without government, I should not hesitate a moment to prefer the latter.

All this was the laudable theory. The government would carry on its actions; a free and independent press would report, comment on, and investigate those actions. The only trouble was that those who propounded the theory were unable to live with it. The result has been fascinating interplay between America's leaders and the men of the press. At times in our history, government and press have been the most savage adversaries imaginable, and at other times they have been such sweethearts that much of the press has been incorporated into the machinery of power.

The gap between theory and practice has been apparent from the beginning.

The Constitutional Convention of 1787 was held in secret. One day a delegate carelessly mislaid his copy of the proposals. It was found and turned over to George Washington, the President of the Convention. He seemed to ignore it, but as the meeting was adjourning for the day, he stated grimly: "Gentlemen, I am sorry to find that some one member of this body has been so neglectful of the secrets of the convention as to drop in the state house a copy of their proceedings, which by accident was picked up and delivered to me this morning. I must entreat gentlemen to be more careful, lest our transactions get into the News Papers and disturb the public response by premature speculation."

Secrecy in government soon took on the color of doctrine. One of the most enduring official concepts, Executive Privilege, was established in 1792, when a committee of the House of Representatives was investigating the "St. Clair Disaster," one of the most resounding defeats in battle in American history. Major General Arthur St. Clair's troop, which was camped at the headwaters of the Wabash River, was attacked by Indians and lost six hundred men. The House committee called for the original letters and instructions bearing on the expedition. Washington and his Cabinet rejected the request and replied:

> "We had all considered and were of one mind 1. that the House was an inquest and therefore might institute inquiries 2. that they might call for papers generally 3. that the Executive ought to communicate such papers as the public good would permit, and ought to refuse those the disclosure of which would injure the public."

But Washington was eager for the public to read that which reflected credit on his Administration. He said to Alexander Hamilton regarding the Farewell Address: "The doubt that occurs at first view is the length of it for a News Paper publication. . . . All the columns of a large Gazette would scarcely, I conceive, contain the present draught."

Realizing that they cannot win popular support without a communication system, and having none in the government, officials have always sought to use the press. For decades their method could be best described as "the party press." When one faction established a newspaper as its party organ, another retaliated by imitation.

While a member of President Washington's Cabinet, Jefferson led the opposition to Hamilton's Federalists, who had already established the *Gazette of the United States* at the new capital in Philadelphia. Eager to develop an editorial voice for anti-Federalism, Jefferson tried to enlist Philip Freneau, a talented journalist who had become famous as "the Poet of the Revolution."

Freneau declined the first offer. Lamenting the rejection, Jefferson revealed in a letter to Madison how much favoritism he was ready to bestow on an editor who would echo Jefferson's own views: "I should have given him the perusal of all my letters of foreign intelligence & all foreign newspapers; the publication of all proclamations & other public notices within my department, & the printing of all laws. . . ."

Later, the itch for a newspaper that would speak for him led Jefferson to woo Freneau by letter again: "The clerkship for foreign languages in my office is vacant; the salary, indeed, is very low, being but two hundred and fifty dollars a year; but it also gives so little to do as not to interfere with any other office one may chuse. . . ."

The sinecure lured Freneau. He established the *National Gazette,* which immediately became the loudest anti-Federalist voice and the most incisive critic of President Washington. The attacks were "outrages on common decency," the President protested. He questioned Jefferson closely regarding Freneau's reason for coming to Philadelphia. Jefferson replied that he had lost his translating clerk and had simply hired Freneau to replace him. "I cannot recollect," Jefferson told Washington, "whether it was at that time, or afterwards, that I was told that he had a thought of setting up a newspaper." In any case, Jefferson pointed out, he could control his employee in the clerkship, but Freneau was a free agent in editing the *National Gazette*.

How effectively such tactics worked is suggested by the success of the party organ, the *National Intelligencer*, when Jefferson became President. The editor of a rival newspaper, the *United States Telegraph*, announced that he had hired a Washington correspondent:

> We congratulate the readers of the *United States Telegraph* upon an arrangement by which the editor is able to obtain earlier, and he trusts *more full and accurate* information of the proceedings of Congress and the measures of government, than can be had from the Washington papers. We have hitherto been obliged to depend principally upon the *National Intelligencer* for reports of the proceedings of Congress; a paper which is conducted with very considerable ability, but with very little candour, inasmuch as the wishes of the president and his particular friends must be consulted in whatever representations are there made. . . .

The minimal value of out-of-Washington newspaper correspondents in the country's early days is suggested by the fact that the *Telegraph*'s man lasted only a few months. He could report on Congress, but no avenue to the Presidency was available, and *he* was soon reduced to reading the *National Intelligencer* to determine what Jefferson was up to.

None of the next three Presidents—James Madison, James Monroe, and John Quincy Adams—could manage the news as astutely as Jefferson. Madison and Monroe, however, did continue the *National Intelligencer* as party organ. Adams used a new paper edited by Peter Force, the *National Journal,* and revealed the extent of his control with this entry in his diary: "P. Force called to say that Mr. McLean, the Postmaster-General, was desirous of publishing in the *National Journal* an article in answer to a published letter addressed to him by J. Binns in the Democratic Press. I told him I could have no objection to this. . . ."

Andrew Jackson used the party press so astutely that one noted historian holds that Jackson actually ruled the country by means of newspapers. The best of the many editors who served the President was Francis P. Blair.

Jackson did quite as much for Blair. Federal officeholders who made more than $1,000 a year were expected to subscribe to his *Globe*. It quickly reached a circulation of 4,000 as a semi-weekly. Then, fed by federal printing contracts, it became a daily. The value of official printing was made clear by Duff Green, who, after finally bowing out as Administration editor, reported that he had "bade defiance" to Jackson, "well knowing that I would, in consequence, lose the printing of Congress and the Departments, then worth $50,000 per annum."

Meanwhile, Congress, which had opened its doors to the public in 1795, found it far more difficult to use the press. Dominant factions maintained a degree of control by awarding printing contracts to key Washington papers and by holding secret sessions. But the leaders were never able to shroud entirely the fishbowl of Congressional debate. For years, reporters prowled about the Senate chamber at will, many of them taking down minute-to-minute stenographic accounts. In this atmosphere, only the most adept Congressmen could compete in the arena of public opinion with Presidents who were adroit at managing the news.

It was almost impossible for a member of Congress to promote a clear national image. Even Henry Clay—daring, magnetic in debate, a thin, molten figure before a crowd and a man greatly gifted at exciting intense personal enthusiasm—could not fight through the network of newspaper animosity and draw enough of the people to him to win his golden ambition, the Presidency. For a Senator might find his speech described by a friendly reporter as "full of marrow and grit, and enunciated with a courage which did one's heart good to hear. No mealy-mouthed phrases . . . but strong and stirring old English, that had the ring of true metal." But then another paper would give itself over to savagery in description: ". . . a soft, catlike step; a keen, snaky eye; a look and address now bold and audacious, and then cringing and deprecatory; his whole air and mien suggesting a subdued combination of Judas Iscariot with Uriah Heep."

To add to the complications, some of the correspondents of that time were eminently bribable. One critic charged, in fact, that their principal mission in Washington was to negotiate terms with "those who stand in need of newspaper assistance." With the President controlling some and bribing others, it was no wonder that independent Congressmen found it difficult to put together a coalition of newspaper support that would allow them to move out of their provincial constituencies and onto the national stage.

Significantly, the end of the era of Presidential government and the beginnings of Congressional government began with a change in the press which came soon after the Jackson Presidency. His successors—Van Buren, Harrison, Tyler, Polk, Taylor, Fillmore, Pierce, and Buchanan—were seldom able to manage either the press or Congress. There was little they could do; Presidential control of the news was gradually eroding. Powerful dailies had grown up in many cities, and now their editors were sending probing reporters to Washington. By 1841, James Gordon Bennett, publisher of the New York *Herald*, was spending $200 a week to maintain a corps of Capital correspondents that was abler than the entire staff of any newspaper published in Washington. Bennett himself, who had earlier been a Washington correspondent, conducted the first recorded Presidential interview, a conversation with Martin Van Buren. As the dyspeptic commander of the powerful *Herald*, he was not a man a President could ignore.

The Associated Press also contributed to the decline of tightly controlled Presidential news by establishing its first Washington correspondent in 1843. AP, which began as a coalition of like-minded publishers, had not yet begun to build the structure of "objective reporting."

And so it was that when the colorless Presidents who followed Andrew Jackson named their party organs, they were impotent. The little Washington dailies and weeklies could not compete with the Washington bureaus and the AP reports. It was a situation made to order for the stentorian editors of nineteenth-century America.

Two events of 1860 marked the formal funeral of the

party press. The Government Printing Office was established, all but destroying the printing-contract patronage that accounted for the survival of so many financially weak Washington papers—and President-elect Lincoln arrived in the Capital. Lincoln listened civilly to several editors who tried to persuade him to make their papers his official journal. Then he rejected all offers. It was a wise decision and altogether characteristic of his shrewd approach to shaping public opinion through the press.

It is an unfortunate fashion of historical writing to picture Lincoln at bay, the press bent on bringing him down. And it is easy to find slashingly negative comments on his great speeches, the First and Second Inaugural and the Gettysburg Address, in the partisan journals of that time:

> New York *Express*: The President holds out, except in words, mere words, very, very little of the olive branch. . . .
>
> Richmond *Enquirer*: . . . couched in the cool, unimpassioned, deliberate language of the fanatic.
>
> Trenton *American*: It is very evident . . . that he feels all the perplexity of his position and his incompetence to shape his own course.
>
> Hartford *Times*: This wretchedly botched and unstatesmanlike paper. . . .

But it is also easy to find examples of high editorial praise for the same addresses:

> Philadelphia *American*: Its language is so direct, its tone so patriotic, its honesty so unmistakable, that all will feel the earnestness of its author and the significance of his words.
>
> Buffalo *Republic*: . . . certainly one of the most important addresses ever issued from Washington.
>
> New York *News*: . . . an able and statesmanlike document.
>
> Washington *Star*: . . . a state paper of great force and reasoning.
>
> New York *Courier & Enquirer*: The address is a noble one. . . .

The truth is that in a time of strength and savagery for American newspapers—a time of unavoidable and deep controversy for the American people—Lincoln came off quite well, largely because of his own insight. He knew the extent of the political power that resided in the great editors of the mid-nineteenth century, and he pointed out: "In this and like communities, public sentiment is everything. With public sentiment, nothing can fail; without it, nothing can succeed. Consequently, he who moulds public sentiment goes deeper than he who enacts statutes or pronounces decisions."

Lincoln was especially sensitive to the criticism of the greatest editor of the time, Horace Greeley of the New York *Tribune*. Greeley was often critical; the President was usually conciliatory. Lincoln once asked a Washington correspondent for the *Tribune* why the impatient Greeley—who often wanted what the President wanted, but faster—could not "restrain himself, and wait a little." The answer was noncommittal. The President sighed, "Well, I don't suppose I have any right to complain. Uncle Horace is with us at least four days out of seven."

Lincoln went to surprising lengths to win Greeley's cooperation. For a time, the *Tribune* had a secret inside line to the White House. The President would give information to Robert J. Walker, a special advisor in the Department of the Treasury, and Walker would pass it on to Greeley "for the use or guidance of the *Tribune*." Later, when the Civil War campaign of 1864 began and Greeley's editorial tone became sharp, Lincoln wrote to him: "I have been wanting to see you for several weeks, and if I could spare the time I should call upon you in New York. Perhaps you may be able to visit me. I shall be very glad to see you." There was no response. Lincoln turned to a mutual friend, praising Greeley and expressing regret that he had not named the editor postmaster, adding that he could have the position if Lincoln was reelected. The editorial tone of the *Tribune* promptly became more favorable.

Lincoln also went far out of his way to placate the arrogant James Gordon Bennett, whose New York *Herald* was influential in Europe as well as in the United States. The President sent an emissary to Bennett—an editor named Thurlow Weed, who had a profound sense of political journalism. Weed persuaded Bennett to slant his editorials in Lincoln's favor. Later, when a *Herald* reporter who had been refused a pass down the Potomac by Secretary of the Navy Gideon Welles went over Welles' head to the President himself, Lincoln was in haste to oblige; he wrote Bennett a "private and confidential" letter of apology.

None of this should suggest that Lincoln made the basic mistake of surrendering to the powerful editors. He granted many of their requests and demands, but just when it appeared that he had capitulated, he would refuse a favor and ignore their editorials. Few editors realized how subtly Lincoln used them. The celebrated Emancipation Proclamation, for example, was as much publicity weapon as it was a declaration of the national conscience, a fact that is emphasized by Lincoln's own account of issuing it two months after it had been written: "Things had gone from bad to worse, until I felt that we had reached the end of our rope on the plan of operations we had been pursuing; that we had about played our last card, and must change our tactics, or lose the game. I now determined upon the adoption of the emancipation policy. . . ."

None of the nineteenth-century Presidents after Lincoln could match his subtle command. Indeed, the entire period from Lincoln's death to the beginning of the twentieth century can be termed atomized. There were many centers of press power over the United States, and no public official could hope to master public opinion for long. When Greeley made his try for the Presidency, he met such fierce opposition from some of his fellow journalists that he said later that he was sometimes uncertain whether he was running for the Presidency or the penitentiary.

The press was still atomized, with many clusters of power scattered across the nation, as the era of Theodore Roosevelt began. As Colonel Roosevelt firing the horseless "Rough Riders" into their dash up San Juan Hill, he had demonstrated how a leader with a flair for drama can overshadow the comic-opera flavor of an absurdity like the Spanish-American War. (Years later, Roosevelt himself commented, "It wasn't much of a war, but it was the best war we had.") As Governor of New York, he had promoted his many causes through twice-a-day meetings with the small corps of Albany correspondents. Then he was maneuvered into accepting the Vice-Presidency, where the Old Guard of his own Republican Party was happily certain his political career would die. But President William McKinley was assassinated in 1901—"Roosevelt luck," one of his despairing detractors called it—and TR, who had been chafing in the tranquillity of presiding over the United States Senate, was suddenly thrust into his sternest test as a shaper of public opinion.

Mark Hanna, who had manipulated McKinley's nomination and become Republican National Chairman, was certain that "that damned cowboy" would disgrace the Republican Party. It was not an improbable prediction. Roosevelt was so various a man that an English weekly derided him as

A smack of Lord Cromer, Jeff Davis a touch of him;
A little of Lincoln, but not very much of him;
Kitchener, Bismarck and Germany's Will,
Jupiter, Chamberlain, Buffalo Bill.

But the new President fixed shrewdly on two important facts. First, the great press associations, which served many papers of varying political persuasions, had been forced during the latter part of the nineteenth century to develop "objective reporting" so that any paper could safely use any story. Except for the few remaining yellow journals, the giant dailies that used dispatches from their own reporters in Washington had been shamed into reporting most political news relatively impartially. The partisan publishers were relying largely on acid editorial pages to shape opinion. That was ideal for the theatrical Roosevelt, who knew quite well that a strong President can promote an indelible image through the news whatever the editorials say about him.

Second, the Age of the Reporter had been ushered in by romantic figures like Richard Harding Davis and by Lincoln Steffens, Jacob Riis, and the other "muck-rakers"—a term Roosevelt himself had coined—with the result that some of the power that had resided in the thundering editors and publishers back home was passing to the correspondents on the scene. The political reporters of TR's day were much more independently powerful than the newspaper "agents" of nineteenth-century Washington.

And so Theodore Roosevelt set about managing the news more adroitly than any President before him. The thrust of his method was orchestration; both courting the correspondents and commanding them. One day he saw a small group standing outside the gates interviewing departing visitors and ordered an anteroom set aside for them. This became the White House Press Room. He developed a subtly effective press conference, long before Woodrow Wilson established it on a formal basis, by regularly calling in the three correspondents whose reports were most widely circulated: David Barry of the New York *Sun*'s Laffan Agency, Charles Boynton of the Associated Press, and Ed Keen of the Scripps-McRae Press Association (now United Press International). Everything the President said was off the record, which allowed him a maximum range of comment and no responsibility for anything they used. The day Keen joined the group, Roosevelt loosed an especially virulent view of his own party's Old Guard, then made the system clear to the newcomer with: "If you even hint where you got it, I'll say you are a damned liar."

Roosevelt's press relations were always a fascinating mixture of apparent impulsiveness and tight control. He was, one correspondent wrote, "the master press agent of all time." He sometimes gave reporters the run of the White House and often overwhelmed them with news. When Lincoln Steffens had completed his exposés of corruption in municipal and state governments and turned to Washington, he was given open access to the Executive offices and saw Roosevelt daily at the barber's hour. "I always came into the room," Steffens wrote, "primed with a question that I fired quick; and he went off." But one thoughtful correspondent, Charles Willis Thompson of the New York *Times*, has written, "He was never interviewed, in any proper sense. He gave out many statements, some of them in the form of interviews, and sometimes, too, he was actually interviewed, but in such cases he always dictated the form the interview should take . . . he never said one word more than he had decided to say. Impulsive? The thousand reporters who have tried to catch Roosevelt off guard and make him say something he did not expect to say will laugh. . . ."

Guiding the correspondents whenever he could, Roosevelt often suggested news items and sometimes wrote them personally. Once, during a Senate fight over a railroad bill, a Standard Oil attorney telegraphed several senators to pressure them into voting Standard's way. Senator Stephen Elkins of West Virginia showed his wire to the President. TR not only gave the story to the press, but, according to David Barry, "wrote the preliminary item that was sent to the afternoon papers."

Roosevelt was understanding when a correspondent disagreed on political matters, but one who abused a privilege was assigned to the Ananias Club. Oscar King Davis, who headed the New York *Times* Bureau in Washington during TR's Presidency, has written, "When he gave his confidence to a correspondent, he gave it completely, and trusted to the correspondent's judgment and sense of propriety as to the use that was made of it. Mr. Roosevelt trusted a confidant until something happened to make him think his confidence had been misplaced. Then he ceased entirely to give his confidence to the man who had not respected it. It was all or nothing with him."

In that heady time of growing strength for the Washington press corps, it is doubtful that any other President could have used the news as adroitly as TR did. Dynamic, eruptive, vigorous of physique and intellect—he never seemed to tire physically or mentally—Roosevelt invested every issue with his own enthusiasm for American life in a way that made it seem that the opposition was subverting democracy. He was already famous, too, as a forceful writer whose mark on the literature of public affairs might have lingered even if he had never become President. The correspondents, whose respect for any colorfully articulate politician was almost automatic, were naturally lured by a man whose sense of visual language led him to speak of "trust-busters" and "malefactors of great wealth," to announce his intention to run with "My hat is in the ring," and to define his foreign policy as "speak softly and carry a big stick."

Theodore Roosevelt was himself a "journalist type," as he often admitted, which may account for the fact that throughout his Administration there was an intimacy with the Washington correspondents that had never existed before. Even the august Department of State was affected. In 1904 a Mediterranean bandit named Raisuli had captured and was holding for ransom a wealthy American, Ion Perdicaris. Secretary of State John Hay had completed the drafting of a diplomatic note designed to win the release of Perdicaris through the Sultan of Morocco. Associated Press Correspondent Edwin Hood walked into the office. Secretary Hay handed Hood the note, which was long, formal, and heavy with the phrasing dictated by diplomacy, and asked for an opinion. Hood read it, shook his head, and said, "I'm afraid you're slipping, Mr. Secretary." Then he scribbled five words that later went to the Sultan of Morocco: "Perdicaris alive or Raisuli dead."

It is clear that Roosevelt won the correspondents' support for his multiple causes not only because of his own magnetism but also because of his respect for the power of journalism and his admiration for those who used it well. Most Presidents had paid lip service to the press, but TR's sincerity was obvious. He castigated some newspapers and magazines for "mendacity, slander, sensationalism, inanity, vapid triviality"—which made the more genuine his tribute: "In our country I am inclined to think that almost, if not quite, the most important profession is that of newspaperman."

This conviction helped make Theodore Roosevelt the first President since Lincoln to use the press astutely—and the last for a quarter of a century to manage the Washington press corps.

It was one of the perplexities of American politics at the beginning of the Administration of William Howard Taft that he did nothing to win the Washington correspondents. Ponderous but genial, Taft was TR's hand-picked successor, with a full opportunity to learn from Roosevelt. Moreover, Taft had once worked as a reporter in Cincinnati, and when serving in Roosevelt's Cabinet had been the favorite news source of many correspondents. While he was Secretary of War, they developed the habit of "going Tafting" every afternoon at four o'clock, and he often helped them dig news out of other Executive departments. An unguarded spokesman in those days, Taft sometimes had to be protected from himself. Once, when Taft had been especially outspoken, Arthur Wallace Dunn of the Associated Press urged him "to place the injunction of secrecy on us" to prevent "disastrous consequences to yourself." Taft was grateful then and again when he became the Republican Presidential nominee in 1908 and saw that many correspondents were passing up stories that might have hurt his chances. But his new relations with his old friends were forecast on Inauguration Day. Several correspondents called at the White House to pay their respects. A secretary said that Taft would not see them then and was not likely to be seeing them very often in the future.

Much later, it became clear that this was no simple case of a new President going high-hat. To put it plainly, Taft was afraid. Always envious of Roosevelt, he knew that he could not match TR's confident command, and so he took the worst possible course, doing nothing. Archie Butt, who was an aide to both Roosevelt and Taft, wrote:

> There are a good many leaks about the White House. Neither the President nor his secretary gives out anything of real interest, nor do they understand the art of giving out news. In consequence, the papers seek their information from whatever source they can find and therefore print rumors which, if printed a month ago (during the Roosevelt Presidency) would have resulted in a clean sweep of the Executive offices. Not able to find out much of the political intentions of the President or his Cabinet, they are turning their attention to the class of news known as bedroom politics. . . .

Into the vacuum came that which Taft most feared—criticism. TR, dismayed by his successor's floundering, prepared for what some correspondents termed "The Return from Elba." And for a time Taft's chief pleasure was reading the New York *Sun*'s lampoons of Roosevelt. He would not even look at the critical papers. One night in 1911 when he asked if the New York papers had arrived and Mrs. Taft handed him the *World*, he snapped, "I don't want the *World*. I have stopped reading it. It only makes me angry."

"But you used to like it very much," said Mrs. Taft.

"That was when it agreed with me, but it abuses me now, and so I don't want it."

"You will never know what the other side is doing if you only read the *Sun* and the *Tribune*," she rejoined.

"I don't care what the other side is doing," Taft said.

It is easy to suspect that the turbulent Presidential politics of 1912, which had Taft opposed for reelection by TR as well as Woodrow Wilson, are a monument to his bewilderment about the network that forms public opinion.

Wilson's Presidency began with loud applause from the Washington press corps. Wilson inaugurated the formal Presidential press conference and announced this credo: "I, for one, have the conviction that the government ought to be all outside and no inside. I, for my part, believe that there ought to be no place where anything can be done that everybody does not know about. . . ."

It was laudable theory, but those correspondents who had experienced the shrewd manipulations of Theodore Roosevelt wondered whether a President following Wilson's policy of "pitiless publicity" could compete meaningfully with a Congress operating outside this enlightenment.

Wilson was not naturally suited to the public relations role he had established for his Administration. Actually, he was warm and human, a lover of vaudeville who once confessed that he also liked fishing, baseball, wrestling, and such intimate sports as running to fires behind clanging engines, gossiping with policemen on their beats, reading grisly crime stories, and watching dogs fight in the street. But none of this came across. He was outwardly a cold man whose only excitements were intellectual. His phrases were stiff: "Open covenants, openly arrived at," "a little group of willful men," and the like. His approach to the Presidency was unrelaxed. He shielded his family from publicity and went to extravagant lengths to avoid informal pictures of himself. Photographers were not allowed on the White House grounds and were rebuffed when they sought to picture the President playing golf. Annoyed by their persistence, Wilson's Secret Service chief seemed one day to acquiesce, took them out to a "shack full of knotholes" near one of the greens where the President would be putting, and crowded them in. The photographers found when their eyes became accustomed to the darkness that there were no knotholes and the door was padlocked. The President played undisturbed —and many a voter continued to think of Wilson as the epitome of austerity.

Meanwhile, the National Press Club, which was then over

Affleck's Drug Store, was becoming an informal home for Congressmen as well as correspondents. Great powers—among them Senator Thomas Gore of Oklahoma and Senator Boies Penrose of Pennsylvania—were letting their hair down in antic Press Club debates like the one that examined the question, "Resolved: That bow-legs are a greater menace to navigation than knock-knees." Later, fourteen senators and representatives engaged fourteen correspondents in a spelling bee at the Press Club, and won. It was a time of growing comradeship between the men of the press and the men of Capitol Hill.

Many reporters retained their high regard for Wilson, but he soon demonstrated that he was not really willing to practice his theory of pitiless publicity. Like Taft, he was supersensitive, and he blamed the correspondents for reporting criticisms of his Administration voiced by Congress. Resentment grew in the press corps when it became known that the President was, in private, a harsh critic of the reporters. "I am so accustomed to having everything reported erroneously," Wilson told Senator J. W. Stone of Missouri, "that I have almost come to the point of believing nothing that I see in the newspapers." He gradually withdrew into a shell of persecution. Press conferences were more widely spaced, then, as the United States was drawn into World War I, were no more.

When Wilson returned to the publicity front after the war, the press corps demonstrated how strong it had become. Wilson was straightforward in promoting his League of Nations; Congress and some of the correspondents were not. Columnist Ray Tucker has described the way a small group of correspondents:

> . . . conspired hourly with the "irreconcilables" and performed service far beyond the call of newspaper duty. They tipped off most of the Congressmen to Wilsonian statements and maneuvers, and started Congressional counterattacks before the War President could unlimber his orators. They wrote phillipics for the Borahs, Johnsons, and Reeds, cooked up interviews . . . carried on research into the League's implications, dug up secret material. Their dispatches bristled with personal hostility

to the League, and carbon copies which they distributed to pro-Wilson writers affected even the latter's supposedly favorable articles. The covenant was defeated by the Senate press gallery long before it was finally rejected by the Senate.

It is easy, and perhaps right, simply to condemn the correspondents. But David Lawrence, Wilson's best friend and most devoted admirer in the press corps of the time, suggests that much of the fault was the President's for his bad relations with the press. "They constituted a series of misunderstandings and unfortunate clashes," Lawrence has written. "The growing tendency in recent years in America to anticipate the news and to discuss future events or the processes by which conclusions are reached, were deeply resented by Mr. Wilson. His theory was that nothing is news until it was completed."

Having discovered the full thrust of their power, it is not surprising that the correspondents used it during the ripe days of the Harding Administration. The era was epitomized by the Pulitzer Prize chronicle of corruption written by brilliant, erratic Paul Y. Anderson (who was later to descend into an emotional whirlpool and commit suicide). First, Anderson's reports in the St. Louis *Post-Dispatch* pushed the Senate into a full-dress investigation of Teapot Dome. Then, during the hearings, he and other correspondents supplied many of the searching questions that were used by Senators Thomas Walsh and Burton Wheeler to cut through evasions in the testimony of Administration officials. Warren Harding's name became almost synonymous with Presidential ineptitude.

This was, in a way, a surprising dénouement. Harding, an Ohio newspaper publisher and United States Senator who liked being around reporters, was protected better by the press during his early days in the White House than any other President. He began well by restoring the press conference to the place it had during the early months of the Wilson Presidency. If he was a bit pompous in answering questions during the formal conferences, he won the correspondents with warmth and an openly friendly feeling after hours. He was an attractive man—"No one ever looked more Presidential," one reporter wrote—who privately confessed his limitations; he told the correspondents that he knew he could not be the greatest President, but he wanted to be the best loved.

Unfortunately, Harding sometimes did not know what he was talking about. He had been in office only a short time when he was asked during a press conference whether the Four Power Pacific Pact that had been drawn up during the famous Washington Conference for the Limitation of Armaments involved the protection of the Japanese Islands. The President said that it did not. Actually, it did, and Harding's answer raced around the world, creating an international sensation. Secretary of State Charles Evans Hughes, his chin whiskers bristling, rushed to the White House to get an official correction. Then he prevailed upon Harding to agree that only written questions submitted well in advance of press conferences would be answered. It was a crushing backdown for a President who was warmest and most expansive in talking to newspapermen.

Toward the end, as the correspondents and the Congress revealed more of the scandals of his subordinates, Harding seemed to withdraw from life. He died in 1923, leaving a memory of a man who was only gradually becoming aware that he had surrounded himself with thieves.

The Administration of Calvin Coolidge was a frustrating time for the Washington press corps. It is doubtful that Coolidge, the inert beneficiary of national prosperity, could have been affected by anything. He presided over a time of repose, napping often and boasting of sleeping soundly for eleven hours every night. It was dismaying for reporters on the lookout for an angle. As Leo Rosten put it, "The most striking characteristic about the new President was his lack of a striking characteristic."

Although the President was a little huddle of a man— Coolidge conquering the tense and controversial times that enveloped his successor is almost unimaginable—it is also true that he calculated his actions. Much later, he revealed in his autobiography that a kind of philosophy dictated his tight-lipped image:

> Everything that the President does potentially at least is of such great importance that he must be constantly on guard. . . . Not only in all his official actions, but in all his

social intercourse, and even in his recreation and repose, he is constantly watched by a multitude of eyes to determine if there is anything unusual, extraordinary, or irregular, which can be set down in praise or blame.

Coolidge did little, and many of the correspondents simply ignored him. Raymond "Pete" Brandt of the St. Louis *Post-Dispatch* said that his group "never covered Washington in the 'Twenties. We covered the Senate. You wasted your time downtown." Those who were responsible for covering Presidential news inadvertently built the image of a President of strength and silence. Henry Suydam, who was then a correspondent for the Brooklyn *Eagle*, has written that President Coolidge would observe laconically, "with respect to a certain bill, 'I'm not in favor of this legislation.' The next morning Washington dispatches began as follows: 'President Coolidge, in a fighting mood, today served notice on Congress that he intended to combat, with all the resources at his command, the pending bill, etc.'"

Thus did the correspondents divert themselves in the quiet days of the Coolidge Era.

The press corps reawakened during the Administration of Herbert Hoover, and for a time mastered both President and Congress. It had been the custom in the Senate since the time of George Washington for reporters and spectators to leave the chamber during votes on Presidential nominations. But Paul Mallon of the United Press and his assistant, Kenneth Crawford (now a columnist for *Newsweek*), decided to destroy the system. They began checking with friendly senators after the executive sessions and publishing the secret roll-call votes.

In 1929, President Hoover sent up to Capitol Hill a highly controversial nomination: Senator Irvine Lenroot of Wisconsin to be a federal judge. The senatorial votes on Lenroot's nomination were certain to affect the elections in a number of states in 1930; the Senate took extraordinary precautions to ensure secrecy. But Mallon made his usual rounds afterward and published the complete senatorial box score. It showed that several senators had been talking one way in public and voting quite another way behind closed doors. Mallon was subpoenaed and questioned sharply by a Senate committee, but he would not reveal the sources of his information. The Senate gave up then, virtually abolishing executive sessions. The Senate has gone into executive session less than a dozen times in the last four decades.

Hoover's own relations with the correspondents were a carbon copy of Taft's. As Secretary of Commerce under Harding and Coolidge, Hoover had been the best news source in Washington, and he and the correspondents formed a mutual aid society. Hoover gave the reporters what Paul Y. Anderson described as "a perfect gold mine of graveyard stuff." They gave him a national stature that no Secretary of Commerce since has ever been able to attain. Gradually, Anderson has written, the impression pervaded newspaper editors and the American people "that Hoover knew more about the affairs of government and the actual condition of the country and the world than any other man in the administration." But then Hoover entered the White House on a wave of respect and liking, and promptly changed. Instead of continuing his impartial news policies, he began to play a few favorites among the correspondents so blatantly—Mark Sullivan was a particular pet—that they became known as "trained seals."

One Sunday afternoon when Hoover was relaxing at his mountain retreat on the Rapidan, news of a sudden development sent him racing back to the White House at sixty miles an hour—dangerous speed on the Virginia roads of those days. The White House correspondents, who were not allowed to stay at the camp, were at an inn several miles away and learned of Hoover's trip too late to catch up with him. But the next day the New York *Times* carried a front-page story on the President's breakneck run to the White House. Convinced that there must have been leak from his staff, Hoover ordered the Secret Service to investigate. Then it became known that Turner Catledge of the *Times* had simply worked a problem in arithmetic involving the distance covered and the time consumed in making the trip, and wrote the story merely to emphasize the foreign-affairs emergency—but Hoover's fury added to the correspondents' belief that he had become a sour and resentful man.

Through much of his Presidency Hoover's relations with the men who covered his actions were strained and humorless.

The President invited publishers to the White House to complain about their Washington men and caused several correspondents to be transferred or fired. When leaks from his disenchanted subordinates reached print, Hoover announced that "only such news as is given out through the stated channels of the executive offices should be printed by the newspapers of the country." This was actually an effort to cut down on the leaks, but with the clear implication that the Chief Executive should rule the press as well as his Administration.

Finally, unable to exert any control, Hoover began to lie stupidly. He required that press conference questions be submitted twenty-four hours in advance. Then, when he bypassed the pointed questions and was asked about them, he would say that they had not been received. During the London Naval Conference, the President stated that the United States was holding up the building of three cruisers. Harold Brayman of the New York *Post* and Phelps Adams of the New York *Sun* then proved that construction was continuing.

The most damning incident came in 1931, when Hoover denied knowledge of a letter from Governor Franklin Roosevelt of New York on negotiations with Canada for a St. Lawrence waterway project. Roosevelt promptly announced that he would make public his copy of the letter. Then Hoover admitted that the letter had been received but denied that he had denied knowledge of it and denied that there had been any negotiations. At that point, many of the few friends he had left in the Washington press corps deserted him.

When panic grew after the Great Crash of 1929, Charles Michelson, a former New York *World* correspondent who had become publicity director of the Democratic National Committee, fired broadside after broadside at the hapless Hoover. Considering the President's ragged relations with the men who wrote about him day by day, it is not at all surprising that, having the option of using Michelson's charges or ignoring them, they played them up. In Hoover's abortive reelection campaign of 1932, crowds booed him, men ran into the streets to thumb their noses at him, and the most widely repeated remark ran, "If you put a rose in Hoover's hand, it would wilt." The President became morose. Driving to the Capitol with his successor on Inauguration Day, he said nothing.

Like his cousin Theodore, Franklin Roosevelt* both courted and commanded the correspondents. His task was more difficult; the press corps grew to more than three hundred reporters during his Presidency. Like most Democratic Presidents, he won the working reporters even though he was opposed by their publishers. It was sometimes a testy relationship, as is indicated by an exchange between Roosevelt and Lyle Wilson, who was Washington manager of United Press. Roosevelt was unhappy about disclosures made by UP, and he engaged in this colloquy with Wilson:

> ROOSEVELT: It wouldn't be very dignified for the President of the United States to have a feud with the United Press.
> WILSON: No, it wouldn't, Mr. President.
> ROOSEVELT: But if I had a feud with UP it wouldn't hurt me but it would hurt UP and it would hurt you.
> WILSON: That's right, Mr. President, it would hurt UP and it would hurt me, but what would hurt us even more is if word got around that you said to kill a story and we did it.

All in all, though, Roosevelt was one of the firmest friends of the Washington press corps, winning scores of reporters for his policies and programs—to his great advantage. Far too much has been made of the influence he exerted through his few Fireside Chats. Too little attention has been given the fact that he held 998 press conferences as President and was overpoweringly effective from the very beginning. At the end of his first Presidential press conference, the correspondents gave him the first standing ovation any President had ever received from them.

Harry Truman won fewer reporters—many fewer—than

* The relationships between the Washington press corps and Presidents Franklin Roosevelt, Harry Truman, Dwight Eisenhower, John Kennedy, and Lyndon Johnson are covered in the author's *The Opinionmakers* (Beacon Press, 1965). At the risk of oversimplifying, it is enough here to sketch the interplay in each case.

Roosevelt won. His relations with the press were nearly always testy. But even those who thought him inadequate and those who felt the cutting edge of his tongue were reluctant to condemn him. He was abrasively strong and positive about everything, and detractors as well as supporters laughed admiringly at an anecdote (perhaps apocryphal) which made its way around the press corps. Traveling through his native Missouri with Mrs. Truman and one of her lady friends, the President would remark often on the quality of the crops and say that agricultural success was because of the manure. It was the way Missouri farmers used *manure,* he said often, which made it one of the great farming states. After much of this, Mrs. Truman's friend whispered, "Can't you get him to say *fertilizer?*" Mrs. Truman responded, "You have no idea how long it took me to get him to say *manure!*"

When, a decade after Truman's retirement, a poll of the leading American historians showed that Mr. Truman was considered a "near great" President—well ahead of Dwight Eisenhower, just behind Washington, Lincoln, Franklin Roosevelt, and the other great Presidents—the talk in the National Press Club was approving.

Federal press agentry had grown enormously under Roosevelt and Truman. It grew even more under Eisenhower, who was so shielded by his assistants from the criticisms of the intellectual community that he was startled at the poll of the historians which showed him ranking well behind Truman and the other "near great" Presidents. He had believed *Time* magazine, which somehow concluded that the Eisenhower Presidency represented "eight distinguished years." Eisenhower's men protected him and misled the reporters. It is no accident that the phrase "news management" was coined during the Eisenhower regime. Much more than "management" was involved, of course. Joseph and Stewart Alsop, who were then writing a newspaper column together, described the "insidiously indirect censorship" of the Eisenhower Administration:

> A reporter obtains and publishes nationally significant information about, say, the grave lag of the American air program behind the Soviet air program. He has seen no secret papers. He has written nothing which was not already fully known to Soviet intelligence. He has merely

posed a major public issue, with a vital bearing on the Nation's future.

Nowadays, however, even the most trivial information has been classified by someone or other, in some dim Pentagon corner or other. Furthermore, the reporter has given no pleasure whatever in high quarters, by posing this major issue which the leaders of the Administration had been hoping to keep under the rug. So a "security investigation" is ordered.

The fact that a reporter is the subject of one of these investigations does not mean for one moment that he has broken the law. Even less does it mean that there is the slightest danger of prosecution. . . . The security investigation, in truth, is nothing but a kind of indirect reprisal against the reporter who shows inconvenient curiosity about facts of national interest.

The reprisal takes three forms. First, while the investigation goes on the reporter must assume that his telephones are tapped and that listening devices may be planted in his house and office. . . .

Second, the reporter's official acquaintances and friends are subjected to the most shameless harassment. It does not matter whether there is a tittle of evidence that they are the source of the reporter's information. It does not even matter if it is well known that they have never discussed the subject in question with the offending reporter. The real object is not to locate the reporter's source, but simply to strike at the reporter through the men he knows in Government.

Then third and finally, the word is passed in Government that the offending reporter lies under the grave displeasure of the powers that be; and that it is therefore a risky thing to see him. Thus the attempt is made to prevent the reporter from doing his job as a reporter thereafter.

The charges of "news management" that were born during the Eisenhower Presidency became more intense during the Kennedy Administration. But there was a stark difference that blunted most of the attacks on Kennedy. It could be seen during the 1960 campaign, especially in Theodore White's *Making of the President, 1960*. Kennedy's aides were quite solicitous. White reported that the three Democratic press assistants "gave off a sense of joy when they greeted a correspondent joining or rejoining the circuit, as if they had waited for him, and him alone, to arrive—and then whispered to him a little nugget of color or some anecdote that his particular magazine or newspaper would especially want."

White's report reveals the little touches that endeared the Democratic candidate to the correspondents:

> Kennedy would, even in the course of the campaign, read the press dispatches, and if he particularly liked a passage, would tell the reporter or columnist that he had—and then quote from its phrases. . . . He would ask the advice of newspapermen—which, though he rarely followed it, flattered them nonetheless. Most of all he was available for quick exchanges of conversation—whether getting on his plane, or in his plane, or by the side of the road where he would stop to drink a Coca-Cola and then chat with the correspondents who clustered round. When presented, say, with a box of apples, he might fling one of them in an underarm pitch to a correspondent, to test whether the man was on his toes. He would borrow combs and pencils from the press—or accept chocolate bars (early in the primary campaigns) when his meal schedule also went awry.

Unlike Taft and Hoover, who grew aloof from working journalists after entering the White House, Kennedy became even closer. He drove to the homes of Washington reporters for parties and meals, he was interviewed endlessly, he established, for the first time in history, an open White House. Never before had the press been granted so close a view of a President at work. It was an affecting experience for the reporters, and it was greatly to Kennedy's advantage in winning public sentiment.

Lyndon Johnson was the victim of the successes of all his predecessors. In dealing with the press, no trick or gimmick that any President had ever tried was beneath him. In the end, hardly a reporter in Washington believed much that Johnson said (and the politicians were not really certain that he had taken himself out of the Presidential race until the Democratic National Convention was over). Eventually, the reporters stopped using euphemisms like "news management" and said quite frankly that the President was lying. Toward the end of the Johnson Presidency, a vicious joke made its way around the Washington press corps (and was printed in *Look* and *The Progressive*):

"Do you know how to tell when Lyndon Johnson is not telling the truth. Well, when he goes like this"—finger beside nose—"he's telling the truth. When he goes like this"—pulling ear—"he's telling the truth. When he goes like this"—stroking chin—"he's telling the truth. But when he starts moving his lips, he's *not* telling the truth."

David Broder of the Washington *Post* has written: "I do not believe that the press of this country ever made it clear to the readers and viewers what the essential issue was in the 'credibility gap' controversy. It was not that President Johnson tried to manage the news: all politicians and all Presidents try to do that. It was that in a systematic way he attempted to close down the channels of information from his office and his Administration, so that decisions could be made without public debate and controversy. Ultimately he paid a high price, politically, for his policy. But because we failed to identify the essence of the issue, we face the peril that another President—perhaps the succeeding one—may adopt the same course, with the same ruinous consequences."

CHAPTER TWO

Nixon and the Press

> *Mr. Nixon has had more than the normal share of trouble with reporters, because, like Lyndon Johnson, he has never really understood the function of a free press or the meaning of the First Amendment.*
>
> *Ever since he came into national politics, he has seemed to think that a reporter should take down and transmit what he says, like a tape recorder or a Xerox machine. He has learned to live with interpretive journalism more comfortably in this campaign [1968] than he did in the campaign of 1960, but he still suffers from this old illusion that the press is a kind of inanimate transmission belt which should pass along anything he chooses to dump on it.*
>
> —JAMES RESTON

> *The best time to listen to a politician is when he's on a stump on a street corner late at night when he's exhausted. Then he doesn't lie.*
>
> —THEODORE WHITE

Although President Nixon has not adopted Johnson's ruinous information policies, it is nonetheless clear that he is on his own collision course with the press. That fact was obscure during the first six months of his Administration. This was in part because Mr. Nixon, who had attacked White House secrecy under Johnson, had promised regular meetings with reporters, and had stated during his campaign that "Only through an open, candid dialogue with the people can a President maintain his trust and leadership," managed to hold only six press conferences during his first six months in office (less than half as many as his two immedi-

34

ate predecessors held in similar periods). Six of Nixon's Cabinet members held even fewer conferences. Attorney General Mitchell, who was to head the heralded "law and order" campaign, did not meet the press until July 11, nearly six months after he took office.

Nixon's coming clashes were obscure too, because any Republican President enjoys an extraordinary honeymoon period with the press, one that stretches much longer than the hundred days or so traditionally granted Democrats. Republican publishers have enough influence to win a full chance for their man. Perhaps more important, the press corps was warily neutral at first because of its savage adversary relationship with Lyndon Johnson.

To put it bluntly, the working reporters were so bitterly opposed to Johnson during his last two years in office that there was no antagonism left for Nixon. But Nixon's policies make it likely that his old experiences with the Washington correspondents are a prologue. Those experiences are worth recalling.

Before he became President Nixon excited both extremes of reaction. On one side were the elements of the press, most of them editors and publishers, who promoted what must be termed a sweetheart relationship with Mr. Nixon. On the other side were the elements of the press, most of them reporters, who were Mr. Nixon's adversaries.

How to be a sweetheart of officialdom is shown by the reporting in some newspapers of the "Nixon Fund," which was a vital issue in the Presidential campaign of 1952. Nixon, who was then a Senator and the Republican candidate for Vice President, had been accepting thousands of dollars from wealthy Californians. Although Nixon claimed that the money was used only to pay extraordinary expenses of his senatorial office, it was nonetheless obvious that the Californians making the payments had unusual leverage with a United States Senator. The issue became so heated that Dwight Eisenhower, the Republican Presidential candidate, considered naming another Vice Presidential candidate. Nixon saved himself only by going on national television with an emotional speech ("the Checkers speech") that has become the single most memorable event of the 1952 campaign.

Arthur Rowse, then a copy editor on the Boston *Traveler*,

subsequently examined the reporting and display of news of the Nixon Fund in thirty-one United States dailies. The title of the book that grew out of his study—*Slanted News*—suggests the results. As Rowse points out, the Nixon Fund story was voted by Associated Press editors at the end of the year as one of the top ten news stories of 1952. Yet it got some strange play from many proud papers in its early days.

Any review of the way thirteen evening papers displayed the Nixon story makes it clear that editors were in no hurry to get the news into the paper. They were even less enthusiastic about getting it onto the front page. Of the thirteen evening papers studied, only four put the story on the front page at the first opportunity on Thursday afternoon. . . . The four papers using the report on the front page included only one pro-Eisenhower paper, the Chicago *Daily News*, which spotted the newsworthiness of (Peter) Edson's column and played it up with a three-column headline on the first page. . . . Three other evening papers used the story the first day but buried it inside the paper. . . . Five evening papers apparently did not use the Nixon story in their editions of record until the next day. . . . One paper, the New York *Journal American*, could not find room on the front page for the story until Sunday, the fourth day the news was available.

Of the eighteen morning papers studied—all pro-Eisenhower on their editorial pages—only eight allowed the Nixon affair on the front page of Friday editions of record. Of the remaining ten morning papers, seven used the story somewhere in their editions of record on Friday. But three omitted it entirely from the issues studied.

Newspapers that were "giving their readers the first glimpse of the story," Rowse points out, "should have included more than just three or four words to describe the cause for all the disturbance." But, Rowse adds, some readers undoubtedly "got such a one-sided picture from the first few stories that they might have wondered what all the defensive statements were about. Thus, the first headline to greet readers of the record edition of the

Chicago *Herald American* WAS: NIXON DEFENDED BY EISENHOWER. The natural reaction of readers might be 'Why not?' as they passed on to another story."

It should be obvious from the foregoing that New York and Chicago readers, among others who were blessed during the 1952 campaign because they were living in cities with competitive newspapers, at least had an opportunity to learn about the Nixon Fund at the beginning. There was enough variation in the treatment of the story in competitive cities to promote diversity of information. But what of Kansas City readers? They are subject to the editorial whims of the Kansas City Publishing Company, which issues both the *Star* and the *Times,* and which is not always eager to have everything up to date in Kansas City.

Rowse found that the *Star* was one of those papers that passed up the chance to carry the Nixon Fund story the first day. Moreover, the *Star* on the following day published a story that was devoted almost entirely to explanations by Nixon, interspersed with charges of "smear" and blasts at what the *Star* called "the Alger Hiss crowd." This was characteristic of the *Star*'s treatment of a news story *Editor & Publisher* assessed as "the biggest news break in the 1952 election campaign." Considering the time lag in getting the story into the paper at all, the conclusion is inescapable that if the story had not become so important—at least in part because of investigative pressures brought by competitive newspapers elsewhere—many of the readers of the Kansas City *Star* might never have heard of the Nixon Fund.

Nixon's relationships with most of the reporters in Washington were quite different. Many who had watched him during the early high points of his career, which included, in 1950, a successful campaign for the Senate during which his opponent was smeared as a Communist sympathizer, were unable to forget his tactics and his opportunism. When the "Nixon Fund" was disclosed, the climax of his appeal to stay on the Republican ticket ran: "Let them [the members of the Republican National Committee] decide whether my position on the ticket will help or hurt. And I am going to ask you to help them decide. Write or wire whether you think I should stay on the ticket or get off." But in 1958, when a reporter disclosed that 80 per cent of the State

Department's mail was opposed to having the United States defend Quemoy and Matsu against the Chinese Reds, Vice President Nixon denounced the official who had released the information. He called the official a saboteur and ridiculed the notion that important issues should be decided "on the basis of what random letters say the people will support in the light of the minimum and often misleading information available to them." Many correspondents agreed with the latter idea and thought at the same time that Nixon changed his convictions as easily as he changed his clothes.

Sharply aware that the correspondents were chiefly responsible for the nickname "Tricky Dick," Nixon decided when he was running for President in 1960 against John F. Kennedy that he would avoid them. The abrasive attitude of Nixon and his entourage toward the journalists who accompanied them may have symbolized the worst mistake of the campaign. Nixon had proved before—notably in going through intensive interviews with Earl Mazo of the New York *Herald Tribune* and Stewart Alsop of the *Saturday Evening Post*—that he could present himself winningly to searching examination. Moreover, the reporting of a presidential campaign is not limited to fashioning news stories from speech notes. It calls for fleshing out a man, highlighting the color and flavor of a personality who is in quest of the nation's highest office, and this is a practice that works to the advantage of any personable candidate. By avoiding the reporters, Nixon made their work difficult and negated a source of his own strength.

As the campaign progressed, some of the correspondents who had followed Kennedy from the beginning had become his friends, many were his devoted admirers, and nearly all diverted themselves by singing cutting songs about Nixon and the Republicans as the Kennedy entourage made its way across the nation. On the Nixon side, the correspondents became fond of composing malicious parodies of his speeches for their private amusement: "GUTHRIE CENTER, IOWA—Vice-President Nixon said today farmers should eat their way out of the surplus problem. . . ."

After Kennedy's victory, the question of whether the correspondents' attitudes shaped and colored their reporting—and affected the election—became a matter of fierce debate. The ardently pro-Nixon New York *Daily News,* which had slanted its own news columns for Nixon, charged in a full-column editorial that many correspondents had:

> ... sabotaged Mr. Nixon and his cause with every dirty-pool device known to dirty-pool newspaper people—of whom, unhappily, there are still too many.
>
> They slanted their dispatches against the Republican candidate. They left out incidents and sidelights which might have been helpful to him. They frequently under-reported the size and enthusiasm of the crowds that gathered to hear him speak. In campaign press conferences with Nixon himself, some of these crooked crusaders for John F. Kennedy badgered Nixon instead of asking him honest and pertinent questions.
>
> Things got so bad in this respect that Nixon called off the conferences several weeks before the election.
>
> When the alleged news dispatches reached the editors of the papers under discussion, they shirked their duty oftener than not. That is to say, they left the slanted, distorted, biased, or downright false statements in the material and passed it on to their readers as allegedly honest or factual news.

Richard Pourade, editor emeritus of the San Diego *Union,* brought an equally severe indictment against the Associated Press and United Press International, saying that "personal feelings have permeated the entire AP and UPI copy." He submitted to the wire services a long report carrying twenty-eight pages of excerpts from their stories. "A cheapness of language," he wrote, "contributed to devaluating a political statement of commitment. The AP dismissed one statement by President Eisenhower as a mere political 'plug.' Nixon 'coaxed' support. He made a 'pitch' in Virginia. In another, Nixon is compared to a 'snapping trout.' Nixon was trying to 'push' himself into the White House. . . ."

These charges are tempered by the fact that Pourade's own paper, like the New York *Daily News,* did not hide its love for

Richard Nixon. The editor of the *Union*, Herbert Klein, was on loan to Nixon as press secretary, and this story suggests the paper's bias:

ANY VOTER IS ELIGIBLE
TO CAST NIXON BALLOT

Any registered voter may cast his ballot for Richard Nixon.

Registered Democrats and independents can vote for Nixon as well as registered Republicans.

Responsible election officials pointed this out yesterday to clarify possible misunderstandings resulting from misinformation about California's election laws being circulated before the election.

Voters cast their ballots in secret and how each one votes is known only to himself, the election officials pointed out.

Republicans, Democrats and independents alike may vote for Nixon.

Then, perhaps to make the point clear, the *Union* published the same story again the following day.

The defense against charges of pro-Kennedy bias in reporting the campaigns was mixed in quite a different way. Carroll Kilpatrick of the Washington *Post*, which was strongly for Kennedy, called the charges "ridiculous." But J. Russell Wiggins, executive editor of the same paper, conceded that "the struggle to keep reporters traveling with the candidates objective and uncommitted is always a tough one, and I think I would like to avoid a few lapses that we have had in this respect."

Richard Strout of the *Christian Science Monitor* held that the reporting of the campaigns "was fair to both sides." But Theodore White, Kennedy's close friend, wrote: "There is no doubt that Kennedy's kindliness, respect and cultivation of the press colored all the reporting that came from the Kennedy campaign, and the contrast colored adversely the reporting of the Nixon campaign."

Nixon kept his own feelings within a small circle of

friends for two years (although his belief that partisan journalism had cost him the election was reported by Fletcher Knebel in the Minneapolis *Tribune*). Then, the day after he was defeated as the Republican candidate for Governor of California in 1962, Nixon's fury burst forth.

It was a curious scene to be played by a political figure who had once admitted that he keeps his true emotions in tight control by wearing a façade in time of stress. It sprang from impulse. His staff had decided that Nixon should not face the reporters, who were gathered downstairs at the Beverly Hilton Hotel in Los Angeles awaiting a concession statement. Instead, Press Secretary Herbert Klein was to read the statement while the defeated candidate left the hotel. On the way out, however, Nixon made a new decision. Even as Klein was reading the concession, Nixon pushed his way to the platform, his face working. For the next seventeen minutes he alternately frowned and smiled grimly while indulging himself in a monologue so heavy with venom, courage, self-pity, and distortion that Klein was stunned.

Nixon slashed at his opponent, Governor Edmund G. (Pat) Brown: "I believe he is a good American, even though he feels I am not. . . ." He attacked President Kennedy for cutting off White House subscriptions to the hostile New York *Herald Tribune*: "Unlike some people, I've never canceled a subscription to a paper and also I never will" (forgetting that on two occasions of high anger he had canceled subscriptions to the Washington *Post*. A few days later, he canceled the Los Angeles *Times*. For Nixon, this was an acquired distaste. The paper had supported him editorially in every campaign, including the contest for the governorship. But while the *Times* had been lopsidedly for him before, it was scrupulous about giving the Democrats an even break in the news columns this time).

But Nixon's most savage criticism was aimed at the reporters. He was harsh about the coverage of the gubernatorial race, beginning with, "Now that all the members of the press are so delighted that I have lost," ending with a plea that the mass media "put one lonely reporter on the campaign who will report what the candidate says now and then." Nixon attacked the Los Angeles

Times by name. Carl Greenberg was the only *Times* reporter "who wrote every word I said," Nixon charged.*

It was nonetheless clear that Nixon's fury did not spring from the gubernatorial contest alone; he was lashing the correspondents for what he considered hostile treatment throughout his career in public life:

"And as I leave the press, all I can say is this: For sixteen years, ever since the Hiss case, you've had a lot of fun—a lot of fun—that you've had an opportunity to attack me and I think I've given as good as I've taken. It was carried right up to the last day. You won't have Nixon to kick around any more, because, gentlemen, this is my last press conference."

As Nixon stepped down from the platform, he muttered to Klein, "I gave it to those goddam bastards right where they deserved it."

As Norman Mailer has remarked about Nixon's triumphant return in 1968, "America is the land which worships the Great Comeback." That and the fact that the correspondents were weary after battling Mr. Johnson may explain why journalists did so little to expose Nixon's manipulation of his 1968 campaign. It may have been the worst-reported campaign in recent history. Nixon got away with selling out to the South. He got away with announcing that his choice for the Vice Presidency would be the Republican best qualified to succeed to the Presidency, then selecting Spiro Agnew.

How he accomplished these and other manipulations

---

* Greenberg was embarrassed by the accolade, but he need not have feared that he would be suspected of slanting his reporting in Nixon's direction. On at least one occasion, the Republican candidate was quoted as calling President Kennedy a "carpetbagger" for invading California to help Governor Brown. When Nixon denied later that he had ever used "carpetbagger," Greenberg quietly pointed out in print that he had used the word three times.

Several reporters were incensed by Nixon's self-appreciative estimate of his own attitudes toward the press: "Never in my sixteen years of campaigning have I complained to a publisher, to an editor, about the coverage of a reporter." Actually, Nixon had complained only a few weeks earlier about Richard Bergholz of the Los Angeles *Times*.

were explained during the campaign by James Reston, one of the few journalists who made clear what was happening:

> His television performances are masterpieces of contrived candor. He seems to be telling everything with an air of reckless sincerity, but nearly always in a controlled situation, with the questioners carefully chosen, the questions solicited from whole states or regions, but carefully screened.
>
> He is now complaining publicly about how he and Mr. Agnew are misrepresented in the columns of the New York *Times*, but he has been refusing to be questioned on the record by editors of the *Times* and most other major newspapers ever since the very beginning of the campaign.
>
> Mr. Humphrey and Mr. Wallace submitted to questions by C.B.S., but Mr. Nixon sent tapes of replies made in his carefully prepared broadcasts. And his refusal to debate Mr. Humphrey on television is merely one more incident in a long campaign of packaged broadcasts. . . .

There was remarkably little of this kind of reporting during the campaign or during the first six months of the Nixon Administration. As a consequence, he continued to escape press censure. He had said early in 1968 that he had a plan for ending the Vietnam War, but that he would not unveil it then. When he had been in office for almost a year, it became obvious that no such plan had ever existed.

Perhaps the most misleading was that Nixon had seemed at times during his campaign to recognize Mr. Johnson's worst failing. Nixon emphasized: "It's time we once again had an open Administration—open to ideas from the people and open in its communications with the people—an Administration of open doors, open eyes and open minds."

On April 17, 1969, Nixon's Secretary of Defense, Melvin Laird, told the American Society of Newspaper Editors:

> I am fully aware of the special responsibility of those in this audience and others in the communications media to inform the people about what we in Defense are doing

and to call us to account when we make mistakes. . . . As long as I am Secretary of Defense there will be full and free access to all information that can be made available without danger to the nation's security. There will be no coverup, no concealment, no distortion. We intend to put a lot of fill in the credibility gap.

But six days later Correspondent James McCartney revealed just how devoted to concealment both Laird's Pentagon and Nixon's White House had become:

Now, a full week after the EC-121 shooting (off the coast of North Korea), the Pentagon continues to refuse to furnish exact times for key incidents in the crisis, or to describe in detail . . . . Both White House and Pentagon officials have wrapped a mantle of secrecy around the time that Henry A. Kissinger, President Nixon's national security adviser, was notified of the incident at home.

By mid-August 1969, so much doubt had arisen that *Newsweek* published a long catalogue of cases proving that Nixon's "open administration" was "suffering from an advanced case of closed doors."

There were signs, too, of a rebirth of the tough stance many reporters had adopted years before. After watching the Administration bow in quick succession to the American Medical Association, the American Pharmaceutical Association, and the Automobile Manufacturers Association—actually reversing decisions already made—one journalist remarked that Nixon will be in trouble with working reporters for a reason that has always been at the root of his policies: "He worries too much about the problems of people who own yachts."

One point of contention will surely spring from the Nixon Administration's flouting of the Freedom of Information Act, which already has an erratic history.

Born as a result of years of lobbying by the press, finally passed in 1966, the Freedom of Information Act was designed largely to short-circuit the kind of secrecy which was so evident in the Eisenhower Administration. After Eisenhower wrote a letter to his Secretary of Defense commanding him not to present certain testimony before Senator Joseph McCarthy's investigating subcommittee on the ground of Executive Privilege, nineteen other federal agencies began to withhold information from the press, Congress, and the public on the same ground. Moreover, a section of the Administrative Procedure Act of 1946, which had been designed to make more information available, was being used by many Eisenhower appointees to conceal it. They simply crawled through convenient loopholes.

Several members of Congress, led by Representative John Moss of California, began working in 1955 to write the Freedom of Information Act. Representative Moss's Subcommittee on Government Information held 173 public hearings and investigations and issued seventeen volumes of hearing transcripts and fourteen volumes of reports, all of which documented widespread secrecy. By 1966, both houses of Congress had passed the Act. But by the time it became law, it had been through the Congressional mill, and every lobbyist and government official who had a stake in concealing information also had a try at building his own loopholes into the law. Not all of them succeeded, but enough did so that the law is burdened with *nine* exemptions, some of them so broad and vague that they obscure more than they define. The one saving factor is that the law places the burden of proof upon government; instead of requiring that the seeker of information prove his "need to know" before information is released (which was the old rule), officialdom is required to demonstrate a "need to withhold." It is here that the Nixon Administration is running into increasing trouble. For the President has chosen to divorce himself for long periods from the day-to-day actions of government (as did Eisenhower), not only failing to communicate with press and public, but with his own officials as well. In the vacuum created by this aloofness, decisions are left to officials who do not know how far they can go or how much they can say.

The lesser officials are like a captain in Vietnam who is charged with briefing the press. Not quite knowing how truthful the colonel would be were he to deliver the briefing, the captain plays it safe, putting everything in the most positive possible terms to escape censure. The colonel might have been a bit more candid, but he, too, would operate at some distance from the brutal truth, not knowing how candid the commanding general might be in similar circumstances—and *he* can never be certain how close the President might come to the truth if by some alchemy the Commander-in-Chief were to deliver the briefing. One can imagine that on a particular day a President might tell the complete and utter truth about that day's operations. But trying to imagine that a captain at several removes from the ultimate responsibility will be so bold is like imagining February 30th.

It is the same with civilian officials. How can they know how much to say—especially to a press which sometimes seems committed to inaccuracy? Far better to play it safe, look for the most convenient loophole in the Freedom of Information Act, and hope it works. (Suits can be brought under the Act, but few are.)

When one remembers, too, that officials sometimes hide actions that might wilt in the glare of print, the likelihood that the Freedom of Information Act will be abused often becomes a certainty. In one case, the Commander of the Military District of Washington, D.C., attempted to withhold a letter which pressured liquor lobbyists and wholesalers to provide free drinks for 1200 guests at an Army party. His justification was the first exemption to the Act, which protects National Security Information.

Nonetheless, Nixon's old ability to excite sweetheart affections among many editors and publishers seems implicit in one revealing incident. Art Buchwald, whose column appears in the Nixon-loving San Diego *Union*, as well as several hundred other papers, wrote after the election of the activities which would be "in" and "out" under the new President. The *Union* saw fit to delete this paragraph:

"The first thing you have to do is stop calling Nixon "Tricky Dick." That was all well and good during the campaign, but as everyone keeps saying on television, Nixon is the only President we've got for the next four years and Americans must treat him with respect. From now on if you don't agree with him you can call him "Crafty Richard."

The *Union* also deleted these lines from Buchwald's column: "Greeks are in—but Poles and fat Japs are out. ... Buckley's in—Buchwald's out...." Finally, where Buchwald had written, "And last but not least, Spiro Agnew's foot is in," the *Union* gave the columnist's words a 180-degree distortion by making the line read, "And last but not least, Spiro Agnew's in."

In short, although Nixon faces an abrasive adversary relationship with most of the political correspondents, other elements of journalism will show him just what sweethearts they can be.

So much of the press takes the role of sweetheart—not only with federal officials, but state and local officials as well—that we must prize those reporters who challenge officialdom.

The necessity for a challenging journalism does not spring primarily from the fact that officials lie. They do. But far more often, the public is misled because well-meaning, high-minded officials really believe in their policies and programs. They would not be likely to serve well if they did not believe. But believing as devoutly as many of them do, they approach the public interest through a narrow channel and from a narrow perspective. Such men cannot be expected really to *serve* the public interest because their perspectives are so narrow—unless they are called to account by an independent press. The fact that the press has this independent role is part of the genius of the United States Constitution.

These facts have led me to the conclusion that the proper role of the political reporter is that of adversary. That is to say, that however friendly an official and a reporter may seem to be, however often they may drink together or have lunch together, however happily they may remember their college years together, there should be a degree of tension between them when they serve their professional roles. As George Reedy said, the official views public communications in terms of help or hindrance toward a common goal, the reporter views public communications in terms of what he regards as reality. The divergence is inevitable. The politician will seek to promote his strategies and programs by preserving his options and by hiding most political frictions; he usually has a vested interest in tranquillity. If he succeeds, decisions are often made without public debate.

To stimulate public awareness, the journalist must challenge and probe—"submarine," in James Reston's terminology—to move vital issues into the public arena before a decision becomes concrete.

David B. Jones has deftly summarized the relationship with, "The concern of power is unity, or organization; the concern of the press is truth. A press functioning as an adversary does not combat power, but rather seeks out abuse of power."

If we grant that there is a necessity for a degree of challenge in a political journalist's stance as he deals with officialdom—if we grant that democratic government is well served by such a stance—there remain several questions: Is there no limit to the pugnacity a reporter should display? Is there no way for an official to fight his way free of enveloping antagonism? Is there not a balance point on the spectrum of tension beyond which a journalist should not move?

Surely a proper adversary relationship is a delicate balance of tact and antagonism, cooperation and conflict.

How well do political journalists maintain their balance?

The rest of this book is an effort to answer that question—first in a series of reports (most of them by my students) on the adversary relationship, finally in a chapter that uses the reports to define the limits of adversarity.

CHAPTER THREE

The Professional Persuaders

Honest opinion? No military man can give you an honest opinion.

—A MARINE

Let us all resolve to minimize the rumor problem as much as possible by not talking to members of the press, either on or off the record, about the actions or appointments of the National Committee. All announcements will be made by the Chairman through the Public Relations Division.

—*Confidential "Memo to All Staffers"*
from the REPUBLICAN NATIONAL COMMITTEE

Reporters get beaten to death by ladyfingers. Once you get softened up by rubbing elbows with the lords of creation at cocktail parties on Embassy Row, you never want to go back to your roots. The subtle impact of Washington can turn a simple bumpkin into a self important statesman, or a pedestrian news reporter into a pretentious journalist.

—*Correspondent* ED LAHEY

All government handouts lie. Some lie more than others.

—JOSEPH ALSOP

All officials carry many weapons into the area of public opinion. In addition to their obvious power to make their views known—usually through the very media with which they may be in conflict—the federal government now spends more than $400 million on public relations and public information. The Executive branch, in fact, spends more on publicity, news, views, publications, and special pleadings than is spent to operate the entirety of the Legislative and Judicial branches. All together, federal expenditures on telling and showing the taxpayers are more than double the combined costs of newsgathering by the two major United States wire services, the three major television networks, and the ten largest American newspapers. Although this dwarfs the similar efforts of state and municipal governments, they, too, are so convinced of the need to engineer consent that the news media are all but enveloped in public information efforts.

How the hard-sell part of the federal system works has been sketched fascinatingly by Erwin Knoll and Jules Witcover in an analysis of the beginnings of the Office of Economic Opportunity. Established during the Johnson Administration, the authors report, when the new President leafed "through the pending-business basket of the Kennedy Administration for something dramatic to call his own," the program was termed an "unconditional war on poverty" in his first State of the Union message. The $962,500,000 Johnson requested from Congress fell considerably short of being unconditional—and that has epitomized the chief problem ever since: The program has always done a better job of promising than performing.

The selling began with the "War on Poverty" name and its accompanying imagery: Sargent Shriver was "the field general," his subordinates were "poverty warriors." An "inspector general's office" was established, "war maps" flourished on office walls. There was much talk of "weapons," "target areas," "delivery systems," and "alternate strategies."

The chief salesmen were the forty-six staffers working under Herbert J. Kramer, the director of public affairs. Knoll and Witcover wrote that the public affairs staff "supported by a massive Xerox copying machine with a firepower of 2,400 handouts an hour, trumpets the smallest victory in the poverty trenches, conducts seminars for the press, and in general works hard and long to accentuate the positive. . . ."

Accentuating the positive meant much more than issuing magazines and press releases and reprinting for the guidance of reporters who might want to write about the War on Poverty all the favorable articles that others had written on it, although the public affairs office did all these things well. The office seemed to specialize for a time in rebutting the charges of congressional critics, sometimes deviously. When Congressman Adam Clayton Powell attacked, War on Poverty administrators dispatched to their seven regional offices a series of statements by business leaders supporting Shriver. "Suggest these telegrams, together with story guidance, be given immediately to local newspapers and editorial writers as good weekend story indicating that among people who really know administration, Shriver is tops," the regional offices were advised by Washington headquarters. "Important that we try to get this story across."

Officials in the office in Kansas City were so eager to get the story across that they spent $2,900 dispatching three-and-a-half-page telegrams praising Shriver to forty newspapers, including five in Kansas City itself.

Eliminating the negative also seemed to be a constant concern of the War on Poverty, Knoll and Witcover discovered. Often the agency would announce a policy or procedure, be forced to rescind it, fail to announce the change, then call it an insignificant matter when reporters uncovered it on their own. Appointments to the agency were announced with fanfare, resignations were accepted in silence.

When Joseph Loftus of the New York *Times* and Tom Joyce of the Detroit *News* tried to verify reports that VISTA volunteers in Alabama were carrying arms for self-protection, the reports were denied. But Loftus and Joyce later found that the reports were true. The agency also denied that Rutgers University consultants to one Job Corps center were dissatisfied with the center's operations. Then the consultants issued a scathing report on the center. When the agency released figures on Job Corps cost per enrollee and found them challenged in Congress, new, higher figures were released.

There was much more to this analysis of War on Poverty propaganda. The agency harassed reporters who wrote critically and agency employees who might have given information to such reporters. The agency director seemed accessible when the news was good, unavailable when the news was bad, glib and vague in glossing over the bad news when he was caught in negative times.

The use of the testimonial device—the War on Poverty specialized in luring folksingers, star quarterbacks, and cowboy actors to speak for it—was never more astutely employed on Madison Avenue. Except that the salesmen were slicker than most of those in government, the only essential difference between the War on Poverty sales program and a hundred others is that two perceptive reporters analyzed it.

How the real military fights its political wars with public relations was revealed by the Washington *Post* during the 1969 controversy over the antiballistic missile system. Instead of proposing the system, then letting the Congress decide whether it should be implemented, the Defense Department spent millions on these ploys:

The Pentagon organized favorably disposed scientists to manufacture magazine articles supporting the system; senators and congressmen were given classified briefings by high officials; industrial firms and civilian contractors who would benefit were mobilized to swing public opinion toward the ABM; leading citizens in "impacted" communities were the targets of persuasive campaigns; portable display exhibits, pretaped voice commentaries, information packets, and visual aids were employed to convince the general public and officialdom that billions spent for ABM might reduce casualties in a nuclear exchange from 100 million to 40 million.

The Pentagon makes certain that its spokesmen are equipped for the war of words. One who received special training, Martin F. Nolan,* has written:

> Back in 1946, General Dwight D. Eisenhower, then chief of staff of the U.S. Army, wrote to theater commanders noting that "The Army is being subjected to considerable criticism on its postwar program. This has always been the case following a war and the Army desires to do something about it." He added that "An active

---

*Martin Nolan is a Washington columnist and bureau chief for Boston *Globe*. He wrote this article for *The Reporter* magazine (now defunct), worked as a Washington correspondent for *The Reporter,* then returned to the *Globe*.

public relations program should be carried on in all echelons. . . . A well qualified public relations officer can do much to lessen and counteract adverse criticism."

A day before the general wrote of his concern, the U.S. Army Information School graduated its first class of eighty-two officers, who went forth to lessen and counteract. For two postwar decades, the school, renamed the Defense Information School in 1964, has had the mission "to train officers and enlisted personnel of all services in methods of disseminating information about the services to the service and the general public." That is the definition, at any rate, given in the Standard Operating Procedure (SOP) handed each new enlisted faculty member and "published for the information, guidance, and compliance with [sic] of all enlisted personnel."

For fourteen years, from 1951 until 1965, the school's home was Fort Slocum, New York, originally a Civil War fortress of handsome brick buildings on an eighty-acre island in Long Island Sound. With Madison Avenue seventeen miles away and the suburban pleasures of Westchester County within a ten-minute ferry ride, the post was not only an ideal site for learning the black arts of P.R. but also a dogface's dream—or so I thought in September 1963, when I arrived, duffel bag in hand, from basic combat training at Fort Dix, New Jersey.

A collegiate atmosphere prevailed, from the ivy that covered the walls where five "departments" were organized to the academic jealousies and politicking of the faculty, as intense as any described in a C. P. Snow novel. The "college president," a colonel, was the commandant, his assistant a lieutenant colonel. The "dean"—the director of instruction—was also a "light colonel" exercising tenuous authority over the department chiefs, most of whom were of equal rank. There was also an "educational adviser," a civilian, whose job was to keep the uniformed faculty informed of the latest pedagogical techniques.

The conflict between military discipline and the frozen-smile approach of P.R., compounded by academic pretense, made life at Fort Slocum alternately amusing and exasperating. At DINFOS (Defense Information School) the battle cry was "Full Disclosure with Minimum Delay." The slogan was omnipresent. "Full disclosure with minimum delay is the basic Army doctrine," we were told in classes on "Policy and Plans." The instructor, a major, spoke earnestly and sincerely: "In all of our dealing concerning the release of external information, we advocate the doctrine of maximum disclosure with minimum delay." Then, with just a trace of nervousness in his earnest smile, he added: "Of course, we also have to face reality."

Reality appeared in five "limitations" on the full-disclosure doctrine. One was security in the handling of classified information, a reasonable enough tether. Another was "national policy," a factor of concern to General Curtis LeMay, Major General Edwin Walker, and other "muzzled" military men, but of little bother to students who were lieutenants, sergeants, and privates. A third limitation was called "procedural," involving "level of release." This meant, we were told, that a regimental public-information officer (PIO) had better not release anything in the province of the division's PIO, or that a post PIO shouldn't talk about news that would be released from the Pentagon. A fourth limitation looked suspicious. It encompassed the bounds of "propriety, accuracy, and good taste." "Means just what it says," the instructor said, although we never found out what constituted propriety and good taste until we got to photography class. There we were told never to allow a picture to be taken of an officer holding a cocktail glass, "full or empty," because it would violate propriety and good taste.

The fifth limitation was labeled "commander's policy." "This simply means," the instructor said, "that if your commanding officer tells you not to release something, you don't release it. Believe me, it's the toughest thing you'll have to live with." By the time we reached this limitation, even the densest of us could get the message. So the grand doctrinal design of "maximum disclosure" inevitably descended with each class into Fort Slocum's standing joke of "minimum disclosure with maximum delay."

Comparatively little of the student's time was devoted to the metaphysical exercises of "Policy and Plans." The school's main aim was to teach students how to express themselves clearly, a task hampered by the school's reverence for redundancy. The speech department, for instance, was called "Oral Communications," changed under the efficient McNamara regime to "Research and Oral Communications." When a student was shipped to advanced infantry training because he had cheated, a memo to faculty members explained that the soldier "has been relieved from the Information Specialist Class this date for the use of unauthorized assistance in the preparation of academic matter."

More than half of the DINFOS course was devoted to what the Army called "Applied Journalism"—"the best kind, I always thought," one of my fellow draftees remarked. Possibly because I had been a Boston *Globe* reporter, I was assigned after I had successfully completed the course, still a private, as an instructor in the Applied Journalism department, which presented more than two hundred hours of journalism to each enlisted class. The first few hours were given over to lectures on "general principles." These were delivered by officers, since enlisted men were ineligible to theorize. (Enlisted instructors occasionally lectured before officer students but never, never graded their papers. Officers were segregated into classrooms where they were taught by fellow officers.) The officers, few of whom had journalistic experience, presented their basic theories in the first few days of the course. Their work was preceded by a tautologically sparkling address of welcome by the mustachioed commandant, since retired. "Your first job—and it is a continuing one—is to always plan in advance. We must anticipate ahead at all times," he exhorted. Then the officers laid down their general principles, including "ten basic ele-

ments of news." These elements, treated with all the pedagogical solemnity accorded to chemical elements, would
baffle most reporters and enrage city editors. The effect on
the students was hypnotic. "Immediacy, Proximity,
Consequence, Prominence. . . ." On and on the instructor
droned as the students drifted into torpor.

Happily for the morale of the students, they spent most
of their time in less formal sessions called newswriting
exercises, conducted in miniature city rooms. There they
wrote news stories from data sheets given by instructors.
The writing was supposed to meet the standards of release
for a civilian newspaper or for any post newspaper. The
students and instructors were kindred spirits. Some were
college graduates; many were college drop-outs who had
joined the Army "to get it over with." These enlisted students often were better able than our superiors to spot the
characters we had written into plots of fictional news stories. Joseph Heller's *Catch-22,* with its picture of absurdi-
ties in the wartime Army Air Corps, was favorite reading
among many students, who were delighted to see the
novel's hero turn up in a practice release as Airman First
Class Thomas Aquinas Yossarian of Wintergreen, Ver-
mont, "just named Airman of the Month."

Instructors in other departments were generally more
soberminded, since they dealt with weightier subjects
such as "Policy and Plans," "Research and Oral Communications," and "International Relations and Government." The International Relations teachers were mostly
civilian, perhaps in deference to the memory of General
Walker's "troop information" indoctrination programs.
They compressed an almanac of information about America and the world into thirty-three hours, six of them
devoted to Communism. This instruction enabled students to give "troop information" lectures about current
events in company dayrooms the world over.

The forty-one hours of "Policy and Plans" handled the
heavy stuff of "Psychological Warfare" and "Information
Support of Cold War Activities." Whereas the Interna-

tional Relations Department approached Communism in a fairly straightforward fashion, the Policy people viewed the problem with considerable alarm. We learned about "defense against psychological warfare" through Ian Fleming, acronyms, such as "DIRT"—Divisions, Indoctrination, Rumor, and Terror—and "SCARS"—Shifting Fronts, Censorship, Association, Repetition, Symbolization. The PIO's job overseas, we learned, "is to project the image of our nation, the U.S. Army, and the American soldier." Another primary responsibility is "to expose the threat of international Communism." The course glossed over information activities in combat, since the Army in Vietnam was then still in its adviser days. We did learn, however, a "Glossary of Counter-insurgency Terms," a glossary expunged from the curriculum when counterinsurgency became a bad word to use about Vietnam. We were also advised on methods of the "Field Press Censorship Unit," a complicated vehicle designed more to confuse the news than to purify it.

Basic instruction at the school was supplemented by the biweekly appearance of guest lecturers. General Eisenhower led a parade of experts in various fields, from George F. Kennan to Francis Cardinal Spellman to Harry Golden. After Arthur Hays Sulzberger, publisher of the New York *Times,* came, he was referred to in school pamphlets as "father and mother of the Army Information School." The arrival of the eminent guest lecturers was always a grand event. An elaborate memorandum outlined duties for each escort officer, who was to "impart information on the school's missions and accomplishments" and "arrange latrine visit, if needed, before meeting with Commandant."

In February 1964, a lady sociology professor from New England told the class how to use "a community power structure" in community-relations activities. She pointed to a case in a western city where a professor had formed a committee against the installation of missiles between the city limits and a nearby base. "What did the commanding officer of the base do?" the lecturer asked. "Through his contacts made in clubs and civic organizations of the community, he approached the civic leaders who were trustees of the college, asked them to tell the college president to tell that professor to get out of the newspapers and public forums and get back into the classroom and teach. This was done and the problem was solved."

The availability of guest speakers was a weapon in the school's own lobbying effort to forestall Secretary McNamara's order to close Fort Slocum and move DINFOS to Fort Benjamin Harrison, Indiana. But the effort was to no avail. "McNamara thinks this place has been closed for two years," an officer said in despair. Indeed, the Secretary had ordered the post deactivated in 1962, along with several other island outposts along the eastern seaboard. The move to Indiana, completed in September 1965, was confirmed by Arthur Sylvester—"the Honorable Arthur Sylvester," as the Assistant Secretary of Defense for Public Affairs was always introduced to us—when he arrived in July 1964, to inaugurate the Defense Information School.

Sylvester also used the occasion to chew out the school administration and faculty for "not thinking big enough," and ordered more emphasis on magazine writing, as if sergeants and lieutenants could easily burst into mass media by extolling military virtues. Earlier he had ordered more feature-writing exercises, apparently for the same purpose. Under this order, students wrote only one practice news story involving violence—a training accident, referred to by Policy and Plans people as "an unusual incident."

It should be emphasized that most of the students and teachers at DINFOS are honorable and intelligent men, many of whom take their guidance from a forthright directive of May 31, 1961, issued by Secretary McNamara:

"As President Kennedy has observed, the challenge of our times imposes 'two requirements that may seem almost contradictory in tone, but which must be reconciled and fulfilled . . . the need for far greater public information ... the need for far greater official secrecy.' ... We are under a special obligation to disclose mistakes and ineffective administration and operations. The public has at least as much right to bad news as to good news."

Still, anyone who observes the flow of news from the Pentagon or the training directives at DINFOS must conclude that McNamara's "full disclosure" doctrine has been subject to Sylvester's "limitations." After twenty years of an Army-run journalism school and a good five years of Army-dominated news from Vietnam, the "considerable criticism" General Eisenhower mentioned in 1946 shows no sign of ebbing. That year he was given a report by civilian advisers who had been asked to help launch the Army's information program. The report's conclusion, once printed as a preface to Army information guidebooks, does not appear in the DINFOS Policy and Plans handbook. It said:

"If the Army is good, the story will be good—and public relations will be good. If the Army is bad, the story will be bad and the result bad. In the end, public opinion about the Army reflects what the Army itself is. That is the whole secret of Army public relations.

"All any public relations group of the Army can do, in the long run, is to present the Army as it is, not as it ought to be. No more than that can be expected, or achieved."

Although it is doubtful that including these paragraphs in the DINFOS handbook would really have encouraged public information officers to present the army as it is, it is clear that military information men are devoted to painting rosy pictures. Charles Mohr* reported from Vietnam:

A steady stream of misinformation about the war in Vietnam is reaching the American public. The case is easy

*Charles Mohr is a reporter for the New York *Times*. Long a *Time* magazine correspondent in Vietnam, he resigned from the magazine because of its slanted news policies on the Vietnam War. He has since reported the war in Vietnam and United States politics and government for the *Times*.

to document. When the American Special Forces camp at Pleime came under siege in October 1965, military spokesmen reported early in the fight that 90 enemy bodies had been counted and that some of them were hanging on the camp's barbed wire. This report was displayed prominently in many newspapers, including the New York *Times*.

Later, when a reporter reached the besieged camp, still under fire, and said he wanted to photograph the bodies on the barbed wire, the grimy, bearded, exhausted defenders broke into bitter laughter. They said that there had never been bodies on the wire and that they had never made the original count of 90 enemy dead.

Earlier in the autumn of 1965, Lieutenant Colonel George Brown, the American command's official briefing officer, described an ambush suffered by troops of the First Infantry Division northwest of Saigon. He said the Vietcong guerrillas had allowed the "forward security elements" and the head of the truck column to pass through the ambush site and had then struck the second half of the column. He said the troops had dismounted to fight the attackers.

A reporter who visited the unit later was upbraided for "the way newspapers get things fouled up." The First Division troops said that the trucks had in fact been sent to pick up foot soldiers on an operation and that the ambush had begun while soldiers were milling around and preparing to board the trucks.

"The report was totally misleading, even though it did make us look better than we deserved," an officer said. "We made a mistake by parking those trucks too long on the road, where they attracted attention."

A few days earlier, the military spokesman described an ambush against "a night patrol returning home." The troops involved told a reporter indignantly that it had been a daylight patrol just leaving camp. Such points raise questions not only about the briefing officer's knowledgeability and accuracy, but also about how such distortions occur.

More serious errors arise. When enemy suicide squads penetrated the American helicopter field at Marble Mountain, near Danang, and destroyed a number of helicopters, a briefing officer in Saigon left the impression that mortar shells were believed to have done the damage. Many newspapers carried this information. But earlier that day, Major General Lewis W. Walt, commander of the United States Marines in Vietnam, told reporters in Danang that all the damage had been caused by satchel demolition charges carried onto the base.

There has also been a tendency to put the best possible face on military reports through variations in vocabulary. In describing a fierce battle by the 173rd Airborne Brigade, the briefing officer explained that the paratroopers and the Vietcong guerrillas had been so closely intermingled that it was impossible to use artillery or air raids and that the airborne units had therefore "readjusted their positions." The briefing officer angrily rejected questions suggesting that this meant the paratroops had "pulled back." A reporter with the troops that night recounted the incident to a group of airborne officers, who exploded with a string of obscenities about "Saigon commandos." "Of course we pulled back," they said.

In the early days of a prolonged battle in the Iadrang River valley between units of the First Cavalry Division (Airmobile) and regular North Vietnamese troops, a battalion commander in the field told a reporter that he had counted about 160 enemy bodies in two days. He also said it was impossible to count others under fire. That night, the American command's information office in Saigon announced that 869 enemy bodies had been counted. It was clear to men near the battlefield that many hundreds more Communist soldiers had died than had been counted, but there is a distinction between such an assumption and a statement that the bodies have been counted.

So great is the pressure for body-count figures, which often cannot be realistically obtained, that soldiers of the Airmobile Division began to joke about Saigon's request for the "WEG," or "wild-eyed guess."

In some areas of tension, the United States Information Service seems to be staffed with representatives who went through the Defense Information School. Cheryl Roosevelt Volmert* has written of the USIS in West Berlin:

> Headed by Dr. E.E. Ramsaur, the USIS exists to defend American policy, to keep morale high on both sides of the Berlin Wall, and to answer the queries of both German and American journalists. Reaching across the wall with RIAS, Radio in the American Sector, USIS broadcasts objective news around the clock to the people of the East. USIS staffs the Amerika Haus in Berlin, a center which offers the German public a wide range of both books and lectures to clarify United States policy all over the world. Aside from these two major concerns, USIS officials must also keep track of the news and the "news-that's-yet-to-happen," calling background conferences with the press when necessary, circulating "fillers" which boost the American image, and issuing statements on information which could be detrimental to the United States position in Europe. "In short, the USIS," Bud Ramsaur insists, "operates with one major objective: to inform the public. We pursue a policy of 'open disclosures' here. We give the press the facts—all the facts—if they aren't classified." Ramsaur describes press-government relations in Berlin as "totally satisfactory" and "workable." "It's a give-and-take situation: we help the newsmen out all we can and they, in turn, bring our attention to articles in the Soviet papers which we might have overlooked."

While the picture of reciprocation between the USIS and the Berlin press corps which Ramsaur paints is one of harmonious blending, press-government interaction and cooperation in the city is, according to James O'Donnell, *Newsweek* foreign correspondent, "far from optimum." He vehemently argues that rather than operating to dissem-

---

*Cheryl Roosevelt Volmert holds the B.A. in German from Stanford. A Phi Beta Kappa, she has published other articles and now teaches German at Dublin High School in California.

inate "the facts," USIS often works to suppress them. During a private interview with nine Stanford students, the cocky reporter loosened his rakish bow tie, propped his feet up on his magazine-littered desk, and spoke cogently, forcefully, about growing governmental control and manipulation of the news media. "The informational texts distributed through USIS are like throw-away mail—just about as valuable. The State Department officials here process information, all right—they take the news and change it!"

Government officials in Berlin readily admit that they often squelch stories which might be detrimental to the "American image" in Germany. Colonel Jackson, Information Officer for the United States Army, cites one example of government suppression of news which "we feel justifiable." He tells of a minor skirmish between two soldiers from the United States garrison and a Berlin taxi-cab driver. The Americans "stepped out of line" and "roughed-up" the German. That afternoon calls from a dozen reporters kept Jackson's office buzzing. Some of them asked to interview the men involved. "In cases of this sort we usually make a general statement and hope the whole thing will blow over. Naturally I wouldn't make it easy for the newsmen to get to the individual soldiers. A big write up with pictures on this type of incident only serves to defile the image of the American forces here."

O'Donnell contends that this "jealous suppression of news" to preserve the smiling "American image" often assumes radical and dangerous proportions. In 1963 the Western world recoiled when eighteen-year-old Peter Fechter, riddled with Vopo machine-gun bullets, spent the last hour of his life writhing in his own blood, calling vainly to American soldiers only yards away who could not, would not, help him. "The American public was indignant," O'Donnell reports, "that no rescue attempts were made." Focus centered once again upon the Wall, and criticisms of United States policy, which had permitted the "death strip," resounded with new intensity throughout the West. "The Mission here wanted the story to die as fast as possible—wanted the unfavorable publicity to stop. That's why few people today know that Peter Fechter did not make his race for freedom alone." Another East German boy came with him, succeeded where Fechter had failed, and made it safely across the border. United States officials "put the boy under wraps," purportedly for his own protection, and refused to allow newsmen near him. O'Donnell believes that this instance highlights the Mission's intentional control of news. "The entire United States wanted to know about Peter Fechter. The boy who fled with him could have given us 'the Peter Fechter Story'—but the government was squirming over the Fechter incident and wanted to get it out of print, so they whisked the kid away to God-knows-where." Here is a case, says O'Donnell, in which the government not only deprived the American public of the "right to know," but sacrificed the rights of a specific individual to preserve the shimmering "America image." O'Donnell argues that the boy could have sold his story for a generous sum, gaining the means for a new start in West Germany. The United States government "literally stole" this opportunity from him.

While the overzealous defense of the "American image" ranks high on O'Donnell's list of gripes against government officials in Berlin, he complains most bitterly about "silence" and "news distortion" within the government which spring from "individual self-interest." The inveterate reporter accuses government agencies which "compete for the President's ear and Congressional dollars" of using the news to achieve their own objectives. Specifically O'Donnell condemns the Departments of Defense, State, Treasury, and Commerce for "frequent inaccuracies in their reports to the press . . . They often say what they think the President would like to read, totally omitting any facts which might look glaring in print."

Fears of recrimination and loss of status hang menacingly over United States government officials in Berlin, O'Donnell explains. The Mission officer who takes a newsman aside in confidence to report a procedural or personal slip within the department places his job in jeopardy. He feels safest when he can avoid newsmen completely. The anti-press mentality in Berlin is relatively new, a child born of the McCarthy crisis of the 1950's. O'Donnell remembers the days before the end of World War II when the generals spoke "too freely with trusted reporters"—when Berlin was a "happy hunting ground" for ambitious young journalists. Today the reporters must grapple with the "no runs, no hits, no errors" philosophy of United States officials, a striking and frustrating contrast to the open dealing of the forties.

Nervous officials find comfortable refuge in the ever-expanding United States Mission, O'Donnell continues; here they can easily evade embarrassing questions. While only twelve to twenty people staffed our embassy in Berlin before the War, today's diplomatic decisions emerge from the twisted maze of over one hundred American personnel. Foreign service officers once personally answered the queries of newsmen; now they channel all questions to the stagnant reservoir of information, the USIS. The USIS men, trained to be "suspicious of journalists," cautiously hedge all but the most banal inquiries. "They'll quote their published informational texts with zest," says O'Donnell, but the reporter wants relevant responses, not reiterations.

Confronted with a mute government, the correspondent in Berlin must really dig to unearth the facts-behind-the-facts for the American public. The government forces the conscientious reporter to become a detective, to discover the truth through guile and subterfuge. At the same time, O'Donnell insists, officials "use every trick in the book" to prevent the journalist from printing the product of his independent investigations. "I refuse to attend off-the-record press conferences," states the embittered newsman. "Officials misuse them. When they hear that you're uncovering a hot news item—say, one of the many unreported Mission mistakes—they'll call you in, swear you to secrecy, and intimately tell you the story you already know. Then, as an 'ethical reporter' you're constrained to 'keep confidence' and not print the news that you've ferreted out." Of course the Mission can't foil all journalistic attempts to expose flaws in American policy or official persons; many reach the United States papers. "But the government is so big," O'Donnell rejoins, "that it can repress any story by twenty that contradict it. If today's trend continues, the government can fundamentally ignore the press."

The implications of O'Donnell's statements are darkly foreboding, for both professional newsmen and the American public. Free access to vital information has traditionally been the life blood sustaining both our republican democracy and a dynamic American press. But if United States government officials treasure personal position more than the citizens' "right-to-know," if they have the power to invent and suppress facts to protect their own interests, they can gradually clog the arteries of news dissemination. Self-concerned politicians can—intentionally or inadvertently—change the character of familiar systems without ever alarming the trusting American populace.

The problem is critical because Americans are unaware that they are unaware—few of them realize the extent to which the government controls and limits the news which they receive. Why haven't irate journalists like Jim O'Donnell exposed the authoritarian tendencies of government information agencies? The answer to this crucial question is paradoxical. Fearing total alienation from the few remaining official sources of news, most reporters, like the politicians whom they deplore, are reticent. The newsman who criticizes the practices of powerful bureaucrats destroys his own value as a reporter. Indignant officials exclude him from press conferences; they delete his name from the USIA mailing lists. The reporter completely loses personal touch with the government about which he is supposed to report; he can no longer compete with favored journalists. Ironically, it is self-interest—that attitude which O'Donnell cites as the foremost cause of government news management—which constrains reporters from revealing the increasing difficulty of wresting information from the USIS in Berlin.

Seeking to "inform the American public," American correspondents in Berlin report daily on the bloodless battle raging between East and West. But they do not mention their own important struggle.

CHAPTER FOUR

Your Friendly Neighborhood Reporter

Growing up wanting to be a newspaperman, I thought of "a scoop" as one of the magnificent professional achievements. Now I find it usually comes from "a leak"—something that has a market price: making the leaker look good, either on this story or the next one. You pay it. We accept it. Usually nobody is hurt. Sometimes the casualties are colleagues, competitors, occasionally the truth, always the integrity of the relationship. I'll salute the man on the beat who says to me: "You've got a leak? Don't tell me. Call a plumber."

—**WILLARD WIRTZ**

Cronyism is the curse of journalism.

—**WALTER LIPPMANN**

"I do believe that too close a personal friendship with people in public life puts a burden upon writers, upon reporters, upon columnists, upon radio and TV commentators, that it's extremely difficult to shed when it is necessary to write information and judgment which you know is either going to displease or hurt somebody that you know rather well in government."

—*Columnist* **ROSCOE DRUMMOND**

" 'I have written nothing for Dana because I've not had the money to buy newspapers,' Marx wrote Engels. That remark is instructive, not for what it says about Marx's poverty but for what it tells us about his method. He was the journalist of the most despised credentials, the one who does not have access."

—**MURRAY KEMPTON**

The stickiest problem in journalism is defining the proper stance of the reporter toward his sources. Since news is not manufactured out of air—not often anyway—a reporter must have sources, usually among officials. He must depend upon his sources and at the same time be independent of them.

This is a problem that is as old as journalism, which is emphasized by some of the examples in Chapter One. Quite often the reporter digs up information that, if published, would run counter to the public interest. He is usually importuned by some high-placed source to keep it secret. Whether he does depends upon his own judgment of public interest—and how persuasively his source argues.

How this works is suggested by the experience of Charles Michelson of the late, great New York *World* in the 1920's. Michelson had learned of the plight of a group of Western banks, which were near collapse. He sought out Eugene Meyer, who was then chairman of the Reconstruction Finance Corporation, and told Meyer what he had learned. Meyer responded:

"Your information is absolutely correct. Perhaps their situation is even worse than you describe. You are perfectly safe in printing your story. If you do, every one of those banks will close tomorrow. If you don't, we can save three-quarters of them. Now, damn you, it's up to you."

Michelson later wrote, "Naturally the story was not printed."

All well and good—or so it may seem. But a questing, challenging reporter would not have let the story die. Such a reporter may wonder, first of all, whether Meyer, who was himself a banker, had the proper perspective. Might he not have been protecting his fellow bankers from unfortunate but deserved publicity? Or as chairman of the RFC, might not he have been plunging government funds into a vain effort to save a group of doomed banks when the money could have been used much more fruitfully to rescue other failing businesses? Such possibilities are worth exploring, at least to the point of visiting source after source in an effort to triangulate the truth.

The point is not that Michelson was either right or wrong in his decision, but that he was wrong in allowing his skepticism of official statements to be blunted by one official's judgment.

There are worse examples, of course, of journalistic obeisance to sources. Some of the most striking come from using handouts without checking them, digging behind them—or even substituting the detached phrases of reportorial journalism for the partisan words of partisan sources. This is suggested by two items that were issued in 1963, one from the Republican Congressional Committee, the other in the *Delaware State News:*

Secretary of Interior Udall has become the symbol of the Kennedy Administration—arrogance coupled with overriding, zealous activity to run roughshod over private interests and spread Government control. He is a prime example of the danger of bestowing too much power on Government agencies . . .
—July 17, 1963

Republican Congressional
Committee Release

Secretary of Interior Stewart L. Udall has become the symbol of the New Frontier Administration—arrogance coupled with overriding, zealous activity to run roughshod over private interests and speed Government control of our lives and our properties. He is a prime example of the danger of handing too much power to Federal agencies . . .
—July 22, 1963

Story in the *Delaware State News*

More often, the comfortable relationships of a reporter and his sources are not so evident to the public. NBC correspondent Sander Vanocur told of an occasion when he saved President Kennedy from ridicule by pointing out a flaw in a Kennedy speech:

On the way from Great Falls to Hanford, Washington, reporters were given the advance text of the speech that President Kennedy was to make that night in the Mormon Tabernacle in Salt Lake City. Salinger had been assuring reporters all morning that the speech was not an attack on Senator Goldwater but rather an exposition of the President's views on the complexities of foreign policy. Yet, as I sat in the press plane reading the advance, I came across a passage which deplored the idea that "we pick up our marbles and go home" if we did not get our own way in the world. Salinger was sitting in front of me enjoying a beer, and I leaned forward to remind him that the line was vintage Goldwater. He bolted for the pilot's compartment and got on the radio to Air Force One, demanding to know from a secretary how that line from the original text had found its way into the finished version of the speech. It had been a mistake and he returned to the cabin to advise reporters to substitute a line. . . .

The worst of all this has been developed at length by correspondent James McCartney* in exploring the vested interests of reporters on their beats:

Some years ago in Chicago a dispute arose between the Federal Bureau of Investigation and the Chicago police department over who deserved the most credit for trapping a notorious peddler of narcotics. Each agency was convinced it had played the key role. City editors all over town were getting two distinctly different versions of what happened from their men in police headquarters and those on the federal beat.

The late Clem Lane, city editor of the *Daily News,* finally threw up his hands in exasperation. "Haven't we got anybody around here any more who hasn't got an ax to grind?" he cried.

Lane was wrestling with a phenomenon common in the newspaper business, yet, for elusive reasons, often overlooked in serious discourse on problems of the press. He was dealing with reporters who had developed vested interests in their beats—interests so deep that both had difficulty in taking objective views.

To the police, FBI agents were overpaid "glory hunters." The federal men felt, as they often do, that the police were "dumb cops" who would have let the peddler escape. The reporters sided with their friends and Lane's injunctions budged neither.

The phenomenon would be of little interest if the kinds

* James McCartney is a national correspondent for Knight Newspapers. He was a Washington correspondent for the Chicago *Daily News,* became city editor of the *News,* then returned to Washington to report for Knight Newspapers.

of problems it suggests were no more serious than whether the FBI or the Chicago police should get public credit for trapping a dope peddler. But the fact is that problems growing out of reporters' vested interests can be much more serious. They can be serious enough to have a bearing on great national decisions and the molding of public opinion on some of the most crucial problems of the times. Some of the most influential reporters in Washington, for example, have deep vested interests in their beats or in their specialties—so deep that they have as much difficulty in presenting objective views as the two Chicago reporters. The problem is undoubtedly universal in the news business. . . .

The symptoms of the vested interest are not always easy to detect, but the result in the extreme form is that reporters become spokesmen for their news sources rather than dispassionate observers. They become sloppy about recognizing that alternative views may exist and about digging out and including alternative views in their stories. Over a period of time some might as well be press agents for those they are covering and, indeed, sometimes perform that role, or something very close to it. A strong case can be made that many reporters covering such key spots as the White House, the Congress, the State Department, the Justice Department, or the Pentagon are plagued with problems of vested interests.

Obviously the mere writing of a story that is favorable, in effect, to the source is no sign that a reporter has sold his soul to his sources and lost his objectivity. But when reporting becomes consistently noncritical, when months or years go by without a critical story, it may be that the virus of vested interest has struck.

The difficulty in trying to understand the problem or in doing anything about it lies in the fact that the vested interest is frequently one of the most valuable of human possessions—personal friendship. No reporter can operate successfully without friends. But being objective about friends can be as difficult as being objective about one's wife.

Friendship is not all of it, however, by any means. A reporter may hesitate to take a critical view of regularly tapped sources for the very human reason that he prefers to be greeted pleasantly when he walks into an office, rather than to be treated as though he were poison. His vested interest is in maintaining a pleasant atmosphere. Another dimension to the problem involves the reporter who has come, through deep exposure, to understand and sympathize with the problems of his sources. He may become a sincere convert and advocate of their point of view. If he is reporting in a field where there are sharp differences of view he may be on the verge of losing his usefulness as a reporter. At the same time, however, his expertise may be valuable to his paper.

The price that the press, and perhaps the country, pays for reporters' vested interests can be high. . . . Consider some specific problems along this line in Washington.

In the Pentagon it is commonplace for reporters to make alliances with one or another of the armed services, presenting, by and large, that particular service's views on highly controversial problems of national defense. . . . [An] influential reporter is, for all practical purposes, a spokesman for the Air Force. He may be counted upon to defend the Air Force's desire to maintain the manned bomber or to present, in great detail, Air Force views on strategic necessities for national survival. Both, in effect, have become creatures of the so-called military-industrial complex that President Eisenhower discussed with grave foreboding in his Farewell Address. Of course the Defense Department has its spokesmen in the press corps, too. It pressed many of them into service—without actually drafting them—to defend itself against the onslaught from Capitol Hill when Senator John McClellan (D., Ark.) was investigating the TFX warplane contract.

The result of these practices and habits means that stories from the Pentagon frequently represent points of view of one or another of the Pentagon's warring camps. What is disturbing is that often the stories give no indication that the reporter has attempted to balance the story by obtaining views from other camps. [A friend] of the Navy, for example, rarely mentions that he is writing a Navy point of view and that the Defense Department would disagree wholeheartedly. If the result were only public confusion, the problem might not be too serious, for the public in a democracy is often confused. But often the public is misled—a somewhat more serious infraction.

Such specialized liaisons are relatively simple to detect in the sprawling Pentagon. They become more subtle in reporting from the White House. The White House press corps, by and large, is inclined to take the most sympathetic point of view possible toward the problems of whatever administration may be in power. In part, perhaps, because of the intimacy with which White House reporters live with the presidential press secretary, and depend on him, the White House press tends to be the most docile in town. Although there are exceptions, party ideology doesn't seem to be important. Some of the White House regulars who counted themselves as supporters in print of the Eisenhower Administration managed to switch to Kennedy without outward sign of mental anguish.

Just plain fear may play a role in White House reporting. The awesome power of the presidency is, indeed, something to contemplate and few reporters relish the thought of arousing presidential anger. The tendency even in presidential press conferences is to throw the President homerun balls rather than curve balls. It takes a man of some moral courage to brave the possibility of presidential ire or of presidential sarcasm before a national television audience. But the fact is that controversial questions often are simply not asked at presidential press conferences. If they are, one may be sure that White House staff members will not fail to make a mental note of the questioner. The next time the questioner makes an inquiry for his paper at the White House on a routine matter he may find staff members unavailable—for days. At least one reporter remembers months of difficulty in getting anyone at all to answer a phone call at the White House after writing a story about freeloaders on the President's private plane.

The White House beat presents special problems to a regular who might wish to exhibit a sign of independence. The beat produces so much front-page news without critical reporting that a sycophant can stay in business for years.

Some of the most intriguing problems of all arise on Capitol Hill, with perhaps the most intriguing results. The tendency of reporters who regularly cover the Senate, for example, is—naturally enough—to make friends with the Senate's ruling group, the primary source of important news. By itself this is certainly understandable. But over a period of time there seems to be a marked tendency to report the activities of the ruling group in a favorable light and to make challengers to that group appear as though they are social misfits.

The importance of this tendency to the reading public becomes apparent when one considers the political ideology of the ruling group in the Senate. For many years the power has been in the hands of Southern conservatives, often working in harmony with relatively conservative Republicans. Thus reporting from the Senate tends to have a bias in favor of these groups. Senate liberals—or in fact almost all who challenge the ruling group—are frequently pictured in terms that suggest that they are all but a lunatic fringe, when in fact those outside the ruling group in the Senate include some of the most dedicated and responsible legislators in the nation.

. . . The protective instinct . . . extends to reporters on the House side of the Capitol. Some of the most glaring excesses of House mismanagement have been reported with singular lack of enthusiasm by House regulars. An example was the $100 million House office building, a monstrous monument to congressional eagerness to spend money lavishly when accommodations for congressmen are involved. The facts about the building have been reported, but largely by individual correspondents from isolated papers, not by most of the regulars in the House press gallery. Only a few of them bothered to attend the first formal tour of the building. A nonregular also wrote the first story about plans for an elaborate underground parking garage for congressmen and senators in which the cost per parking space was to be $24,700. The story killed the project, at least temporarily.

Actually, far more outrageous examples of reporters' vested interests in Washington could be furnished. Some reporters have been so closely allied to specific political figures that their copy, for all practical purposes, could be read as handouts. There are others whose identification with one or another political party is just as clear. They tend to represent newspapers with political views that are well known through their news columns, however, and thus can't be considered a general problem.

It would be unfair to suggest that the problems discussed here are unique to the newspaper business. It would probably be more accurate to say that perfectly natural human tendencies are at play.

State Department officials complain, for example, that United States ambassadors to foreign countries frequently fall into the same kind of trap. After serving in a country for a certain period of time and getting to know its officials and its problems they are inclined to become spokesmen for the country rather than spokesmen for the United States.

The U. S. Bureau of the Budget has the same problem with men it assigns to specialize in the budgetary problems of government agencies. Top budget bureau officials find that after a while the men begin to take on the thinking of the agency and pretty soon they are fighting to get it more money. "They try to sell the agency's case to us rather than to sell our case to the agency," said one budget official.

In the simplest sense, on virtually any beat in Washington, or possibly anywhere, there are likely to be two kinds of reporters—the "ins" and the "outs." The "ins" are those who play along with the news sources, handle it their way, tend to overlook minor indiscretions, and in general protect their sources. The "outs" fight their sources, or at least needle them. They get their news by insisting on their right to it or by sheer perseverance. They let the source know that they intend to play it straight. They get their news the hard way, running the risk of being ostracized not only by the sources but by the reporters who are "ins." A good reporter can probably do it either way, depending on the circumstances.

It is a sad commentary in general, however, that the news business in Washington has developed an exceedingly high percentage of "ins"—and far from enough "outs." It may be in part a mere symptom of the age of the organization man, the man who wants, above all, to be loved. But it's a bad thing for the business and it's probably worse for the country.

The trick for the "out," of course, is to retain the respect of his sources. To do that in some places may be no more complicated than simply playing it straight—which, as any experienced reporter knows, is not nearly as easy as it looks from the outside. But the problem in playing it straight can become somewhat more difficult in any situation where the number of sycophants becomes unduly large.

In Washington, where there are literally hundreds of reporters, the number of sycophants on virtually any beat is unduly large. This situation is in part because of circumstances. When a government press agent knows that he can count on a reporter to give him sympathetic treatment, he is not inclined to want to take extraordinary measures to make sure that a man who plays it straight is counted in. Government press agents like to deal with their friends.

Unfortunately, the reporters who are under the most pressure in this kind of situation are frequently those representing the wire services, who supply most of the nation's news. The wire services staff more beats than anyone else and count on routine news for their bread and butter. If the wire service reporter doesn't get the routine news, he is, by the standards of his bosses, not doing his job. Thus he is under tremendous pressure to play along with the government press agent—the source of most routine news.

In defense of wire service reporters it should be added that they normally try harder to play it straight than almost anyone else. You will rarely find their stories slanted. The primary method of slanting in the news business, however, is not in what is written—it is in circumstances. In a flash of independence they may write one good critical story. Then they may have trouble getting routine stories that their offices want for weeks to come.

. . . The increasing complexity of national news, and of news everywhere, has made specialization virtually inevitable. Frequently only an expert reporter is in a position to understand, let alone report, the news. Yet the problem of developing vested interests becomes more acute when reporters specialize. Thus, unless reporters and editors are extremely careful in seeking to avoid the pitfalls of specialization, the trend can easily lead to more noncritical reporting. Snooping general reporters in Washington continue to lead the pack in developing new stories, in delving into untouched fields, particularly in investigative stories. These reporters are often "outs" rather than "ins"—who aren't afraid to call a spade a spade in print. Nor are they afraid to ask critical questions that "ins" tend to shy away from.

Avoiding the trend to specialization cannot be the answer in the complex world of Washington news, although the business will be in a sad state if the general reporter is ever abolished. Some techniques can be employed, however, to avoid some of the pitfalls of specialization. For example, if a man is assigned to cover economics in Washington, it would seem sensible to include both sides of the economics coin on his beat. He might be assigned to be responsible for the Labor Department as well as the Treasury. In that way he would be exposed to varying approaches to problems. Or if a man is assigned to the State Department, it might be wise to make him responsible, as well, for the Senate Foreign Relations Committee, from whence a critical view may come. Neither of these specific examples may be practical, but the basic strategy seems sound. The idea is simply to keep beats broad enough, when possible, so that a man is exposed to conflicting views in his daily routine. Probably the most practical idea would involve the aggressive use of general assignment reporters, allowing them to probe freely on beats or in specializations as a regular procedure.

In the last analysis, however, the conclusion is inescapable that mere devices are not going to do the job. The basic problem must, inevitably, lie with editing and editors.

If a story from the Pentagon reports an Air Force or a Navy point of view, it is certainly sound journalistic practice to require that the story make mention of the fact that the Defense Department violently disagrees. Unfortunately, this seemingly simple practice—to check with the other side—is often abandoned on the so-called "higher" levels of journalism.

If a beginning reporter fails to check both sides, or all sides, of a story, he is certain to incur the wrath of the city editor. But for reasons not always easy to understand, when a veteran political or labor writer, or a Washington correspondent, clearly fails to touch all bases—on much more significant material—the failure is often tolerated. By the same token, if a major scandal were to develop in most city halls under the noses of veteran reporters, heads would be likely to roll. But when a situation that might well be scandalous develops in the United States Senate, a situation that had been in existence for months or maybe years, the attitude seems to be somewhat more tolerant.

The business and the world that we live in need the

application of every sharp and suspicious mind available. They need more reporters who are willing to suffer the indignities of being "outs." They need more editors who read their newspapers with care and are able to pick up the telephone, place long-distance calls, and say: "What the hell!"

Perhaps the chief trouble in reporting the infamous Bobby Baker case is that no one was saying "What the hell!" to Senate reporters. The result is described by Laurence Stern and Erwin Knoll:*

Muckraking, still an honorable form of journalistic enterprise at the city hall and state capital levels, has long gone out of fashion among the elite corps of reporters assigned to the Congress of the United States. The national legislature makes so much news that most of the reporters assigned to it cover only the surface flow of events—such formal happenings as committee hearings, floor debates, parliamentary maneuvers, and the genial press conferences staged regularly by the leadership. A state of symbiosis has grown up between press and lawmakers, enabling both to go about their business in an atmosphere of mutual tolerance. The viability of this relationship is rooted in an unwritten code that the press, and especially the journalistic "regulars" who cover the daily operations of Congress, will behold only the official face of the legislative branch and avert their eyes from the tattletale gray patches of private impropriety.

When the Bobby Baker scandal broke into print in the fall of 1963, it came, therefore, as something of a journalistic anomaly. Stories of personal wrongdoing emanating from Congress about its own members are a rarity in Washington Bureau dispatches. When such scandal

*Laurence Stern is an assistant managing editor of the Washington *Post*. Long an investigative reporter, he continues to write investigative stories for the *Post* and other publications. Erwin Knoll is Washington editor of *The Progressive* magazine. He has worked as a reporter and editor for the Washington *Post* and as a Washington correspondent for Newhouse Newspapers.

flares, it usually centers on a hapless member of the Executive Branch.

At the outset, the Baker affair had a divisive effect on the Capitol Hill reportorial community. "It has the smell of dead fish," grumbled one veteran Senate correspondent about the early allegations. The regular Senate hands, to whom Baker had long been an invaluable news source, responded to the early flow of revelations with skepticism and even a touch of annoyance at those colleagues who persisted along the Baker trail.

This is a point that deserves emphasis. The initiative and enterprise that went into development of the story did not come from the Senate Press Gallery, but rather from a group of journalistic outsiders and irregulars. For example, the story was brought to the surface by Jack Landau, an alert Federal District Court reporter for the Washington *Post,* who recognized immediately the explosive implications of a civil suit to which he had been tipped.

Once the Baker affair surfaced, Senator Joseph S. Clark could not resist twitting the newsmen who regularly covered the World's Greatest Deliberative Body. "Where have you guys been all these years?" Clark needled. Clark's question still haunts some of the newsmen and editors who pride themselves on their grasp of political realities in the Senate. Where, indeed, had they been while Baker—between trips to the Senate floor—was amassing and directing a paper empire that he valued at more than $2,000,000?

There had been clues, to be sure. Some newsmen had been guests at the gala opening of Baker's sumptuous motel, the Carousel, in the seaside resort town of Ocean City, Maryland. Newspapers in the Capital celebrated the event as a major social event of the 1962 summer season—and it was. That a $19,600-a-year Senate employee with no known private resources could plunge suddenly into a million-dollar business venture apparently was accepted unquestioningly by all. The Carousel opening was dutifully recorded on Washington society pages.

A little earlier the same year, John J. Lindsay, of the Washington *Post* (now with *Newsweek*), had disclosed Baker's affiliation with a Silver Spring, Maryland, insurance agent, Don B. Reynolds, who had written $200,000 in insurance on the life of Lyndon B. Johnson (and who was later to become Baker's principal public accuser). Painstaking research among Maryland corporate records had confirmed the story for Lindsay, but Baker had denied taking any active part in the firm's affairs. Reynolds subsequently testified that he had paid Baker some $15,000 for helping to bring in business from his many Capitol Hill acquaintances. After a one-shot story, there were no follow-throughs.

By the time of the Carousel opening, a diligent examination of public records could have provided a catalogue of Baker financial affiliations that included: a motel partnership with a fellow Senate employee, Small Business Committee clerk Gertrude C. Novak; a $54,000 Small Business Administration loan for repair of hurricane damage at the motel; a thriving Washington law practice; and an active insurance business. Further investigation into the law firm might have revealed such additional affiliations as the Serv-U Corporation, a fast-growing West Coast vending machine firm; the celebrated Quorum Club on Capitol Hill; and a travel agency, Go Travel, Inc.—all listed in District of Columbia records as enterprises incorporated by Baker's law firm.

If Baker's name emerged in the news during this period, it was only in occasional profiles of a bright young man on the way up the Washington social and political ladders. In these appreciative pieces tribute was invariably paid to Baker's acumen as a Senate headcounter, to his personality, and to his devotion to duty. One exception was an article by Chicago *Daily News* correspondent Jim McCartney, who related Baker's boast that he controlled ten senators.

Nonetheless, the genesis of the Baker case, insofar as the

press is concerned, must be dated September 12, 1963. That was the day when the Washington *Post* published on page 3-C, deep in the local section, a story by District Court reporter Landau that was headlined: "Senate Official Is Named in Influence Suit." Baker's name was not mentioned until the third paragraph, but Landau's article gave the details on the civil suit filed against the Senate official and two associates by a vending machine operator, Ralph L. Hill. Hill claimed, in effect, that he had bought Baker's influence to get a lucrative vending concession in a defense plant and that Baker's influence was subsequently used to break the contract.

There had been considerable initial soul-searching by the *Post*'s editors on whether news of the suit should be reported, since it was a complaint in a private dispute. Finally, the executive editor, J. R. Wiggins, and the city editor, Ben W. Gilbert, decided to clear Landau's story without so much as a call to the newspaper's counsel.

Following publication of the initial story, additional manpower was assigned to the Baker story by the *Post*. The result was a page-one story published on September 22, 1963, that identified for the first time Baker's heavy financial interest in the Serv-U vending concern, which did most of its business in defense plants. At this point, the *Post*'s only direct competition on the story was a little-known trade publication, *Vend* magazine, organ of the vending machine industry. Both published the story of Baker's affiliations with Serv-U on the same day. It was one of those rare instances when a highly specialized trade journal became a newsstand sellout in Washington.

After September 22, reportorial curiosity was further whetted by a sudden freshet of leads from disenchanted former associates of Baker, from casual acquaintances who could speak of specific episodes, and from anonymous telephone tipsters. Those who professed to know hinted darkly to newsmen of call-girl operations on Capitol Hill, of abortion rings, and of clandestine business deals in which prominent Congressional figures were alleged to have participated. One of Baker's former associates passed out the telephone number of a prostitute who boasted to several newsmen of a list of patrons almost large enough to constitute a quorum of either House. Her confessions were tape recorded by a Washington private detective who subsequently granted paid audiences to newsmen who wanted to hear the recordings. (Stories based on the tapes were eventually published in the Hearst papers, the New York *Daily News,* and the New York *Post.* Only the *News* named the woman—and printed her picture.)

Some of the initial reports that came to the press from the gossip mines of Capitol Hill later proved to be substantially accurate; others turned out to be distortions or utter fabrications. Nevertheless, to the small corps of newsmen who were pursuing the story and trying to sift fact from fantasy, the Bobby Baker affair was assuming a new importance. This stemmed, in part, to be sure, from Baker's close relationship with Lyndon B. Johnson. But there was also the additional suspicion that a far bigger story lay beneath the surface of the Baker case. One news magazine correspondent made this memorable observation at the time: "What we have here is the story of the invisible government of the Senate—of how things are really done in Washington." The way things were really done in the world of Bobby Baker, reported Julian Morrison in the Washington *Daily News,* included the use of Senate limousines on private business and the juggling of Senate pageboy salaries.

Only a handful of newsmen was engaged in the lonely, investigative stage of the inquiry preceding Baker's resignation on October 7, 1963. Without the early stories, it is doubtful that Baker would have resigned or that the Senate would have directed the Rules Committee on October 9 to embark on a full-scale investigation.

While the Rules Committee made leisurely preparations for an investigation—an activity that was foreign to its normal housekeeping role—disclosure was heaped upon disclosure by a growing phalanx of reporters devot-

ance Corporation of Milwaukee (MAGIC), which later favored him with the opportunity to buy valuable stock at below-market prices (Washington *Evening Star*); Senator Olin D. Johnson of South Carolina had interceded with Dominican authorities for a gambler constituent whose investments were endangered after the downfall of Trujillo (New York *Times*); Senator John J. Sparkman, second-ranking Democrat on the Banking and Currency Committee, had bought stock in a newly chartered Washington national bank with a one-third down payment (Los Angeles *Times*); a cargo airline had provided free transportation for Capitol Hill staffers and lobbyists to a Las Vegas fund-raising dinner in honor of Senator Howard W. Cannon, Democrat of Nevada (Scripps-Howard).

Lyndon B. Johnson's accession to the Presidency imposed heavy inhibitions on newsmen who had been exploring the nature of the relationship that existed between Johnson and Baker. The press reflected the national desire to maintain unity in the wake of catastrophe. On the morning of November 22, insurance man Don Reynolds gave Rules Committee investigators the first evidence injecting Johnson's name into the Baker inquiry. Although the details of Reynolds' session with the committee staff were known to several reporters, the story did not appear in print until January, 1964.

Of all the private sources of information, Reynolds knew the most about Baker's business dealing and had the most documentation to back up his assertions. As a witness, he provided some of the most damaging testimony—although only in the form of published transcripts, since the Rules Committee never called him in open session. He became the center of the Johnson Administration's first news management controversy.

"Persons within and close to the Johnson Administration have attempted to use secret Government documents to impugn the testimony of a witness in the Robert G. Baker case," Cabell Phillips reported on page one of the

New York *Times* on February 8. In the background of the controversy were Reynolds' allegations that he had been pressured into buying advertising time on the Johnson family's Austin, Texas, television station, and that he had paid for an expensive gift stereo set for the Johnsons. After Reynolds had given his testimony at two executive sessions of the Rules Committee, publishers and other key newspaper executives began receiving telephone calls from high figures in the Johnson Administration who pictured the insurance agent as an unreliable witness and cautioned against publication of his charges.

Phillips reported, and others confirmed, that "in several instances, individual newsmen and news executives have been read excerpts from what purported to be reports by either Air Force intelligence or the Federal Bureau of Investigation. These reports purported to contain derogatory information on Mr. Reynolds' background and his reputation for veracity."

The effect of these calls was varied. The Washington *Evening Star* revised a story about the stereo gift after a White House call, only to acknowledge later that its reporter had been right in the first place. The Hearst Headline Service, first to publish the story, made its decision to go ahead after a frantic round of telephone calls between Washington and New York. The Washington *Post* decided to await the expected release by the Rules Committee of Reynolds' testimony about the stereo set and advertising kickbacks to the Johnson station.

In any event, the Reynolds charges were widely publicized in all media when uncensored transcripts were released by the Committee, although they had to compete for news play with the concurrent release of President Johnson's budget measure.

At this point, columnist Drew Pearson and his associate, Jack Anderson, began to publish a series of sharp attacks on Reynolds, quoting extensively from what they described as official records. In one instance, Pearson appended to his column the text of an Air Force memorandum on Reynolds' war record that bore a January 1964 Pentagon stamp. In a "confidential report to editors," according to one published account, Pearson wrote: "For your information and because of possible concern over libel in columns on Don B. Reynolds, I am giving for your private information a copy of an Air Force report on Reynolds' background. Information contained in columns is from various sources, though the following is a fairly good summary."

The White House denied that it had any part in compiling or releasing the dossier on Reynolds. The Justice Department also denied any complicity in the leak. The Defense Department refused to make any comment on the episode, even in response to Senatorial inquiries.

The source of the leaks remains a mystery to this day. And the problem of how to handle unattributable, derogatory information from official files—a problem posed in its most acute form during the McCarthy era a decade ago—remains unresolved. In dealing with the Pearson revelations, the Washington *Post* twinned the first critical column with an answering statement by Reynolds. Other Pearson subscribers carried only the column. In a few instances the Pearson column was killed.

A chronic problem underscored by the Bobby Baker affair is the strong pressure on Congressional beat men to confine their reportage to the visible legislative surfaces. Admittedly, covering the Senate is a complex and exacting assignment—one that is competently performed by most of the mature professionals in the Press Gallery. It is argued that Senate reporters are too burdened with daily coverage responsibilities to ferret out corruption in the legislative branch. However, the disclosures of the Baker case drive home the harsh truth that self-interested actions concealed behind the parliamentary façade are an intrinsic part of the story.

One Senate aide paid tribute to the role of the news media in the Baker case with the observation that "without the newspapers this would have been over long ago."

He alluded to the fact that press disclosure provided the frame of reference for the Rules Committee investigation. Unarguably, the press did itself credit in the Baker affair, displaying the investigative initiative it can bring to bear once its interest has been whetted.

Still, the question propounded by Senator Clark— "Where have you guys been all these years?"—remains a perplexing one. Had it not been for a seamy business squabble that spilled over into the courts, how long would it have been before the press recognized that the private financial interests of the Senate's number one news source were also news?

CHAPTER FIVE

Adversaries and Sweethearts

> *A political leader is essentially an advocate—a man who is seeking to shape the world toward ends he considers worthy. . . . A newspaperman, on the other hand, is one whose job is to chronicle daily events and to place the facts before the public in some reasonable perspective. Events and facts have a life of their own. They are independent of the dreams and desires of men. . . .*
>
> —GEORGE REEDY

> *A high appointed city official will say, "I didn't want to tell your city hall reporter this because . . . well, he's a nice guy but he doesn't understand how these things work. But I know you'll understand from your days on the beat why we'd like to play down. . . ."*
>
> —ART NAUMAN,
> *Managing Editor, Riverside (Cal.) Press*

> *If the idea of democracy should ever be invalidated, it will be because it came about that more and more people knew less and less that was true about more and more that was important.*
>
> —WILLARD WIRTZ

The problem of the reporter's relationships with his sources is even worse at the county and municipal levels than it is in Washington or in the state capitals. In Washington, and to a lesser extent in the state capitals, sheer numbers of reporters may provide some protection for the public interest. When hundreds of reporters cover the federal establishment and dozens are at work covering the state establishments, there is a fair likelihood that the hidden facts will be brought to light. But many county and municipal governments are covered by only one or two men, especially in this age of monopoly newspapers. Almost nowhere can the public which is served by a weak-willed city hall or county government newspaperman count on radio or television reporters to probe and investigate in his stead. With few exceptions, radio and TV do not nurture challenging reportage. Nor are their men assigned to the grinding beat work—again with a few exceptions—which alone will enable a reporter really to understand what is going on in the halls of local government.

The local government reporter for the newspaper thus carries a crushing responsibility—and not often very well. Unless his skepticism is deep-grained and his skin quite thick, he will take the easy course of accepting what he is handed, which may bear only a faint relationship to the truth.

Sometimes the reporter has little choice. With the burgeoning of local governments and the growth of special districts, not to mention the ever-increasing entanglement of other local institutions in governmental affairs, the reporter is unable even to accomplish the minimum: attend all the meetings that will enable him to comprehend the rudiments.

In one community that seems typical, less than 50 per cent of the meetings of governmental bodies and civic organizations are attended by a reporter from the only daily in town. Some of the others are "covered" by making phone calls to officials and officers after the meetings, or by asking someone who plans to attend to call the paper if anything newsworthy occurs. Granted, most such meetings yield little more than petty wrangling and grandiose planning, and avoiding them may improve a reporter's disposition. But this is a sure system for ignoring the threads that tie a community together. It is worse. An official who is truly devoted to the public interest is frustrated in his best resolves by the absence of news coverage. An official who is pushing his own interests likes nothing better than to pick up a telephone and act as his own reporter. One need not be a cynic to suspect that the absence of coverage promotes private interests.

Most important in developing challenging reporting at the local level is the leadership provided by the editors and the publisher. At the top level, newspapermen are usually familiar, if not actually friendly, with all the First People of the community. It must be made explicitly clear to reporters that the acquaintances and friendships of newspaper executives—and those of the reporters as well—are not to influence reporting. It is especially necessary to make it clear that the paper's editorial policies and crusades should not influence factual reporting.

This kind of leadership can be provided through words, but actions are more convincing. An example was provided by Tim Hays, editor and co-publisher of the Riverside (California) *Press* and *Enterprise*. When one of his reporters, George Ringwald, was deep in a controversial series of stories telling how California Indians were being cheated (the stories later won the Pulitzer Prize), Hays himself was in trouble. Superior Court Judge Merrill Brown was in charge of the Indian guardianships and conservatories in question, and although he was not the chief villain, he was embarrassed by the series. Judge Brown ordered Hays to appear in his court. It would have been easy in such circumstances for Hays, who is himself a lawyer, to obey and apologize for any embarrassment the stories caused Judge Brown. But Hays responded, "I would be reluctant to appear without some understanding of the reason for my appearance." Judge Brown then wrote:

"1. Your presence will be required at 10:00 A.M. on Friday, November 3rd, 1967;

"2. If there are transportation problems, I will arrange for the Sheriff to bring you; and

"3. As an officer of the court you are ordered to appear at that time."

Hays responded:

"I have received your communications indicating your desire that I appear in your court tomorrow in connection with the estate of Winifred Patencio Preckwinkle. I know nothing of this estate, and you have given me no basis for my appearing either as a witness or an attorney. In the absence of regular processes of court, I see no reason to leave my obligations here and appear."

Judge Brown then instructed his clerk to issue a warrant for Hays's arrest. The clerk checked with his superior, the County Clerk, who in turn consulted the County Counsel, who then declined to issue the warrant. The judge responded by ordering the County Clerk and the County Counsel to appear in court. All this occurred on a Friday, and Hays, the Clerk, and the Counsel were to appear on Monday. But Judge Brown thought better of it over the weekend and backed away from his own order.

Such examples encourage sub-editors and reporters to question and challenge authority. The managing editor of one of Hays's papers, Art Nauman, is encouraged to resist the overtures of officials who call the Riverside *Press* asking that reporters be pulled off stories or beats because the reporters are adversaries rather than sweethearts. They call, Nauman says, and argue, "You know, your reporter, Fred, does a great job, but how about assigning John to our story because . . . well, he *understands* us better." Rather than a convincing argument, Nauman considers this an unintentional warning that John will be a far less effective guardian of the public interest than Fred is.

Every day, somewhere in this land of boost and uplift, a reporter or an editor hears a plea that reporting facts, however dispassionately, will injure the community. Often in recent times, the argument is advanced by community leaders that reporting the rallies, demonstrations, and conflicts that accompany the demand for minority rights will be injurious. Some journalists listen and acquiesce. The more thoughtful among them point out that one of the reasons for the current conflict is that journalists ignored the need for correcting basic injustices for too many decades.

Even more often, community leaders argue that news affecting local business and industry—especially lures for new industry—should be handled discreetly, if at all. One editor has described such a case:

> Three or four months ago our city manager went before the city council to urge that they take certain steps to prepare the way for a prospective new industry. These were matters of utility service, or zoning, or something of that order. He did not intend to name the industry, but inadvertently did so. Then he and others present tried to per-

suade our reporter that he should not include the name in his story. They said that our city was competing with two other cities for this desirable industry and the officials of the company had indicated that the city's chances would be jeopardized if their identity were revealed.

Next I got a call from the city manager, who put the case very strongly. He felt that my values were false and he couldn't understand how I could threaten this kind of injury to the community. Then the head of our leading bank called my partner who asked me to return the call, and I had the task of explaining my position to a good friend who was in no mood to understand.

It's irrelevant but perhaps interesting that the industry did decide to come to our city.

In 1967, John Mayo* set out to determine the differences, if any, between state capital and municipal reporting by looking at the press relations of the new gubernatorial administration of Ronald Reagan in Sacramento and Mayor John Shelley in San Francisco.

Since Mayo's report was written, the principal figures in his account have gone on to quite different troubles. Then-Lieutenant Governor Robert Finch, who in Mayo's report is admirably detached and philosophical about the role of the press, became Secretary of Health, Education, and Welfare in the Nixon Administration. As the most liberal member of a basically conservative Administration, Finch has had problems, especially because the press has been trying to trace the decision processes which resulted in withdrawing two appointments of officials who were to be highly placed in the HEW organization.

Mayor Shelley left office after an unhappy term, and the San Francisco *Bay Guardian* charged that his retirement was the result of a deal with his eventual successor, Joseph Alioto. (As for Alioto, *his* troubles with the press are now in the courts; he brought a $12.5 million libel suit against *Look* magazine in 1969 for an article which linked him to Mafia leaders.)

* John Mayo is a candidate for the Public Affairs Ph.D. in the Department of Communication at Stanford. A former Peace Corpsman in Colombia, he is now working on a television research project in El Salvador.

Finally, Mel Wax, whose actions as a San Francisco *Chronicle* reporter and mayor of Sausalito are sketched here, has become editor of the most highly acclaimed news program on educational television, "Newsroom of the Air," which is presented by KQED-TV in San Francisco.

Mayo wrote:

> In Reagan's first two months, three major issues sprang to banner headlines: a 10 per cent across-the-board budget cut, a proposal to charge tuition at the state's universities and colleges, and the dramatic firing of University of California President Clark Kerr. Each action was met by strong and usually negative comment in much of the press. It seemed natural to expect from Lieutenant Governor Robert Finch a lingering hostility, resentment, or at least wariness.
>
> Surprisingly, he saw nothing disturbing in press coverage. "There is a pyramid effect with important decisions always coming to and from the top," Finch pointed out. He said that it was inevitable that the press should concentrate at this level of the decision-making process and that it should concern itself with the officials who occupy the top ranks.
>
> Finch stressed, however, that the channels through which decisions arrive at the top are also critically important both to the Governor's staff and the press: "The problem is that lower officials often vie for and seek out opportunities to sound off." He used Governor Reagan's tuition proposal to prove the point. Reagan and his advisers were not prepared to fight the tuition issue so early in the new administration. They had distributed a memorandum to key officials asking for ideas and offering suggestions for alleviating the staggering cost of maintaining California's superb system of higher education. Finch said that "some civil servant picked it up and decided to make political hay out of it." It got into the headlines before Reagan was ready to fight, and he lost—at least for the time being. As a result, Reagan and his staff took action to insure that subordinate officials will no longer be able to feed stories to

journalists or even be privy to the Governor's thinking.

Despite the tuition incident and the embarrassment it caused the administration, Finch was philosophical on the matter of leaks, and he seemed prepared to accept them as an inevitable handicap of public office. He cited Reagan's press conferences as proof that leaks are unavoidable: "Only rarely do the Governor's press conferences serve as a platform to announce new policies. More often than not, the important stories have leaked and the press conference actually serves as a reaction situation in which the reporters try to probe the controversies already stirred up by premature disclosures." However, what disturbed Finch the most is what he called "black and white reporting," the tendency on the part of some reporters to view issues and personalities in extreme terms. On the sensitive issue of the Kerr firing, Finch said that, "It was perfectly clear where Governor Reagan and I stood, and yet, because a majority of the Regents voted with us, it was automatically assumed that we had engineered the thing." Despite his annoyance with the way the Kerr story was treated, the Lieutenant Governor does not appear willing to chastise the press. He cited the need for more background and in-depth reporting and he feels that once the newspaper morgues are automated, journalists will be able to avail themselves more readily of more historical and general reference material and their coverage will improve accordingly.

Finch's adversaries, the men of the Capitol press corps, are ensconced in a complex of crowded offices located a short distance from the spacious quarters of the Lieutenant Governor.

Jack Welter and Jack McDowell of the San Francisco *Examiner* have forty years of cumulative experience covering the state government in Sacramento and are senior members of the corps. Both men were pleased with their budding relationships in the new administration, although they qualified their optimism. "They need to smooth out," says Jack Welter. "Brown's boys were old pros after eight years here." "We still can't call up and get a straight answer," said Jack McDowell. "These fellows are new to government and just don't want to stick their necks out." The reporters agreed that once the new administration got a few more months under its belt, access should be easier and a lot of time would be saved.

Regardless of the period of adjustment which was under way in Sacramento, Welter and McDowell claimed they were busier than ever. Not only must they establish new contacts and renew old ones, but the reporters are forced to contend with a horde of freshmen legislators. "These guys are bugging us like hell," says Welter. "In the old days they would swamp you with handouts. Now, with the new facilities, every damn one of them is calling a press conference." Moments later the phone on Welter's desk rang. He picked up the receiver, nodded and grunted for a few seconds, then slammed it down and exclaimed, "See there, some idiot's office just called to tell us that their man's having a press conference tomorrow to give his opinions on the Powell case. Dammit I've got better things to do!"

Welter and McDowell did indeed have better things to do. During the first crucial year of the new administration, they must nurture the contacts which will provide them with stories in the years ahead. They must find ways to split and enlarge cracks in the pyramids of power, cracks which will lead to valuable insights into the thinking and policy-making processes of the Governor and his top associates. "There are no secrets in Sacramento and we aim to keep it that way," quips McDowell.

In the sense that politics is "the art of the possible" and, as such, a constant process of bargaining, persuasion, and compromise, it would seem impossible for a reporter in Sacramento to be anything but a superior breed of the *homo politicus*. Assisting in the preparation of individual bills, editing speeches, and occasionally giving more than customary attention to a particular legislator's pet project are among the arsenal of favors which the political journalists rely upon to gain access to the inner thoughts and machinations of important legislators and civil servants. According to McDowell, it was a senior civil servant, whose name he refused to disclose, who leaked the story of the administration's tuition inquiries. "This is how we do the public's business," adds Welter, "and few politicians expect anything different."

San Francisco Mayor John F. Shelley displayed a defensive hostility in his encounters with the press, in contrast to the assuredness with which the Reagan administration seemed to handle its press relations. At one daily press briefing, the Mayor allowed himself to be constantly rattled by City Hall reporters Russ Cone and Mel Wax. The important issue of the day was the Mayor's forthcoming trip to Washington on behalf of his city's effort to persuade the Republican National Committee to select San Francisco as the site for its party's 1968 convention. When rigorously questioned regarding the reasons for San Francisco's bid, Mayor Shelley's rather awkward responses were countered with under-the-breath but clearly audible comments such as "That's wrong" or "Why in God's name do we want them here in the first place?" With each question, it became increasingly difficult for the Mayor to put forth his justifications for wanting the convention trade. The interview progressed, the Mayor's face reddened, the level of his voice rose, and soon he was completely unable to seize the initiative from the two reporters who also were growing restless over what Mel Wax later termed "this morning ritual of evasion and misinformation."

On the basis of the press conference, it appears that at least a part of the Mayor's inability to work with the press and the press' resulting dissatisfaction with the Shelley administration was attributed to the Mayor's concept of himself in office. It was Shelley's first journey into the executive branch of government. He returned to San Francisco after fifteen years in Congress and, before that, he served as a state senator and president of the California Federation of Labor, two posts which required minimal contact with reporters. In his current office, Mr. Shelley evidently found the daily scrutiny of the press a novel and extremely unwelcome experience.

Vernon Williams, the Mayor's press agent, known as confidential secretary, feels that his boss suffers because of the reporters' unceasing efforts to squeeze out decisions and to stir up controversies. "Obviously the Mayor was not exposed to this treatment in Washington," Williams admits, "and he is determined to avoid embarrassing commitments here." What seems to emerge from Williams' remarks and Shelley's actions is a nostalgic reaffirmation of the deliberative function of government. In other words, as a result of his many years of legislative experience, Shelley learned to cherish time, privacy, and quite possibly obscurity as prerogatives of the decision-making process. He chose to avoid public disclosures of his thoughts, partly out of instinct and partly for the simple reason that he has never been held so immediately accountable for them in the past. This habit has undoubtedly been perpetuated by the fact that neither of the major San Francisco newspapers has a correspondent in Washington. Obviously, this permitted Shelley and other northern California congressmen to operate with maximum license at a considerable distance from their constituents. Regrettably, it is the reinforcement of this propensity for detachment which undermined Mayor Shelley's effectiveness in City Hall.

Mel Wax of the San Francisco *Chronicle* offered the harshest critique of Mayor Shelley and his administration's press relations. "He (Mayor Shelley) gives us the impression of a guy who can't make up his mind," complained the reporter. Wax, who is the Mayor of Sausalito, has covered City Hall for six years. He seems uniquely qualified to assess the responsibilities of a public official to the press and vice versa. "The Mayor should be using us," says Wax, "not to tell us that the sun will rise and set today, but for real ideas and opinion." This reporter and his companion, Russ Cone of the *Examiner,* also regard Shelley's legislative background as a possible explanation for his behavior, although they refuse to mollify their judgments in light of it. Again in Wax's words, "The executive is a different bird and a mayor must take positions. He has got to be ready to make quick decisions and to let those decisions be known." In short, he has to take the initiative.

Neither Wax nor Cone is blind to the fact that premature disclosures and publicity can, at times, hinder a public official's effectiveness. In fact, they seem willing to grant the Mayor the privacy he would need to deal in his own way with sensitive issues such as appointments and certain contract negotiations. The acquisition of the famous Brundage art collection during the administration of Shelley's predecessor, Mayor George Christopher, is an example of this point. According to Wax, a public airing of the bargaining process which resulted in the awarding of the famous collection to San Francisco could only have hindered the city's efforts to resolve privately the donor's preconditions for making the gift. Similarly, the reporters cited the tricky course of events involved in the Giants' move to San Francisco in 1960 as another instance when the press withheld premature disclosure and comment out of good faith and an understanding of Mayor Christopher's intentions and need for flexibility.

What irritates Wax and Cone is that Shelley, unlike his predecessor, does not make himself "open and available" to the press. "With no understanding we can no longer give concessions," says Wax. The breakdown in communications has not only impaired the Mayor's effectiveness, but it has also fostered a difficult hostility in their working relationship. This has led to a crippling mistrust of the Mayor's policies by the City Hall press corps.

The contrast between the press relations of the Reagan administration and those of Mayor Shelley reveals a number of important factors which are applicable to a more generalized approach to the existence and function of the adversary system. Above all, it seems clear that while political prejudices and sympathies will inevitably color a reporter's evaluation of a particular decision or action, detachment and the cold eye of objectivity must be retained by the adversaries if the relationship is to have utility and be productive for both the government and the press. Disruptive imbalances result when either the public official or the press fails to perceive the divergent objectives which motivate each other's behavior.

The Reagan administration and the Sacramento press corps have so far achieved a productive working relationship. Despite the controversial nature of many of the Governor's decisions, the adversaries in this case acknowledge and, more importantly, act upon an essential awareness of the responsibilities which distinguish each other's tasks. Balance and mutual adjustment have resulted. At the other extreme, Mayor Shelley and his staff have not understood the press' role and, as a result, the Mayor's suspicion of the City Hall reporters has led to bitterness and frustration on both sides. Shelley has also failed to alter his leadership style to the context of City Hall politics and the public has suffered from a diminishing volume of news. In his refusal to be drawn into a dialogue with the press, the Mayor has denied himself the potential rewards of an adversary relationship. Ironically, by insisting on his right to "go it alone," the press—out of spite—seems to have granted Mr. Shelley his wish.

Cincinnati's leaders are not likely to suffer Shelley's fate, but Emily McKay's* report on that city makes it clear that Cincinnati journalists are quite content to let the adversary system fail:

Cincinnati is an old, conservative, German city, with diverse industry supporting a metropolitan area population of over one million. In 1925, it was listed as one of the ten worst-governed large cities in the United States, with a 32-man, ward-dominated council, a strong mayor, and a tremendously effective—and dishonest—Republican

* Emily Gantz McKay holds a Master's Degree in Journalism from Stanford. A Phi Beta Kappa, she divides her time between working as a program and manpower specialist for the Pittsburgh Poverty Program and freelance consulting and writing.

machine headed by a duo of bosses who ran the city from
the second floor of the Mecca Saloon. In 1926, with the
help of a crusading newspaper, Cincinnati became a
reform-government town, with a city manager–city council system, a nine-man council elected at large (the mayor
chosen from among the council members), and proportional representation (the party with, say, two-thirds of
the vote elected two-thirds of the council). For years after,
Cincinnati was considered one of the best-governed large
cities in the United States. The city manager was chosen
by the council but enjoyed nearly complete autonomy in
running the city administration, which used the Civil
Service merit system.

In 1957, proportional representation was voted out,
and since then the Republicans have held a majority of at
least five on the nine-man council. The bi-partisan Charter party split, and the other four seats were usually
divided between Charterites and Democrats, 2–2. In 1967,
the Republicans increased their strength to six, allowing
them for the first time to pass legislation requiring a two-
thirds majority without the support of any minority party
councilmen.

The complexion of Cincinnati city government has
now changed. Since 1967, Cincinnati has again become
almost a one-party town. On two recent occasions, the
Civil Service Commission was bypassed when appointments were made. The professional city manager chosen
by the council before 1969's Republican victory was
forced out, and the new city manager has been called a
political appointee. Observers say that Richard Krabach,
former Finance Director for Ohio Governor James
Rhodes, was chosen by party leaders, and his selection
announced to the press before all the Republican councilmen had gotten word to support him. One Republican
councilman reportedly asked during council committee
meetings, "Why are we having these meetings anyway?
We have nothing to say about who gets chosen." Another
highly respected Republican councilman said privately
afterwards that he did not favor Krabach, but had "no

freedom of choice; I couldn't hold out any longer" and finally had to give in to the GOP policy committee decision. The new city manager is not professionally trained for the job, and reportedly is not in fact responsible to the council. He has been criticized by minority councilmen for failing to attend council Finance Committee meetings, and even council meetings.

During the summer of 1969, the city manager began a reorganization of the city administration, in the name of efficiency and decentralization—bringing government to the people. In fact, say critics, it separates people further from the downtown decision-makers, and increases the number of party appointees to be named by the city manager. Veterans of the 1926 reform movement fear the re-establishment of the ward system and the potential for bossism.

Big business supports the Republican domination. According to Betsy Bliss of the Cincinnati *Enquirer*, business leaders often control political organizations, selection of candidates, and party fund-raising. "It's kind of a United Appeal agreement." A former councilman says businessmen are the "shadow government" in Cincinnati. It is not, however, a bossism situation today, but rather a coalition based on similar interests. One young man aspiring to political office observes that "you have to be a Republican to be in politics, if you are in business. If you want to get involved with the Democratic party, and work for a bank, you get fired. If you work for Procter and Gamble, you get admonished."

Veteran reformer Murray Seasongood, first mayor under the 1926 Charter administration, feels that the similarities to those days of Boss Cox are marked. As reported in the *Enquirer,* he feels that the present administration "is just as bad as Boss Cox's reign in terms of domination by a small group of businessmen. They just have a higher type of henchman now."

In an effort to counter the Republican domination of the council, Democrats and Charterites in 1969 established a coalition, their first in 12 years. Their platform stresses the unresponsiveness of the present administration, its complete domination by party chiefs—not elected officials—and the necessity to return to the nonpolitical city manager system. It will not be easy. As Thomas Brush, Coalition candidate for the council explains, "You don't have signs of physical neglect. Examples of graft and corruption would make our job easier. But instead of corruption, you have apathetic, unresponsive government. People are apathetic, too. So the task is enormous." Cincinnatians are so accustomed to honest government they do not realize they are in danger of losing it. They do not realize the city is no longer being run by its elected officials.

The newspapers in Cincinnati are apathetic, too. During years of reform government, the adversary system was probably less needed than elsewhere, because of many internal checks on government. Even today, there are no party labels on the ballot. If there are ten candidates for a given set of offices, names are listed alphabetically, with a different name first on each ten percent of the ballots—so that no positional advantage is given to any one candidate.

More important internal checks were provided by the independent city manager–overseen administration and the bi-partisan council. As the city manager has become a political appointee only nominally responsible to council, and the council has become so majority-dominated that the minority no longer has a significant voice, the newspapers have failed to provide the necessary adversary function.

An original study of Cincinnati newspapers in 1967 and a second check in 1969 show a superficial coverage of city government which has failed to improve as its responsibilities to the people have become more crucial.

Cincinnati is a two-newspaper town (until several years ago a three-newspaper town), although both morning and evening offerings are now owned by Scripps-Howard. In order to avoid a monopoly suit (an effort which failed; the case is still pending), Scripps-Howard has left the *Enquirer* under the control of a long-established citizens board of prominent, conservative Cincinnatians, which ran the paper before Scripps-Howard gained control. Thus the *Enquirer* has its own publisher. The *Post and Times-Star*, on the other hand, is strictly a chain organ.

Both papers are poor. Their local news coverage is especially weak, superficial, and frequently slanted; their editorial positions lifeless to downright reactionary. Veteran newsman Forest Frank, executive director of the Cincinnati Charter Committee, in 1967 termed local journalism "third-rate." Enlarged Charles P. Taft, senior councilman and Charterite, "If I want to get something published, I write it out. If I really want to get it in, I write two paragraphs, no more—and make it lively." Republican Willis D. Gradison, Jr., agreed: "If you want to get it in, generally the best thing to do is write it out and take it to them." One discouraged Cincinnatian, particularly displeased with the lack of leadership, defined the papers' editorial policy: "They love motherhood and hate the housefly." During one four-week period in 1967, the tally of local-government–related editorials included only five, two concerning the county Probate Court, one urging modernization of county government structure, one an appreciation of Councilman (now Mayor) Eugene Ruehlmann, and one jokingly rebuking Councilman Taft for urging the Cincinnati Symphony Orchestra to perform Leopold Mozart's "Beagle Symphony" using live beagles. Only the last two concerned city as opposed to county government. During this same period, five editorials supported various charity drives. To summarize the problem, said the Charter director, "The newspapers show no discrimination, no superior knowledge—which they should possess."

Cincinnati's press, especially with regard to its reporting of local politics and government, satisfies neither party men nor councilmen nor citizens. Where and why does it fail? Its failure could best be viewed as a breakdown of the adversary system resulting from the following factors:

1) publisher bias
2) reporter bias
3) lack of reporter independence from local government
4) lack of reporter accuracy and skill

Both the *Enquirer* and the *Post and Times-Star* are biased, but in different ways. The *Enquirer* bias comes mostly from above, from the often ultra-conservative citizens board. *Post* bias comes somewhat more from below, though it is present at both ends of the hierarchy. It should be made very clear that editorial partisanship does not, in and of itself, represent what is meant here by bias. A paper may support Republicans on its editorial page and still give fair coverage to Democrats, so long as reporters are not pressured openly or otherwise to give prejudicial coverage to one side of any issue. The Los Angeles *Times* is said to be proof of this distinction.

Seven years ago, the *Enquirer* editorial page began printing all the "kook" letters that came in. Liberals canceled their subscriptions as liberal columnists all but disappeared. In 1965, Francis Dale, then president of the Ohio Bar Association, became the publisher. He instituted a new policy: no two letters from any one person were to be printed within thirty days, and preference was to be given to letters which opposed views taken in the editorials—encouraging controversy between newspaper and reader rather than among readers. This change did not make the *Enquirer* less conservative, but did make its policies less "irresponsible" from the liberal's point of view.

Since 1967, this editorial page trend seems to have continued; letters represent a variety of views, and both liberal and conservative columnists are carried. Observers expect the paper to carry out a careful policy regarding councilmanic endorsements, backing six Republicans, one Negro, Charterite Taft, and one "safe" coalition candidate.

Such a policy, though perhaps not overly "enlightened," is hardly likely to incite demonstrations from aggrieved liberals.

Whatever its editorial views on an issue, the editorial-page staff of the *Enquirer* has remained fairly independent of the rest of the paper. Indeed, *Enquirer* City Hall reporter Gilbert Sands has little but derision for the editorial writers, complaining that they "don't consult the source very much," usually taking statistics out of news stories or using "their own imagination. Once our editorial writers used some 'facts' out of the competition— which weren't accurate." Generally speaking, Sands concludes, editorials "usually aren't cluttered with too many facts."

Lack of editorial-staff pressure, however, does not prove an absence of news column bias. Taft noted in 1967 that to get a story into the *Enquirer*, he should ideally take it to the assistant city editor on a Sunday afternoon. "Fixed prejudices are less likely to take hold then."

Taft's dissatisfaction with news coverage in the papers had by 1969 caused him to pay for his own five-minute radio program each day, on WNOP in Newport, Kentucky, just across the Ohio River from Cincinnati. During the broadcast, he discusses current problems that he feels would not otherwise receive sufficient attention.

For the *Enquirer*, especially, ties with big business, via the citizens board, tend to reflect themselves throughout the news pages. As a Charter Research Institute report, prepared for the International City Managers Association, noted, "On the subjects touching private enterprise —for example, utility rates or off-street parking—newspapers have tended to handle the news gingerly. On the other hand, any hint of irregularities in the conduct of a city employee has usually been followed up thoroughly." Similarly, a good in-depth reporting job tends to occur "when a policy of interest to the management of the newspaper has been involved."

By 1969, party activities of the Republicans seemed also to be largely off-limits to reporters. It is widely known, for example, that Republican employees at City Hall are required to kick back two percent of their salaries for party campaign coffers, yet neither paper has ever said so.

When Coalition candidates question party practices of the council majority, they also find themselves quoted without comment. One candidate, attacking the proposal to charge students adult bus fares, attempted to determine a typical daily fare under the proposed rate hike. He called the appropriate transit official, received the information, then told the man he would be quoting the figures. At this point, the official became less certain of his figures, and ended by saying he really didn't know what it would cost a student to ride a bus from Clifton to Walnut Hills under the proposals his employers had submitted. The newspapers made no attempt to determine either the validity of the claim or what the cost would be—though it was certainly a matter of concern to many readers.

In matters of party activities, "digging" is equally discouraged. The facts behind the selection of City Manager Krabach were never discussed, though the papers themselves were well aware that their information on his selection had not yet been provided to some of the councilman who were supposed to do the voting.

Big business and the status quo find another friend at the *Post*, though the editorial page situation is quite different. This paper runs canned Scripps-Howard editorials. For local editorials (which appear rarely), there is no fixed staff responsibility; the announced system as of 1967 was a "joint effort overseen by (then Editor-in-Chief) Richard Thornburg." This means that *Post* editorial writing is not automatically in the hands of only one group and independent of the rest of the news staff. The bias, which favors the Right as at the *Enquirer*, tends to come from below as well. When Taft wants to get even an important story into the *Post*, he must take it to Thornburg (or his successor as of 1969, Walter Friedenberg) personally. For a Republican, the situation is easier to handle. Party activities of Republicans are well covered, the Democrats get coverage by making controversial statements, and Charter—bi-partisan and, until autumn of 1969, independent of the Democrats—had to come to the paper. Since the Coalition, minority candidates have found that prepared press releases are printed, and their remarks, especially when controversial, quoted. Laments Thomas Brush, "A candidate could say absolutely anything, about any subject, and his remarks would not be challenged—just published. I would like—and expect—reporters to be a little more probing." As the Democratic-Charterite coalition fights what it considers to be a battle for two-party government and against destruction of the city-manager form of government, the *Post* City Hall reporter, Leo Baron, and other newsmen, reportedly come to the Coalition candidates complaining that "there are no issues; why don't you bring out some issues?" Says one candidate in disbelief, "They just don't understand that the issue is the danger that goes with one-party domination."

Both papers deny any conscious bias. Leo Hirtl, City Editor of the *Post* and respected as a capable reporter himself, denied in 1967 that "policy" affected him in any way. In fact, he protests too much: "We just diligently avoid discussing what policy might be." He adds, "I know the politics of *one* reporter." To an observer, it would seem that if he is that unaware of reporter bias and policy requirements, he needs more information in order to do his job. *If* there is no pressure, why avoid mentioning editorial-page preferences? A city editor should know his reporters' biases in order to avoid sending a John Bircher out to interview a pacifist or an ACLU faithful to a DAR meeting.

According to one observer of the 1969 councilmanic

race, "Hirtl likes people to come to him, not to the reporters, with information." This puts him in the position of assigning stories according to reporter capabilities—which would seem to include their preferences and prejudices as well as newspaper experience.

In addition to the unadmitted or unconscious bias that leads them to cover Republicans more faithfully than Democrats or Charterites, *Post* staff members also suffer from the familiar Scripps-Howard style of "squeezing" news stories into tiny summaries and, as one disgruntled Cincinnatian observes, dispersing them among "sob stories."

City Hall does receive attention from both papers, though its quality and quantity depend upon the individual beat men. Gilbert Sands, long the *Enquirer* beat man, seems fair and tries to be, stressing that "I don't go out of my way to put anybody's name in the paper," though the "minority bloc is always the more vociferous." Sands has been offered the chance to work as a press agent, but prefers to retain the confidence of all the councilmen. He is extremely proud that he is frequently allowed to attend "executive sessions" of the council. Sands' biases, though sometimes evident in his reports, seem to be largely unconscious.

In 1967, the *Post*'s long-time City Hall man was Charles Rentrop. Unlike Sands, he was not popular with minority party councilmen. At one time, he served as press agent for former Mayor Donald Clancey while Clancey was at once mayor and a candidate for Congress. Rentrop therefore was faced with the task of doing an objective reporting job, as council reporter, on a man who was paying him to make news. Rentrop's pets were not only Republican councilmen; several years ago he reportedly tried to push the council into making the then-assistant director of the Board of Health its new director. Said Charterite Taft, head of the relevant council committee, "Over my dead body!" A man was brought in from out of town for the job, but Board of Health people were still so

angry with Rentrop that the *Post* had to assign another
reporter to cover Board of Health news—the staff there
refused to speak to him.

By 1969, the *Post* had a new City Hall man, Leo Baron.
His style resembles that of Sands: fairly accurate reporting
of what happened in meetings, but no additional
information or interpretation reflecting any investigative
efforts. Baron's wife is head telephone operator at the
County Court House—a political jobholder. Baron himself has been described by one council candidate as an
"old political hack." He has not, however, gained the
animosity once rather enjoyed by Rentrop.

Bias need not be as deliberate as Rentrop's to be significant. A lack of independence from the beat can have
equally deleterious effects. Both Rentrop and Sands were
on the City Hall beat continuously for well over twenty
years. As Republican Gradison has noted, "They have
been referred to as the tenth and eleventh councilmen."
As is Baron, they are "very knowledgeable. They write
much more accurately than the guys who replace them on
temporary assignment. Yet somehow, I detect a certain
lack of flair." They are experienced—and jaded. They do
not dig. They do not investigate. Sands himself has
explained that he confines his contact with councilmen to
covering committees, talking to them while they are at
City Hall, and occasionally calling them. He never visits
their offices outside City Hall, even if they are close by.

Even the papers have recognized this lack of freshness as
a problem. The city editor of the *Post* analyzes the system:
"Tenure gives the beat man an extraordinary number of
sources, but it also has a flaw. A beat man who stays a long
time tends to identify himself with the beat. . . . Perhaps
changing of the guard would be the best method." It gives
the reporter a chance to "refresh his mind—see new stories." Hirtl would favor changing every five or six years,
but is frankly "afraid of rocking the boat too much" and
so rationalizes, "Our beat men all are successful; all held
other beats and were successful on them."

The City Hall men themselves vehemently oppose the rotation method. Said Sands, "It would be a bum move. All my experience and contacts and the way I know my way around" would be wasted. Rentrop was proud of being able to "correct the councilmen"—and there is a kind of power in being so experienced and so well known.

Charter Research Institute disagrees. "A weakness of Cincinnati coverage is the fact that City Hall reporters remain on assignment so long they begin to feel wiser than is consistent with thoroughly objective reporting. This tendency is reinforced by the deference accorded them by councilmen and presiding officers." Perhaps it is this tenure and deference, more than initial bias, which cause a City Hall reporter to try to "run City Hall." At any rate, objective viewing of the stories of the three men suggests that while they know everything that regularly occurs, they do not seek the unusual, the depth necessary if the public is to understand the significance of actions taken by city government. They are too much a part of the world they report to view the councilmen as adversaries whose actions need to be explained and reported— whether the councilman in question favors such coverage or not.

Perhaps much of this failure is due to a lack of investigative reporting. Neither Sands, Rentrop, nor Baron engages in such activities. The *Enquirer* tends increasingly toward specialization, which should be a healthy trend if good reporters consistently cover various stories concerning one general issue (again, assuming that there is eventual rotation). The *Post* still uses a pool system for most beats, so that a man reporting welfare today may be covering the Board of Education or Chamber of Commerce tomorrow. Hirtl is proud of this, believing, "Everybody is an investigative reporter. A good reporter is a good reporter, period."

In practice, this is a difficult system. The rate of turnover is very high at both papers, and so staff men "don't really know a great deal about the town," according to one councilman. If they are constantly switched from one area to another, they also know little of the background on any given topic. Taft has noted that it is possible to read two stories and not recognize that both deal with the same event if one is written by a good specialist (two of the best in 1967 were the *Enquirer*'s Margaret Josten, welfare writer, and Emil Dansker, "Progress and Aviation"), and the other by reporter X who got sent to do a "think piece" on department Y today. One young *Post* reporter finds the pool system "great for a young reporter who needs experience—but in a few years I'll want to specialize, become an expert. When that time comes, I guess I'll move on to another newspaper."

In one area (outside its usual beats), the *Post* does specialize, at least sporadically. It has done exposés on city and county issues. These might have been an attempt to cope with *Enquirer* superiority in in-depth coverage of such current topics as the War on Poverty. In some cases, as with a 1967 Probate Court investigation, the crusades, though sensationalized, are in large part accurate. Unfortunately, sometimes they are not.

A memorable instance of crusading without a legitimate need occurred in the coverage given by both papers to the "Crime Commission" of 1967. The Commission was a publicity stunt launched by a clever Republican councilman named John ("Jake") Held, who got lots of credit, day after day, week after week, for heading a "commission" that did absolutely nothing but hold up selection of a new Police Chief for a month, infuriate various portions of the community, rehash old ideas on crime, and spend $30,000 during the discussions.

Sometimes this failure to check facts or question motives reaches mammoth proportions. A young man named Chester Cruse, campaign manager for the local Republicans in the previous councilmanic election, was announced as a council candidate in 1965 because of his "phenomenal work in the campaign." The Western Hills *Press* printed his biography, and it was duly reprinted by both dailies. According to it, he had organized Operation Doorstep, providing free inoculations and chest X rays for poor people. Not so: the program was initiated and carried out by women volunteers of the Board of Health, who called upon Cruse, as president of the Junior Chamber of Commerce, to provide them with male escorts for evening calls. The papers also said Cruse originated the Robert Taft Institute for Government Study. Actually, the Robert A. Taft Institute was founded by New England supporters of that staunch conservative; and the Cincinnati group, headed by a University of Cincinnati professor, wrote the Junior Chamber asking if any of them wished to take part, since Chamber people were involved in other cities. Seven months after the original letter was written, Cruse became president of the Junior Chamber and said yes, they were interested.

None of these inaccuracies was publicly challenged by the two groups involved, since they did not wish to earn the everlasting wrath of the Junior Chamber of Commerce. Instead, they called upon the Cincinnati Charter Committee to refute the published report. The Charter Committee, in large part a citizens' organization rather than a political party, thus served as a check on local government and on newspaper accuracy, even performing the watchdog function at times. A county auditor who several years ago negotiated a reappraisal contract with a Dayton, Ohio, firm has found Charter the only group to complain loudly that the contract is costing Cincinnati one million dollars more than it should according to the going rates. In a sense, Charter has been performing the adversary function, which has been largely neglected by the newspapers. Once the papers receive information about wrongdoings or controversies, they generally print it, because it will sell papers. But Charter is forced to do much of the preliminary investigating and error-catching. The years and the defeat of proportional representation have been hard on Charter; reformers in Cincinnati are—according to one of them—"pretty beaten down";

the original reformers of the Boss Cox era, "older and tireder." It is hard to get press support and hard to mobilize public opinion.

Even when a reporter is permitted to do an investigative piece on a controversial issue, the issue is all too frequently dropped after the initial story. Jerry White, considered one of the most independent *Enquirer* reporters, did a story several years ago on city purchasing policies. Neither the *Enquirer* nor the *Post* picked up the trail, and no action was taken to change the policies. Says one discouraged observer, "It was like hitting the great pillow; nothing happened. Silence is an effective way to stifle controversy." During the 1969 campaign period, White began to uncover failures and inequities in housing code enforcement. Several candidates picked up the issue, but it seemed to become a political cliché rather than a cause for action.

Failure to carry through a legitimate investigative discovery, as much as unquestioning trust of inaccurate hand-outs, can work to the advantage of unscrupulous men. The papers should know whom to ask for information to determine the accuracy of claims. The *Post*'s Hirtl, for example, can name three of the nine councilmen as men "who know what they know with great precision, whose ideas are always exactly stated. . . . You make friends with the people who know the general picture; you develop those who know the details. . . . Some councilmen have a reputation for honesty and accuracy—because they are honest and accurate."

Certainly this is a laudable formula for insuring that council news is accurate—just check facts with these knowledgeable men. Hirtl *talks* a good paper. Sadly, reporters simply have not done this. Councilman Gradison, one of the three men considered by Hirtl to be most reliable, has complained that often people make incorrect statements about subjects he is expert upon, and known to be expert upon, yet no one calls him to check the facts. Taft, another of the three, receives great verbal support from Hirtl: "Whenever he has something to say, we print it." Half the time he comes to them, the other half they go to him, according to the *Post* city editor. Yet Taft himself specifically describes the extreme difficulty he has had in getting any coverage at all in the *Post* unless he takes a prepared statement to the editor-in-chief.

Add to this no-check policy the inaccuracies that used to creep in because Charley Rentrop never wrote out a story but simply called it in by telephone, and it is perhaps surprising there were any accuracies in *Post* council stories at all. Sands does write stories out and delivers them to the *Enquirer*—doing his own legwork, he calls it—but investigation is left to the haphazard methods of staff men of widely varying ability.

It is interesting to attempt to separate the bad from the not-so-bad Cincinnati journalism on the basis of varying stands on "background only" material. The councilmen themselves differ on this, Gradison not upset by its occasional necessity (though he noted that many of the things he has told newsmen off-the-record they would already have discovered for themselves—and then been free to print—had they been alert), Taft avoiding it whenever possible. According to Taft, if anything not to be used is said at an *Enquirer* editorial conference, "You are absolutely safe." At the *Post,* however, in the days of Thornburg, the editor came "as a newsman, not a policy or editorial man." He looked for news; what a councilman said off-the-record would not be attributed to him, but it would often be printed. The new editor, Walter Friedenberg, evidently has carried on the tradition. After a particularly unpleasant confrontation among school board candidates recently, an agreement was made not to report the meeting's events. The *Post* did run an article on it anyway, incurring considerable wrath by its choice of a headline beginning "RACISM SURFACES . . . ." Such actions could represent a bit of nearly dormant adversary behavior, but are also extremely bad manners journalistically, and may lead to a refusal by candidates to invite the *Post* to background sessions, or exclusion of their reporters from private meetings.

As for the newsmen, Hirtl resents background information, saying, "I try to prevent anybody from saying anything off-the-record." He believes that people use the stipulation to "tie your hands," making reporters feel that they should not report something, even if they got it later from another source. It should be noted that almost all the reporters say they do print a story if another source releases it for publication.

Gilbert Sands does not agree with Hirtl. "I'll accept anything off-the-record," he says, noting that he might not get it at all otherwise. After getting it, he continues to work on the man, and usually manages to "worm it out some way" and get permission to print it. In any case, however, "If somebody gives me something in confidence, I respect that confidence."

Varying views on background information could suggest a difference in view of a journalist's responsibility. If a reporter is to be a proper adversary, understanding what is going on in government and reporting it clearly to the public, he must have background information to put events into context. A newsman who refuses to listen to facts which are not for immediate publication simply is not going to be sufficiently well informed about causes and developments to make clear to his readers the significance of a "public" event.

In those rare instances where the adversary system seems to have been operative in Cincinnati, the reporters have made use of all information available, both the released-for-publication and the for-background-only kind. Crusades, such as that on the Probate Court, often grow from "no-source" tips. When Gradison opposed the Republican organization and his four fellow Republican councilmen and voted with the minority councilmen to defeat Police Chief Stanley Shrotel's bid for the city managership several years ago, reporter Mike Maloney quietly collected the relevant information, both underground political murmurings and public votes, and told all of Cincinnati how Gradison was standing against his party. Gradison, though committed to his dissent, admitted afterwards that he would have preferred to keep the whole thing quiet, but approved Maloney's actions while pointing out that they "stir up controversy." (Reflecting his acceptance of an adversary press, Gradison said he does his part—he does not compliment reporters on a good story, because he would then feel obliged to criticize them, too. He prefers to maintain a no-favors-either-side relationship.)

In a sense, of course, the adversary system depends on a newsman's integrity and independence, as when Sands refused to work as a behind-the-scenes press agent or when he tries to get off-the-record information released for publication, or when Jim Horner of the *Post* bucked advertisers and his own paper's Court House reporter (said to be one of the offending parties) and said that estate appraisers were receiving exorbitant fees and tended to be friends or relatives of probate judges. Horner could easily have accepted some of these plums and supported, by silence, the status quo.

The uneven level of local-government reporting and investigative work by the two newspapers may be just an unfortunate chance, but Gradison does not think so: "I assume it is a matter of policy." The papers could pay well enough to get good men for local reporting; since they do not, he feels that city-government reporting simply has low priority. Certainly, the money problem is important. Two of the best Cincinnati beat men covering local government in recent years, Mike Maloney and Bill Kegler, became a state senator (appointed originally by the Republicans after serving as one of their staff men) and a Kroger Company official, respectively. Young people may sometimes lack dedication, may be unable to resist the offers of well-paid jobs from big business or political parties, or may prefer to work for newspapers which stress political reporting. In any case, the papers tend to be left with someone who, according to Charter director Frank, "has made his peace with the management and is not likely to print what he knows are the facts."

The general lack of an adversary press in Cincinnati has been so long accepted as inevitable that one atypical instance of concerted adversary behavior, in the late summer of 1969, was greeted with as much shock as joy. Betsy Bliss, a young reporter for the *Enquirer,* prepared a series called "The Movers and the Shakers," which named the members of the Cincinnati power structure, described how they ran the town, and discussed their actions as viewed by city planners, educators, "little people," and other critics. The article on the movers in politics, head-lined "REPUBLICAN GRIP ON CITY NURTURED BY POWER ELITE," discussed the role of big businessmen in supporting and determining policy for the Republicans; quoted a critic saying "Big business has been trying to destroy the Charter reforms for years"; allowed reformer Murray Seasongood a number of damaging comments, including that big businessmen "like bossism—because they like to get things done, and it's easier when you don't have to bother with elective processes"; defined the long-range rather than day-to-day control exerted over government officeholders; and discussed Charter-Democratic views on the improper handling of the new stadium and the selection of City Manager Krabach. Seasongood was even quoted comparing today's situation with that of the Twenties—finding many similarities—all this in front of the whole world.

Why did Francis Dale, himself owner of the Cincinnati Reds and a member of the Establishment, run such a series? The Democratic Newsletter in October, a month after the series, agreed with the information in the series, and wondered, "A Republican newspaper was forced to tell the story like it is. Why?" Does this represent a start toward the kind of real adversary press Cincinnati needs to police and improve a Republican-dominated city government?

Most observers, unhappily, think not. A number of explanations have been offered. Francis Dale is, after all, a small-town boy with a strong moral sense; did he feel a responsibility to tell the people what was happening, perhaps to warn them? Probably not, say the nonconservatives. Mr. Dale is a conservative who believes in big business and its powers for good.

What then? Some say the refusal of council to accept the large scoreboard planned for the new stadium—which would have required all advertising to be sold by a wholly owned subsidiary of the *Enquirer;* in choosing the small scoreboard instead, they cost him prestige and money. Yet this does not seem a sufficiently major issue.

The most likely explanation, then, is a more political one. Mr. Dale has reportedly been very interested in running for governor of Ohio; Governor James Rhodes and he are close friends. Many local Democrats believe that local Republicans refused to support Mr. Dale for governor, and that his brilliant "The Movers and the Shakers" series was designed in retaliation for that rebuff.

Whatever the cause, most observers believe the series to be an isolated, though extremely laudable, example of the power of the press. One observer, offering three possible explanations for the general failure of the press, sees the Bliss series as proof of one of them. According to him, lack of press adversary activity in Cincinnati could be due to any of these three factors:

1) They don't know their responsibilities;
2) They don't give a damn;
3) They are controlled by the business-political power structure.

If a newspaper like the *Enquirer* suddenly shows it possesses the knowledge and talents to prepare a series like "The Movers and the Shakers," when it has never shown these abilities before, then it seems likely it had the capability before but preferred not to use it—i.e., control. Mike Maloney certainly was capable of such adversary services; in 1967, every non-newsman questioned singled him out as an example of city-government reporters at their best. Yet never did he attempt anything so closely related to the power structure or political leadership of Cincinnati. Jerry White has shown similar ability, but never in such critical areas. Evidently, the *Enquirer,* at least, understands the techniques and power of an adversary press.

In the past, Cincinnati has fared well even without such efforts. Its reformist history, deeply conservative leanings, and largely bi-partisan–insuring charter seemed to insulate it from the dangers of bossism and corruption. Since 1957, however, stepped-up party activity, and the increasing dominance of a single party, controlled not by elected officials but by party chiefs hovering in the background, have left the city far more vulnerable to graft. Minority councilmen, who no longer have that crucial sixth vote, have become so discouraged that often they do not try hard enough to get newspaper assistance and coverage. And the newspapers, except for that one magnificent lapse, have carefully avoided looking under the rug or even through the almost-closed door for the meat of a story or controversy.

Unless the newspapers change their priorities and loyalties, Cincinnati may soon lapse into bossism. As one Democratic leader is quoted as saying, in one of the Bliss articles, "The absence of debate on public issues is the most salient and most negative characteristic of Cincinnati's establishment. We not only have one completely dominant political party but also sympathetic media. When you have big business, a powerful party and the newspapers and broadcasting participating in the establishment, that's a closed system."

In a closed system, the little people are not kept informed, and power remains with the few. Such an atmosphere—which could not occur if Cincinnati had an adversary press—makes bossism possible.

Just how prevalent the sweetheart system of press-government relationships has become is indicated by an investigation made by David M. Rubin and Steve Landers:*

> Although the Robert Kennedy manuscript entitled "Thirteen Days, the Story About How the World Almost Ended," was easily the most expensive and publicized piece to appear in the November 1968 *McCall's* magazine, another article in that issue stirred up readers and newspaper editors from Maine to Washington, and occasioned a flood of queries, complaints, congratulations, and threats of legal action.
>
> The piece was critical of local water supplies in over a hundred United States cities, and it received widespread, bylined coverage from papers with circulations of from 3,000 to 200,000. Quite frequently national publications level charges of misconduct or inefficiency against individual cities, although rarely on so massive a scale. In such instances each local paper is charged with the responsibility of acting as either public defender or detective. A close study of the *McCall's* case indicates that, for a variety of reasons, papers acting as detectives were few, and investigative methods of local reporters were haphazard and incomplete.
>
> *McCall's* must shoulder part of the blame. The article, entitled "Drink At Your Own Risk," was ballyhooed on the cover, in the magazine's inimitable style, as "Danger In Our Drinking Water: The Alarming Truth About 102 U.S. Cities." It was based on United States Public Health Service (USPHS) data, collected between June 1967 and June 1968, which placed the water supplies of 102 cities in 32 states and Puerto Rico on the "Provisionally Approved" list. The USPHS had found these systems deficient in one or more of the following ways:

---

* David M. Rubin is a candidate for the Public Affairs Ph.D. in the Department of Communication at Stanford. He has written for *Columbia Journalism Review* and the San Francisco *Chronicle* and co-authored with William L. Rivers a study of the San Francisco Bay Area press for the Institute of Governmental Studies at Berkeley. Stephen Landers holds a Master's Degree in Journalism from Stanford, has worked for the Detroit *Free Press,* and is currently a freelance writer and part-time newspaperman.

Water quality was not completely protected from
supply to household tap;

Water was not being taken from the purest possible source;

Bacterial levels were too high;

Bacterial checks were too few;

Regulations to prevent health hazards were
inadequate;

Surveys to detect potential health hazards were
too infrequent;

Chemical impurities were too high;

Nonapproved analytical tests were being used.

Such a rating should inform the city that its supply is
potentially dangerous, if certain corrections are not made.

McCall's presented this information in a rather clever
10 x 13 inch chart (complete with skull and crossbones)
which encouraged readers to look for their city, and gasp
in alarm if they found it. The impression was left on many
citizens that the water they had drunk at dinner was about
to make them sick. This impression was false. The text
following the chart made clear that, in fact, all the named
systems were still safe, but they were dangerously stretch-
ing USPHS safety limits. *McCall's* title and layout tended
to obscure this.

Another problem arose because of poor communication
links between the USPHS, state health authorities, and
local authorities. Some state and local officials may not
have been aware of their "Provisional" status (which
demands corrective action based on a timetable accept-
able to local and USPHS officials). It is also quite possible that many mayors and newspaper editors were not
aware of their local system's problems, since it is not the
sort of thing a waterworks general manager is likely to
brag about.

The article was written at the request of *McCall's*
Norman Cousins by David Peter Sachs, a conservation
and pollution expert who has spoken widely in the San
Francisco Bay Area and was on the planning committee

for a 1969 environmental conference held in Washington, sponsored by the Consumer Protection and Environmental Health Service. Excluding the chart, the article focused on the nationwide problems of environmental deterioration and air and water pollution, as shown in decreasing margins of safety in public water supplies. Sachs also presented a course of corrective action open to concerned citizens. How many readers made it past the chart to this information is a moot point, but it is clear from a survey of local newspaper coverage in the 102 named cities that however much *McCall's* was guilty of sensationalism in its packaging, local editors were even more culpable for the disservice they performed their communities by non-reporting the actual condition of water supplies.

Rather than investigating why their supplies were on the USPHS's "Provisionally Approved" list, editors moved to obscure the data and protect their cities. Reporters collected batteries of denials from sources with vested interests in the issue, assured their readers that nothing was wrong with the water supply, and waded into *McCall's* with fists flying. The mistakes made by the magazine and Sachs (who failed to indicate on the chart precisely what "Provisional" status meant and that a few named cities might have come off the USPHS list in the lag time between compilation and the article's publication) gave editors a cozy out for their communities. The sad thing is that almost all of them took it.

Unquestionably, editors in the 102 cities recognized the potential importance of the article to their communities. Better than four-fifths of these papers carried at least one story on *McCall's* charges, and half ran two or more, often totaling up to sixty column-inches. Of those that carried the story, half played it on the front page and another quarter placed it on a page reserved for local news. Editors assigned trusted reporters to the story, usually a veteran general assignment man or the beat reporter who would normally cover the city's water supply. Although the Associated Press moved many stories about *McCall's* charges, nearly every city on the chart which elected to investigate the story did so with one of its own reporters, including tiny weeklies.

The spirit of coverage that resulted (including the wire copy) can be summed up in one word: hostile. This happened in part because of the defensive posture editors took in response to *McCall's* sensationalism, but more so because of the incomplete and plainly improper investigatory methods of reporters assigned to the story. By far, the sources most frequently contacted for comment were waterworks general managers and local elected officials (such as mayors, who may not have been aware of the "Provisional" status). In response to a mail questionnaire on this subject, 80 per cent of the editors indicated they approached such local sources, and those who did not went to state health department officials, who were only slightly less ego involved in protecting the reputation of the individual city systems. These officials naturally viewed the article as a threat to their jobs and a challenge to their competence, and reporters should have taken this into consideration. Few seemed to.

For example, the Spartanburg (S.C.) *Journal* (Daily, 11,500) quoted city waterworks General Manager John Andrea as follows: "The author is apparently unknowledgeable in the water supply field when his article hits at Spartanburg as having an unsatisfactory water supply. Spartanburg is known for its excellent quality of water and NO unsatisfactory rating has been given it by any health authority." The Topeka (Kan.) *Daily Capital* (Daily, 67,500) offered this from neighboring Salina's Superintendent of Utilities Ron Webster: "For this guy to pick on our water supply, I am inclined to think he doesn't know what is going on . . . I just can't see how some guy can come out and say something like this. This is the same water I drink, that I give my wife and kids— even my dog."

At the state level denials were more polite, but sources

talked around the USPHS "Provisional" rating, preferring to praise the local system, which appears to be what the editors were seeking. They also distorted the meaning of the *McCall's* article by stating emphatically that there was nothing wrong with the drinking water. They ignored how close their systems were to trouble, and reporters were content not to press it.

Dr. Hugh B. Cottrell, executive officer of the Mississippi State Board of Health, issued this statement to the Pascagoula *Mississippi Press* (Daily, 12,938): "The State Board of Health has always had the finest cooperation from local officials on matters pertaining to public health—and this business of water quality control is no exception. Mississippi municipalities (four were named on the chart) have a good record in this regard, and they are to be commended for their interest in public health." In a widely circulated AP story on the water supplies of four Wyoming cities, Director of the State Division of Environmental Sanitation Arthur E. Williamson said the *McCall's* article was part of a "scare campaign" by the USPHS to prompt Congressional action on a public water supply bill. The Sachs article did not mention such a bill. More important, the remark is irrelevant to explaining the "Provisional" rating of the Wyoming water supplies.

Most papers stopped their investigations at the state level. Only one in five editors said they contacted regional offices of the USPHS for clarification; one in eleven went to the USPHS in Washington, from which the figures originated; and one in five turned to local experts not connected with the city water supply for an outside opinion. The numbers contacting the author and *McCall's* editors were negligible.

The Spartanburg *Journal* was one of two papers that did speak with Sachs long distance on two occasions for over an hour. They discussed specifics of Spartanburg's problem, Sachs' background, and the more general national implications of the article. For its time and money the *Journal* produced a piece of only eleven col umn-inches which consisted largely of a statement by the local waterworks general manager. Nothing from Sachs' discussion of the situation was included.

The Nashville (Tenn.) *Tennessean* (Daily, 141,700) attempted to reach Sachs and *McCall's* editors, unsuccessfully, for a Sunday, November 3rd piece. The reporter parlayed this into a rather successful flank attack: "Efforts by the Nashville *Tennessean* and the Associated Press yesterday to locate the author of the article . . . failed. *McCall's* New York Office did not answer the telephone." What the *Tennessean* didn't point out was that *McCall's* failed to answer on a Saturday, when no one is in the office—it is hard to imagine they would be avoiding newspaper reporters anyway—and that the AP hunt hinted at was staged by the same *Tennessean* reporter. Two days after the article appeared, this reporter finally contacted Sachs' secretary, and after obtaining biographical information which was subsequently distorted in a November 5th story, informed the secretary that Sachs had already been "roasted" by his paper.

The *Tennessean* demonstrated its unwillingness to recognize the widespread problem of water pollution in an amusing (or disturbing) juxtaposition of articles on November 5. In one piece attacking *McCall's* they quote Howard Chapman, director of the Environmental Controls Administration in USPHS Region IV, which includes the entire state of Tennessee. He denied the existence of a local water problem. This article ran *side-by-side* with an AP piece out of Chattanooga concerning the death of five cows. It seems the cows were poisoned by ammonia nitrogen from the same creek which feeds the city's water supply. It might have been interesting to hear Chapman's comments on this situation, since Chattanooga was also named on *McCall's* chart.

The Clarksville (Tenn.) *Leaf-Chronicle* (Daily, 10,600) picked up some of the *Tennessean's* material on the unsuccessful effort to reach *McCall's* and Sachs, incorporating it into its own bylined story. On November 8 the Jackson (Miss.) *Clarion-Ledger* (Daily, 55,200) ran *word-*

for-word the story which appeared on November 6 in the Pascagoula *Mississippi Press*. Considering the uniformly poor coverage, is it unreasonable to expect the press to undertake independent investigations?

The general approach most papers took to *McCall's* charges was one of obfuscation. After presenting the heated denials from local and state officials, most reporters did dig into the recent history of the city's water supply, noting any warnings it received or problems encountered. By reading between the lines, and sometimes the lines themselves, it became evident that most water officials were aware that the charges were indeed problems in their own systems which they were trying to remedy. But the officials obviously did not like the publicity, so the admissions were smokescreened with praise for the overall waterworks operation. This left the reader confused as to the veracity of the USPHS data, the quality of the local system, and the magnitude of national water pollution problems.

Reporter John Hughes of the Aberdeen (Wash.) *Daily World* (Daily, 17,000) teased admissions from two city officials that the Hoquiam, Washington, water supply was indeed rated "Provisional," and that an April inspection had produced six recommendations for upgrading the system. His story closed with this statement from an official of the local health department: "The article made some good points about water pollution on the East Coast. But the insinuation was that the people of the Pacific Northwest are drinking polluted water. And that's simply not true." By exploiting *McCall's* sensational approach, the newspaper was leading Washington readers astray. Safety margins had fallen dangerously low in Hoquiam, yet editors, reporters, and officials were cooperating to keep away from a discussion and investigation of the "Provisional" status. Unless they had read the *McCall's* piece for themselves, residents of Hoquiam would have no way of knowing that the USPHS was concerned about margins of safety, not raw sewage flowing from the household taps.

In the last two inches of an eight-inch story, the New London (Conn.) *Day* (Daily, 33,500) notes that the city does not have adequate bacteria checks on its supply, a fact appearing on the chart. It is hoped New Londoners read that far.

Maggie Jones, staff writer for the Wilmington (N.C.) *Star* (Daily, 20,000), spent much time in statistical manipulations trying to disprove some HEW figures appearing in the *McCall's* article. Miss Jones, who spoke only to Wilmington City Manager E. C. Brandon and Director of Public Waterworks Robert Coleman, might not have sounded so much like a public relations woman if she had spent less time attacking *McCall's* and more time following up the admission by Coleman that bacteria counts in Wilmington water have been high.

The Abbeville (S.C.) *Press and Banner* (Weekly, 3,000) went perhaps the farthest astray in its attempts to befog the issue and befuddle the readers. "Air pollution is also brought up in the article," wrote Joy W. Bolen, "but there are no statistics given on the pollution rate for the 100 cities." (There was nothing on garbage disposal either, although this apparently did not bother Miss Bolen.) She continued, "There is no indication here that the smog of Los Angeles is looming over the city of Abbeville or that industrial wastes of Cleveland that empty into Lake Erie are making the city's (Abbeville) water unfit to drink."

Two papers did try to look past the sensational aspects of the article to problems with the local water supply and to show how these problems fit into the national picture. The Chattanooga (Tenn.) *Daily Times* (Daily, 56,700) reassured her readers that there was little immediate danger from the drinking water, but coverage went much farther. On November 10 the paper editorialized: "The publicity (about the water supply) has not been wholly injurious. It has alerted Chattanooga area citizens to very serious pollution along several small streams which empty into the Tennessee River upstream from the City Water Company's intake. It also brought to light the fact that in one instance at least the water company was forced to order additional treatment elements to counteract excessive pollution in the river. Public concern over stream pollution has been measurably heightened here in the past week. This is the first step toward enforcement of existing controls and enactment of more effective prohibitions against stream pollution."

Times City Hall reporter Springer Gibson followed this with a hard-hitting article under the head "No Reduction in Pollution." He wrote, "We rush around crying foul against the *McCall's* article questioning our water supply. And the City Water Co. assuredly is careful to give us safe water to drink. But the Chattanooga *Post* proved to us in pictures and words that we are fouling the waters of the Tennessee River and the tributary, Chickamauga Creek, before it empties into the Tennessee. Even if our water supply were not remotely involved, are we going to keep on permitting our streams and rivers right here in Chattanooga to be fouled with wastes?"

While the Chattanooga *Times* and *Post* choose to use the *McCall's* piece as a base for investigating general river and stream pollution in their area, the Worcester (Mass.) *Evening Gazette* (Daily, 94,500) and *Telegram* (Daily, 62,700) launched a full-scale investigation of the city water supply. An October 22nd article in the *Evening Gazette* reported that state laboratories and city laboratories were differing greatly in the measurement of the bacteria count in Worcester's water. An article on the 23rd revealed that five testing stations were repeatedly showing high bacteria counts because the water was fed to them through old mains. A *Telegram* editorial of the 23rd stated, "There is no getting around the fact that the controversy has brought to light potential hazards in Worcester's water system."

On October 25, a Massachusetts State Health Department official called for a "complete evaluation" of the water supply to check on a coliform group of bacteria which had been discovered; he labeled the supply "suspect" as a disease carrier. And on December 17 the *Gazette* announced that "Worcester's water system is being treated with an extra supply of chlorine on a year-round basis to help keep down non-harmful bacteria counts."

How much of this action is attributable to the work of *Gazette* reporters Theodore Mael and Louis Salome and how much credit is due Worcester city officials is hard to say. But there is no doubt that the forthright manner in which both the Worcester and Chattanooga papers responded to criticism from a national publication was in the best journalistic tradition.

Before passing from papers which covered the *McCall's* piece in exemplary fashion, it should be pointed out that other papers, such as the Grand Junction (Colo.) *Sentinel* (Daily, 21,500), which treated the *McCall's* piece in cavalier fashion, had been doing a steady, competent job of reporting on water pollution. If papers as a group were serving as more efficient watchdogs, however, local water supplies would not be dropping so precipitously in quality.

A number of suggestions have been made along the way which editors might keep in mind the next time their city is the object of attention from a national publication. First, they must avoid the attitude of Will Fehr, City Editor of the Salt Lake City (Utah) *Tribune* (Daily, 188,000), who said: "If we have to rely on a national magazine for guidance, we should start laying our heads on the editorial chopping block." There may be valuable lessons to be learned from an outsider assessing the problems in another area. The local paper may often be too close to the problem for an objective assessment.

It isn't as if editors don't realize the best way to handle such stories. Half the editors of papers involved with the *McCall's* story were asked how they *would* handle a hypothetical story in a national magazine based on United States Office of Education data charging that the quality of public school education in their city was deficient. Nearly 90 per cent said they would give the story at least moderate play; 87 per cent said they would be likely to editorialize on the issue; 36 per cent said they would do an in-depth job of investigative reporting; and 80 per cent said they would at least present a balanced story with quotes from varied sources.

The *McCall's* experience shows national publications that sensationalizing an article is not necessarily the most effective way to get a message across. In this instance, local editors were able, in good conscience, to correct the misimpression created, while never getting at the very real problems of declining water safety margins.

Clearly the vast majority of papers erred in giving sole prominence to officials who were actors in the situation—from whom the newspapers had no right to expect straight answers. Yet many were content to act as an uncritical conduit for the remarks of such officials. A state public health official's statement to the Manchester (Ga.) *Mercury* (Weekly, 2,450) that a plant was "neat and clean" and that "the City of Manchester should be complimented for having operators who take such interest in their work" cannot be allowed to stand as the final word; such statements completely beg the questions posed in *McCall's*, as did much of the coverage. Such sources as local water pollution experts, unaffiliated with the treatment plant, should have been contacted for their opinion. Efforts should have been made to interview the USPHS in Washington, and perhaps the author, if further information was needed.

Rather than respond, as many Wyoming papers did, with charges that the article was hurting the image of the area for industries seeking to relocate or expand, editors might have taken the opportunity, as the Chattanooga *Post* did, to investigate existing pollution from industrial wastes, before inviting more.

Most important, a newspaper editor should remember that to shield his community and readers from outside criticism is a dangerous practice. In a period of increasing media combination and concentration, editors should welcome every voice in the wilderness.

CHAPTER SIX

When Government Controls (United States)

I think the inherent right of the government to lie—to lie to save itself when faced with nuclear disaster—is basic, basic.

—ARTHUR SYLVESTER

Is the public interest best served when the press and government stand on opposite pedestals and snipe at each other across a mythical abyss? I think you will agree that the answer is "No"—and that journalism as well as government is aware of the need for something more.

—ROBERT MANNING

It is true that the Constitution established a free press and made no provision for a government information system. It is also true that the tightly controlled party press of the early period of the United States government is no more. But it is not true that all of the modern press is free to range itself against officialdom in an adversary position.

There is more to this than the secret decisions, the closed meetings, the pressures on journalists, and the huge apparatus of government publicity already described. Although there is no government *newspaper* in the sense of a conventional daily which seeks to inform and entertain a varying audience, hundreds of *newsletters* are issued from local, state, and federal offices. They are specialized, usually touting the accomplishments of an agency, a program, or an official, but so many of them carry facts as well as self-serving information that they are potent. The important matter is that they avoid the brokerage system represented by the press—in which journalists have an opportunity to evaluate and check up on government information—and go directly to millions

of Americans. In addition to this the hundreds of broadcast programs produced by government agencies and officials, and the
publications issued by groups which have a commercial stake in
continuing government programs—Chamber of Commerce publications and the like at the local level, the magazines and newsletters of defense industries nationally—make it clear that the voice
of government is stentorian.

It is an especially loud voice for the millions of overseas
Americans, who are likely to have to rely on the military information system whether they have any military connection or not.
The lure of news from the United States—any news—is quite
strong. Those who want to hear an American voice or radio or see
an American face on television must rely on the radio and television stations established by American armed forces. To read an
American newspaper, many overseas Americans must turn to the
papers published by the local American military post. All this
means that the Armed Forces News Bureau (AFNB) in Arlington,
Virginia, has a hand in informing overseas Americans. Often, it is
a heavy hand, packaging news for 1,500 troop and ship newspapers and 300 military broadcasting operations so as to please the
Pentagon.

So far, the proud European and Asian editions of *Stars
and Stripes*, which are headed by military men but staffed primarily by civilians, have resisted most of the pressures from AFNB.
As *Newsweek* pointed out, "Despite a certain tapioca blandness,
Stripes has traditionally filled an editorial function almost all
other armed forces newspapers avoid like KP—the publication of
serious domestic and foreign news supplied by the two major
United States wire services."

This tradition seemed on its way out in January 1967,
when the AFNB director moved to bring to his headquarters in
Arlington the eight *Stars and Stripes* editors in New York who
send domestic news to the *Stripes* editions in Germany and Japan.
This would have enabled AFNB to select and edit the news
Stripes receives from the United States. But *Stars and Stripes* staffers want to preserve what independence they have. One said
flatly, "The new AFNB center will furnish sterilized news." He
and his protesting colleagues were no doubt thinking of "Galley

Guide," a monthly set of instructions to editors under AFNB control. The "Guide" of the previous month had carried a front-page item on editorials which held: "Steer clear of controversial subjects on which there may be a wide divergence of opinion. An editorial doesn't have to be a bombshell to attract reader interest. . . . ." They may also have been thinking of the newly named deputy director of AFNB, Air Force Lt. Colonel William Coleman. As deputy editor of European *Stars and Stripes* in 1966, he had killed an innocuous Associated Press analysis of Soviet leaders on the ground that, "It implied they were people in gray flannel suits like many Americans. In other words, it watered down the potency of the Communist threat." And even as AFNB was moving to bring *Stars and Stripes* under its control, Coleman was asking, by wire to Germany and Japan, that neither *Stripes* edition publish a long Associated Press feature on the Joint Chiefs of Staff. The feature revealed that Generals Curtis LeMay and Maxwell Taylor often became so "apoplectic" at each other that they refused to speak.

Forty-one *Stripes* editors protested the AFNB takeover attempt to Congressman John Moss. He promised to investigate, whereupon AFNB backed off. But the two *Stars and Stripes* editions have a circulation of more than 300,000, thanks in part to their degree of independence, and it is a real question whether they can continue their present course.

Government news control in a subtler form is evident in the continuing battle in the United States over free press–fair trial. Stated simply, this is an apparent collision of two Constitutional provisions. The First Amendment prescribes a free press. The Sixth Amendment prescribes a fair trial. The clear question is: If the press uses the full extent of its freedom to report and comment on the accused, is his trial fair?

It is not necessary to become embroiled in the current controversies which find the press and the bar in conflict in several states to consider this issue. It is much older than it sometimes appears to be, dating, in fact, from the star-chamber proceedings in Europe of centuries ago in which those accused were often arrested, tried, and sentenced in secret. In the United States, the issue began to reach a wide public when Bruno Richard Haupt-

mann, a carpenter, was charged with the kidnaping and murder of
the infant son of Charles Lindbergh. Because Lindbergh was a
national hero—the first pilot to fly the Atlantic alone—the Hauptmann trial was front-page news and was reported in a highly emotional atmosphere. Hauptmann was convicted and executed. Perhaps for the first time, a famous journalist, Walter Lippmann,
stated the case for government control of such proceedings:

> We are concerned with a situation spectacularly illus-
> trated in this case, but typical of most celebrated criminal
> cases in the United States, which may be described by
> saying that there are two processes of justice, the one
> official, the other popular. They are carried on side by
> side, the one in courts of law, the other in the press, over
> the radio, on the screen, at public meetings—and at every
> turn this irregular popular process interferes with, dis-
> torts, and undermines the effectiveness of the law and the
> people's confidence in it.
>
> Because there are two pursuits of the criminal, two
> trials and two verdicts—the one supposed to be based on
> the law and a thousand years of accumulated experience,
> the other totally irresponsible—the self-appointed detec-
> tives get in the way of the regular detectives, the self-
> appointed judges and jurymen and advocates for the pros-
> ecution and defense get in the way of the officers of the
> law, and the official verdict becomes confused with the
> popular verdict, often in the court itself, almost always in
> the public mind.
>
> We can examine the problems best, I think, by examin-
> ing a few concrete instances. Hauptmann was arrested on
> September 20, 1934, and within a week there was a head-
> line in a New York paper saying that "clues build iron-
> clad case against Bruno, police claim," and a few days
> later it announced that "twelve men and women selected
> at random" by a reporter had decided, according to the
> headline: "BRUNO GUILTY BUT HAD AIDS, VERDICT OF MAN
> IN STREET."
>
> Here we find that the police, unless the newspaper was
> lying, which I doubt, made an appeal to the public to

believe their evidence before that evidence had been submitted to a court of law. That was an interference by the police with the lawful process of justice. It is for a jury to determine whether a case is "iron-clad," and since juries have to be selected from the newspaper-reading public, such a positive statement on the authority of the police is deeply prejudicial. I do not for a moment think that Hauptmann was innocent. But that does not alter the fact that he had a right to be tried before a jury and to be tried nowhere else. Because he was tried in two places at once, thousands of persons came to believe that he was not tried fairly. But in the administration of justice it is highly important not only that the right verdict should be reached, but that the people should believe that it has been reached dispassionately.

In the two headlines I have cited, and you will recognize them as being by no means exceptional, we see the police rendering a verdict on their own evidence and a newspaper establishing a verdict among the potential jurors.

Let us pass to the trial in Flemington. It had, of course, to be a public trial. But if it was to be a reputable trial, it had also to be a trial in which the minds of the judge, the jury, the lawyers, and the witnesses all concentrated on the evidence, were as little influenced as possible by excitement or prejudice. The courtroom at Flemington is said to have a maximum seating capacity of 260 persons. On January 2, according to the New York *Times,* the constables on duty admitted to an already overcrowded courtroom—275 spectators without passes. A few weeks later it was learned that attorneys for both sides were issuing subpoenas to favored friends in order to force their admission as spectators in the courtroom, more than a hundred having been issued for one day's session. The authorities permitted the installation of telegraph wires in the courthouse itself, and one of the telegraph companies alone had to have a hundred men on hand. Although it was forbidden to take pictures during the trial, pictures were taken, and the authorities took no action.

Now there is no use pretending that a case can be tried well in an overcrowded courtroom with every actor knowing that every word he speaks, every intonation of his voice, every expression of his face, will instantly be recorded, transmitted to the ends of the earth, and judged by millions of persons.

This brings us to the actual trial of the case outside the courtroom. As a sample from the press, we may take a report, in which it is said that Hauptmann on the stand "made senseless denials" and he was described as "a thing lacking human characteristics." This, let us not forget, was during his trial and before the jury had rendered its verdict. We should not delude ourselves into thinking that comment of this sort is of no effect simply because the jury is locked up and is not allowed to read the papers. The witnesses read them, the spectators read them, and no newspaper man needs to be told that the sentiment of a crowd communicates itself more or less to everyone. There is no way to isolate a jury in such a way as to protect it from the feeling of the crowd.

We have next to consider the conduct of the lawyers. They began trying the case in the newspapers almost from the day of Hauptmann's arrest. The counsel for the defense, Mr. Reilly, appeared in the newsreels two days after his appointment and declared his belief that Hauptmann was innocent. A few days after the opening of the trial he announced to the press that he would name the kidnapers and that they were connected with the Lindbergh household. Two weeks after the trial, while the case was set for appeal, he addressed the Lions Club of Brooklyn and denounced the verdict, and the next day he addressed a mass meeting at which, during the course of his speech, the crowd booed Colonel Lindbergh.

Hauptmann himself issued newspaper statements during the course of the trial, the statements being given out by his lawyers. The prosecution also tried the case in the newspapers. On January 3, Mr. Wilentz said at his press conference that Mrs. Lindbergh's testimony would be "loaded with importance"; on January 22, he told a reporter that he would "wrap the kidnap ladder around Hauptmann's neck," and so on and so on.

Finally, we cannot omit the Governor of New Jersey, who, on December 5, 1935, while the case was still pending before the Supreme Court of the United States, let it be known that he was conducting his own investigation. I do not criticize him for that. The governor of a state has a right and, I think, an obligation to satisfy himself that justice has been done in his state. But the governor, who is a member of the New Jersey Court of Pardons, a quasi-judicial body, proceeded to try the case not before the court but in the newspapers. On December 8 his investigators let it be known that rail 16 of the ladder had, in their opinion, been planted against Hauptmann, and the governor was quoted as saying that he thought so, too. He also gave his opinion about fingerprints and was reported as saying that his personal investigator was "convinced that Hauptmann is not the man."

Lippmann's account makes it clear that the press is far from alone in trying criminals on the front pages. Indeed, he emphasized, "without the connivance of the regular officers of the law, the abuses of publicity would have been reduced to manageable proportions." The opposing attorneys "by their public statements violated No. 20 of the Canons of Ethics of the American Bar Association." Nonetheless, the press was blamed. In 1937, two years after the Hauptmann trial, the American Bar Association passed Canon 35, which sought to ban photographers and electronic media (meaning chiefly radio, at that time) from the courtroom. In 1952, when television had become strong, it, too, was banned by Canon 35.

Another pivotal event occurred in Cleveland in 1954—the trial of Dr. Samuel Sheppard. The case had all the elements of high drama: Dr. Sheppard was a handsome young osteopath accused of the brutal murder of his lovely young wife. The family was prominent. There was another woman. A mysterious man was alleged to have been in the house on the murder night.

Many of the patterns of the Hauptmann case were repeated. Hordes of reporters and photographers descended on

Cleveland. Information was leaked. Notes were passed to reporters by the accused. Lawyers talked. Self-styled crime experts analyzed the evidence, even added evidence, in public print. Biographies of the accused were published and broadcast. The photographic coverage was extensive. The sex element was played big, and the crime was described in gruesome detail.

There was, of course, wild variation in the way the story was disseminated. As Alan Gould, then executive editor of the Associated Press, pointed out: "You put a crime-and-sex story in the hands of 1,700 editors and you get every color in the spectrum. . . . Some papers are playing it big, with all the trimmings, photos, sidebars, purple phrasing. Others are dead-panning in the writing, but keeping the story on page one. Still others are keeping it inside. There is evidence that a few are ignoring it entirely, or nearly so. To the majority, it's a good news story—but only colossal, as they say in Hollywood."

Dr. Sheppard was convicted and sentenced to life in prison. Then, in 1966, after he had served ten years, the Supreme Court ruled that the "carnival atmosphere" of the 1954 trial had deprived Dr. Sheppard of his Constitutional rights. In an opinion written by Mr. Justice Thomas Clark, the Court held:

A responsible press has always been regarded as the handmaiden of effective judicial administration, especially in the criminal field Its function in this regard is documented by an impressive record of service over several centuries. The press does not simply publish information about trials, but guards against the miscarriage of justice by subjecting the police, prosecutors, and judicial processes to extensive public scrutiny and criticism.

The Court has therefore been unwilling to place any direct limitations on the freedom traditionally exercised by the news media for "what transpires in the courtroom is public property." But the Court has also pointed out that "legal trials are not like elections to be won through the use of the meeting-hall, the radio and the newspaper."

There can be no question about the nature of the publicity which surrounded Sheppard's trial.

Nor is there any doubt that this deluge of publicity reached at least some of the jury . . . . The court's fundamental error is compounded by the holding that it lacked power to control the publicity about the trial. From the very inception of the proceedings the judge announced that neither he nor anyone else could restrict prejudicial news accounts, and he reiterated this view on numerous occasions.

Since he viewed the news media as his target, the judge never considered other means that are often utilized to reduce the appearance of prejudicial material and to protect the jury from outside influence. We conclude that these procedures would have been sufficient to guarantee Sheppard a fair trial and so do not consider what sanctions might be available against a recalcitrant press nor the charges of bias against the state trial judge.

The carnival atmosphere at the trial could easily have been avoided since the courtroom and courthouse premises are subject to the control of court. . . . Bearing in mind the massive pretrial publicity, the judge should have adopted stricter rules governing the use of the courtroom by newsmen as Sheppard's counsel requested. The number of reporters in the courtroom itself could have been limited at first sign that their presence would disrupt the trial. They certainly should not have been placed inside the bar. Furthermore, the judge should have more closely regulated the conduct of newsmen in the courtroom. . . .

Secondly, the court should have insulated the witnesses. . . .

Thirdly, the court should have made some effort to control the release of leads, information, and gossip to the press by police officers, witnesses, and the counsel for both sides. . . .

The judge should have at least warned the newspapers to check the accuracy of their accounts. . . .

The prosecution repeatedly made evidence available to the news media which was never offered in the trial. Much of the "evidence" disseminated in this fashion was clearly inadmissible. . . . The newspapers described in detail clues that had been found by the police, but not put into the record.

It is clear from all this that the Supreme Court held the trial judge chiefly responsible. But this should not be allowed to obscure the role of the news media. The Court cited the Cleveland *Press* for a vicious series of headlines and news accounts, and among the many prejudicial reports was a broadcast carried by station WHK in Cleveland in which Bob Considine likened Sheppard to a perjurer and compared the episode to Alger Hiss' confrontation with Whittaker Chambers.

The Supreme Court decided that Dr. Sheppard should be retried promptly or granted freedom. A retrial was held in November 1966 under closely controlled conditions, and Dr. Sheppard was found not guilty.

The chief result of this and similar cases has been much stricter supervision of court proceedings. If that were all, we might consider it a lesson well learned. Unfortunately, local law enforcement officials and judges in many areas were frightened or confused or both, and overreacted. In Phoenix, a judge suppressed the right of the media to report what occurred in open court. In Wake County, North Carolina, two Superior Court judges issued a rule concerning publicity and due process which suppressed virtually all police news. These and similar actions were fought successfully, but they illustrate a national tendency to take the Supreme Court's decision further than it was intended to go. Ironically, in attempting to preserve the defendant's rights by restraining the press, officials are endangering the Sixth Amendment itself. The reason for the guarantee of a fair trial springs from the bitter experiences of the colonists with star chamber proceedings, where closed courtrooms enabled officials to make capricious decisions.

Such considerations were so convincing that it seemed for a time that court trials might be opened to the machine media. In

Portland, Oregon, a presiding judge made news in 1954 when he permitted photographers to cover a sensational murder trial. He specified that no flashbulbs were to be used and that the photographers were not to move around the courtroom, but should remain in their reserved seats in the front row of the spectators' gallery. Each Portland paper took more than one hundred pictures, and parts of the trial were also filmed for later television broadcast. No one complained about the trial being disrupted in any way. The judge expressed his pleasure that the photography "was done honestly and decently without interrupting or bothering anyone."

The outlook for more such experimentation was bright. New engineering developments were making it possible to cover hearings, trials, and assemblies without disrupting them. Cameras had been developed which would take interior shots without flashbulbs, and cameramen had learned to restrict their movements as well as their equipment. The bar associations in most states were continuingly opposed, but news photographers and television cameramen found a convincing way to suggest that their machines could be unobtrusive. In state after state, members of the bar and representatives of the mass media would meet to discuss the issue, and only after the meetings were adjourned would the attorneys be told that cameras had recorded every minute of the meetings.

Then, in 1962, a swindler named Billie Sol Estes who had already been convicted in a federal court and sentenced to fifteen years in prison was tried in a state court in Texas on additional charges. Although Canon 35 of the American Bar Association was still in force, it is not law; and Judicial Canon 28 of the State Bar of Texas permitted news photography and radio and television broadcasting at the discretion of the trial judge. Estes' attorneys argued before the pre-trial hearing that television, radio, and news photography should be banned from the courtroom. But it was a case that attracted national attention, and the judge denied the motion. Estes was found guilty.

In 1965, the Supreme Court reviewed the case and reversed Estes' conviction. In a decision written by Mr. Justice Clark, the Court held:

> These initial hearings were carried live by both radio and television and news photography was permitted

throughout. The videotapes of these hearings clearly illustrate that the picture presented was not one of judicial serenity and calm to which petitioner was entitled. Indeed, at least twelve cameramen were engaged in the courtroom throughout the hearing taking motion and still pictures and televising the proceedings. Cables and wires were snaked across the courtroom floor, three microphones were on the judge's bench and others were beamed at the jury box and the counsel table. It is conceded that the activities of the television crews and news photographers led to considerable disruption of the hearings. Moreover, a venire of jurymen had been summoned and was present in the courtroom during the entire hearing but was later released after petitioner's motion for continuance had been granted.

. . . Pretrial can create a major problem for the defendant in a criminal case. Indeed, it may be more harmful than publicity during the trial for it may well set the community opinion as to guilt or innocence. Though the September hearings dealt with motions to prohibit television coverage and to postpone the trial, they are unquestionably relevant to the issue before us. All of this two-day affair was highly publicized and could only have impressed those present, and also the community at large, with the notorious character of the petitioner as well as the proceeding. The trial witnesses present at the hearing, as well as the original jury panel, were undoubtedly made aware of the peculiar public importance of the case by the press and television coverage being provided, and by the fact that they themselves were televised live and their pictures rebroadcast on the evening show.

When the case was called for trial on October 22, the scene had been altered. A booth had been constructed at the back of the courtroom which was painted to blend with the permanent structure of the room. It had an aperture to allow the lens of the cameras an unrestricted view of the courtroom. All television cameras and newsreel photographers were restricted to the area of the booth when shooting film or telecasting. Here, although there was nothing so dramatic as a home-viewed confession, there had been a bombardment of the community with the sights and sounds of a two-day hearing during which the original jury panel, the petitioner, the lawyers and the judge were highly publicized. The petitioner was subjected to characterization and minute electronic scrutiny. . . .

In a 5 to 4 decision, the Supreme Court ruled that Estes deserved a trial without such extravagant coverage by television. Mr. Justice Potter Stewart entered a vigorous dissent: "The suggestion that there are limits upon the public's right to know what goes on in the courts causes me deep concern. The idea of imposing upon any medium of communications the burden of justifying its presence is contrary to where I had always thought the presumption must lie in the area of First Amendment freedoms." The majority stopped short of the kind of ruling that would suggest to judges in lower courts that cameras are never welcome in any trial, but it is clear that the cause of electronic communication lost ground.

Considering the activities of the mass media during the Estes and Sheppard trials, it is not surprising that the outlook for resolving the free press–fair trial issue seems more distant than ever.

Everything points to stronger restrictions on law enforcement coverage by all the media. One might recall the occasions when reporters went wild and judge that restrictions will serve them right. But there should be sober second thoughts: Would a white civil rights worker arrested in rural Mississippi benefit if reporters for the wire services and wide-ranging papers like the New York *Times* were restricted in reporting what happens to him? And what of the fact that many a man who has been convicted of a crime has later been found innocent because a reporter was free to investigate the processes of justice? The real dangers have been spelled out by Nicholas Horrock, a reporter for the Baltimore *Sun* who holds that "prosecutors, police and other mechanics of the law enforcement business spend much of their time and effort now in endeavoring to conduct their business with as little public scrutiny as possible." Recalling his days as a cub reporter in New Jersey, Horrock told of the arrest of a Newark Negro for the rape of a suburban housewife. He and a veteran reporter were at the police station when the Negro was brought in at 2 A.M. Said the veteran: "Look around—do you see any lawyers—anybody from the ACLU? Sure you don't. You and I are it."

In short, protecting the right to a fair trial is an aspect of government control of information which seems laudable. And then on the other hand. . . .

Clearly, it is necessary for press and bar to work out rules for trial coverage in a spirit of accommodation. This will not be simple unless they approach the First and Sixth Amendments with the belief that both are designed to accomplish the same purpose. For surely the design of the First Amendment was to bring the truth to light. The design of the Sixth Amendment, opposing as it did secret court proceedings, was the same.

Government controls of another kind have been encroaching on another aspect of the freedom of the press in recent years, but it is likely that the public interest is well served by the encroachment. This is the area of commercial practices, and it is represented fairly typically by a successful suit under antitrust laws against monopolistic advertising by the Kansas City *Star*.

Perhaps the most important commercial case was brought under the antitrust laws against the Associated Press. The AP, which is cooperatively owned, had long protected its members by refusing to sell its service to their competitors. The new Chicago *Sun*, competing in the morning field with the Chicago *Tribune*, was unable to obtain AP service, and its suit became pivotal. The fact that the *Sun* supported Franklin Roosevelt against the Roosevelt-hating *Tribune* added emotional overtones. Robert Lasch described the struggle:

> Almost to a man, the publishers of America interpreted the filing of this action as a foul assault against the First Amendment, and with frightening unanimity exerted all their power to impress upon the public that point of view.

"We see in this, not the end perhaps, but surely the greatest peril, to a free press in America," said the Detroit *News*. From the citadel of its monopoly position in a city of 600,000, the Kansas City *Star* cried: "This is the sort of thing that belongs in the totalitarian states, not in a free democracy." "In the event of a government victory," said the New York Daily *News*," the press services of the United States will be under the thumb of the White House."

These were not extremist positions. They represented a fair sample of the opinion handed down by the press, sitting as supreme court, long before the government brought its case to trial and won the first round in the United States District Court of New York. The Associated Press proudly published a volume of the collected editorial judgments for the instruction of the country.

The country rode out the storm with equanimity. Dimly or otherwise, the people perceived that the newspapers, once again, had proved unable to separate their commercial privileges from their civil rights.

In retrospect, the press outcry seems a bit silly. The government won the case, the *Sun* got AP service, the White House did *not* put its thumb on the wire services, no newspaper was restrained or censored. The question was commercial: whether a news service could be withheld from some newspapers for competitive reasons.

The dangerous element in all this is that the press puts itself in the position of crying "Wolf!" when it is threatened by a rabbit. It helps neither public understanding of freedom of the press nor public respect for the First Amendment to associate them with problems of newsboys' pay or restrictive membership in a news service. It is not that the newspapers were wrong in fighting these issues, but there is considerable doubt whether they should have been fought on grounds of press freedom.

Now the press is fighting another battle with government encroachment. Again, the antitrust laws are pivotal. The question is whether, as the numbers of large metropolitan newspapers diminish, the remaining giants should acquire suburban papers in the same area. The Department of Justice has stepped into several such acquisitions, objecting that competition is diminished. It is not yet certain that the government will be able to establish guidelines for ownership to which the press must adhere, but magazine and book publishers are watching the developing battle between newspapers and government with keen interest and some fear that a formula may be established which will prevent wholesale acquisitions and mergers. Obviously, this is not so much a question related to historical concepts of freedom as to the press as a business institution. And the danger of a press controlled by conglomerates which have many interests that do not square with free information is obvious.

In 1967 certain elements of the press moved strongly to try to exempt some of their business practices from government regulation. This first took the form of the "Failing Newspaper Act," then the "Newspaper Preservation Act," which is still being debated in Congress. This would have the effect of giving newspapers freedoms from antitrust action which other businesses do not enjoy. What its proponents in the press may not realize is that if the bill becomes law, it will certainly work to their commercial benefit, but it may make the press vulnerable to laws of another kind which could restrict editorial freedom. This threat is likely to come from the growing sentiment for "right of access" legislation. Many groups, especially racial minorities, are demanding that the media grant them sure access to columns and programs so that their voices may be heard. They have the support of some thoughtful and civil libertarians, and there are not a few legislators and Congressmen who doubt that the media provide a full opportunity for a free marketplace of ideas. But the point is that if the press promotes its own special-interest legislation of the sort sought in the "Newspaper Preservation Act," it will be difficult for lawmakers to think of the press as anything but fair game for other kinds of legislation. If the press is so eager for legislation, in short, legislation will come flooding in.

The heart of the problem of government regulation of the media lies in broadcasting. This industry experiences most of the kinds of encroachment which are visited upon the other media, and more. Programs are frequently attacked for their "indecency" or their "political content." Broadcasting has long been a subject of antitrust actions. Congress takes a keen and continuing interest and from time to time has investigated broadcasting for alleged Communists, for monopoly, for violence in programs, for political prejudice in news coverage, and the ratings systems which help determine program schedules. The point of all this is that each threat to broadcasting is the stronger because the industry is under the continuing regulation of the Federal Communications Commission.

To understand the atmosphere of broadcasting, one must imagine newspapers, book publishers, and film companies as being required to obtain a federal license before going into business and to renew it—giving proof of good public service—every three years. Such a requirement would be intolerable, and it would be bitterly resisted as contrary to our concept of free communication and undoubtedly in violation of the First Amendment.

The chief problem, of course, is that there are too few channels; or, more correctly stated, too few *desirable* channels. When broadcasters choose their own, as they did in the early 1920's, they cluster around the same channels, and the air becomes so filled with competing sounds that listeners often hear only a cacophony of squeals and distorted programs. Moreover, entertainment broadcasters are not alone in using the air. The military, the police, the transcontinental telephone and teletype, shortwave communication from and between automobiles and trains, the forest service, the rural electric service—all these and many others have a stake. The need for the Federal Communications Commission to lay out the boundaries and guard the fences is obvious.

The necessity for commercial broadcasters to obtain licenses from the FCC creates a peculiar problem for a country that has been grounded in libertarian communication theory. The nub of the problem is how the FCC should select the licensee when there is competition for a channel—and it is especially spirited in television. Vast potential profits ride on the decision, not to mention many thousands of dollars which must be spent on legal fees to prepare for the hearings. The FCC, represented by an examiner, must sit in judgment. The Communications Act has given the examiner an almost hopelessly broad yardstick to judge applicants: the standard of operation is the "public interest, convenience, and necessity." The meaning of these words has filled countless thousands of pages of hearings and debates.

Court action is a less frightening prospect to broadcasters today than is Commission action, and Commission action is in turn less frightening than Congressional action. "If the threat of Congressional action hung over us in radio times, it hangs one hundred times as heavy now that we are in television," one network head has said. This is because the political potency of television makes it a constant concern of officials, and because the broad investigative powers of Congress and the possibility of restrictive legislation are constant realities to broadcasters.

All this severely limits broadcasting as an adversary, as John Jennings* makes clear:

> Some two hundred years after it was fairly well established what a newspaper should be, radio first tested its lungs by performing a newspaper function, reporting the returns of the Harding-Cox presidential election in 1920. Soon, radio was borrowing the traditions (and the performers) of other media: the music hall, the vaudeville theatre and the motion picture. Radio added pictures and television arrived, borrowing not only the traditions and performers of the motion picture industry, but the product as well. With such a curious parental mixture, it is not surprising that television is at times neither fish nor fowl.
>
> Having inherited so many different traditions and functions from so many different media and trying to live with them all, television has developed an advanced case of schizophrenia. It is never quite certain whether its prime purpose is to provide escapist entertainment, or to insure that every American armpit is sprayed with a proper deodorant, or to serve as a newspaper with pictures that move.

* John Jennings is a candidate for the Public Affairs Ph.D. in the Department of Communication at Stanford. A former broadcast journalist, he now teaches radio and television journalism at the University of Texas.

There is no question, however, that the entertaining and selling functions occupy far greater time and consume more network and station energies than does the news-editorial function. At those times when television does operate as a descendant of the newspaper, it is usually content to provide brief summaries of events or to become a neutral observer of events. The instances of television's filling the adversary function are so rare as to receive widespread attention at the time and to be long remembered—Edward R. Murrow's devastating program on Senator Joseph McCarthy, CBS's "Harvest of Shame" (again Murrow), Howard K. Smith's "political obituary" of Richard Nixon, Seattle broadcaster Stimson Bullitt's editorials opposing the war in Vietnam, CBS's "Hunger in America."

Television's reluctance to play the role of adversary is, of course, in no small measure due to the medium's commercial structure and the resulting fear of alienating prospective sponsors or viewers. An additional and perhaps more important inhibiting factor is that every television station in the United States operates at the sufferance of the federal government.

A newspaper publisher owns the building in which his product is produced, the presses on which it is printed, and the trucks that deliver it. The television broadcaster usually owns the building in which his station operates and the transmitter that produces the signal, but he does not own the means to deliver his message. He is granted a license by the federal government to use a delivery channel owned by the public. That license can theoretically be yanked if the broadcaster's operation is not in keeping with "public interest, convenience, and necessity."

Congress, in the Communications Act of 1934, created the Federal Communications Commission to issue licenses and regulate those who use them. The relationship between the broadcasting industry and the FCC alternates between a love match and a backroom brawl, depending upon the shifting membership of the Commission. When the FCC actively attempts to be more than a traffic cop for the electromagnetic spectrum to keep television signals from interfering with each other, when it attempts any action that might affect a station's programming or its cash register, a virtual state of war exists between the regulator and the regulated. The brief periods of war are interrupted by long stretches of inactivity or indecision. When James Landis, former dean of the Harvard Law School, was commissioned in 1960 by a Senate subcommittee to look into the working of the federal regulatory agencies, he did not like what he saw at the FCC:

> The Commission has drifted, vacillated, and stalled in almost every major area. It seems incapable of policy planning. The available evidence indicates that it, more than any other agency has been subservient to the subcommittees on communication of the Congress and its members. A strong suspicion also exists that far too great an influence is exercised over the Commission by the networks.

The FCC's constantly shifting interpretation of how the broadcaster can best serve the "public interest" is perfectly illustrated in the Commission's attitude toward editorializing. Twenty-five years ago editorializing was forbidden. In 1941 the FCC renewed the license of a Boston radio station, WAAB, that had broadcast editorials, only after it had been assured that the station had given up the practice, that it did not intend to resume it, and that it had no editorial policy. The language was unequivocal: "A truly free radio cannot be used to advocate the causes of the licensee. . . . It cannot be devoted to the support of principles he happens to regard most favorably. In brief, the broadcaster cannot be an advocate." Eight years later the Commission reversed itself and said that a broadcaster might editorialize, but only on the condition that he give those who disagree with him a chance to be heard. After

Newton Minow became chairman of the Commission in 1961, the broadcaster was told that he not only had the right to editorialize, he had the duty to do so. At the same time, the broadcaster was told that not only should he allow opposing voices to be heard, but he must "seek out, aid and encourage" those who disagree with him to step forward and use his microphone. This "Fairness Doctrine" applies to all expression of opinion, not just a station's formal editorial statements.

It would not be surprising, therefore, to find broadcasters staying altogether clear of controversy in an effort to avoid starting an interminable chain of argument and debate. A survey by the National Association of Broadcasters shows that only about one-third of the country's 600-plus television stations editorialize at all, and fewer than half which editorialize do so on a weekly or daily basis. (One would be hard put to find more than a handful of weekly or daily newspapers without at least one editorial in every issue.) About half of the stations which editorialize admit that they stay away from "political issues," but apparently are vigorous in opposing litter on the street and death on the highway or supporting the Community Chest and the arrival of Spring. (Louis Simon, a Group W Vice President and editorial reader for KPIX in San Francisco, believes most of his editorials should be "positive" rather than "critical.")

A distinction should be made between "editorials" and "commentary." An editorial represents the opinion of the station management, while commentary is a personal statement by an employee of a station or network. Louis Simon of KPIX is an editorialist, Eric Sevareid is a commentator.

Those few stations whose acceptance of the adversary tradition is reflected in their reporting and editorials usually take out promotional ads in all the trade publications pointing with pride to their accomplishments when they have been effective in bringing about needed change in state or local government. That such performance is

treated as something "beyond the call of duty" is an indication that the role of adversary has not been universally
accepted by the television industry, that it is, in fact, somewhat rare.

Broadcasters must not feel that it is necessary to be an
adversary in order to garner praise, or at least approval
and respect. A survey by Elmo Roper has revealed that
more people tend to trust the news they hear on television
than the news they read in their daily newspaper. When
Richard Nixon called a news conference after his defeat
by Pat Brown in the 1962 California gubernatorial election to announce his "retirement" from political life, he
complained bitterly of having been "kicked around" and
generally abused by reporters and newspapers, but he said
he had been treated "fairly" by television.

If regulations of the FCC make it difficult for television
to be as active an adversary as its printed cousins, the relationship between the Congress and the electronic media
poses a problem of practicality rather than legality. The
Congress contains some of the best friends that the broadcasting industry could ask for—not only friends, but in
some cases members of the family. More than thirty members of the House and Senate own broadcasting stations or
own stock in one or more stations. One member of the
House Commerce Committee, Representative Clarence J.
Brown, Jr., of Ohio, is president of a radio station in
Urbana, Ohio. His committee writes the laws that regulate broadcasting.

Congressional friendship has worked to the broadcaster's advantage time and time again, especially during periods of threatened FCC activity. When the FCC began
toying with the idea of charging a higher fee for the broadcaster's license to use a valuable piece of public property
to deliver his messages, broadcasters let their displeasure
be known, and the Senate Commerce Committee crisply
told the Commission to drop the matter. It did. When the
FCC proposed the adoption of regulations to limit the
length and number of commercials on radio and televi-

sion, the broadcasting industry loudly pleaded "The First," accusing the Commission of trying to become a censor. The House heard the cries of all those friendly stations back home and quickly began consideration of a bill to prevent the FCC from carrying out its proposal. The proposal was dropped before the bill could get to the floor of the House for a vote.

There is yet another relationship that exists between one segment of broadcasting and the federal government: a customer-merchant relationship between two of the networks and the Executive department. The parent company of one network (NBC) and a subsidiary of another (CBS) develop and manufacture electronic equipment that is useful in missiles and artificial satellites. Space and defense contracts provide a considerable share of the business of these arms of the broadcasting giants.

It is understandable that networks are sensitive to criticism or complaints from the Executive branch of government. The broadcast by CBS of an interview between Edward R. Murrow and Soviet Premier Khrushchev brought a telephone call of complaint from President Eisenhower to CBS Board Chairman William Paley. The Defense Department let CBS know of its displeasure in 1965 when CBS correspondent Morley Safer did an emotional piece about United States Marines putting the torch to Vietnam villages, leaving old women and children without shelter. CBS got back in the good graces of the Pentagon two years later however, when it aired "Vietnam Perspective: Bombing in the North," fifty-five minutes of which were devoted to interviews with military men supporting the bombing and five minutes of which were devoted to those who oppose the bombing. It is difficult to long remain an adversary of one of your best customers.

If networks, with all their power and wealth, are so sensitive to criticism and pressure, it seems foolish to expect more from an individual station. To become a true adversary, a station must overcome the pressures of friendship with the Congress, the pressures of the cash register, the fear of the FCC. Perhaps it is too much to ask.

It is little known that government is heavily involved in the book business as well. Geoffrey Wolff* has written:

"Words are loaded pistols," says Sartre, and official voices in this country have come to fully acknowledge the dictum. In the months before the 1964 election, for example, eighteen of our fifty senators were working on one or more books, most of which would be ghost-written and published under their names. The publish-or-perish syndrome is even more prevalent in the Executive branch: we have had platoons of books and nonbooks about the Peace Corps, introduced by Sargent Shriver; the Defense Department has been endlessly chronicled, as have NASA, the diplomatic corps, the Internal Revenue Service, and the rest of the Establishment's interests. A story often heard in Washington had President Kennedy looking ahead to the 1964 election and huddling with his lieutenants to come up with a campaign issue. In one of the meetings, the story goes, he asked if there was anything of substance in Michael Harrington's study of poverty, *The Other America*. Assured that there was, Kennedy called for memorandums, documents, and ideas. Shortly thereafter, poverty books came forth by the dozens—many written by persons who were part of or close to the Administration. Magazine articles followed; silence and ignorance gave way to public clamor; an issue was born, and the War on Poverty began.

In principle, there is nothing alarming about public officials generating books to further their political ideals and careers. In practice, however, political expediency has made many writers so arrogant that they scorn facts and ignore their duty to learn and the reader's right to know. There is much evidence that books are used increasingly

*When he wrote this article for *Book Week*, Geoffrey Wolff was book editor of the Washington *Post*. He is now books editor of *Newsweek* and is the author of a novel, *Bad Debts*.

as engines of propaganda, that highly placed persons are precensoring books they find repellent or embarrassing, and that they are commissioning and controlling the writing of books without disclosing the facts of such control. If we believe that truth has a more exclusive claim to our attention then partial truth or falsehood, and if we believe that openness and disclosure of the circumstances surrounding the writing, publishing, and marketing of a book are requisites of a free access to ideas, then we must be alarmed at the sham, illegality, and indirection that have infected much of what is sold as objective reality.

Recently, for example, Mr. George Carver wrote for the highly respected periodical *Foreign Affairs* an article supporting our official policy toward North and South Vietnam. Mr. Carver is with the C.I.A. but this crucial information was not related by *Foreign Affairs*. Worse, it is possible it was not given to the magazine. It is illegal for the C.I.A. to operate as an intelligence-gathering or intelligence-disseminating organization in the United States. The same restrictions apply to U.S.I.A., which is bound to confine itself to propaganda activities abroad. Yet its officers admitted several months ago in hearings before a subcommittee of the House Committee on Appropriations that part of the activity of its "Book Development Program" has been the *secret* production of manuscripts, published by private companies which the U.S.I.A. subsidizes, and sold in this country without any government *imprimatur* or other acknowledgment of the circumstances of their origin.

Reed Harris, appearing before the subcommittee in his capacity as director of the U.S.I.A. Information Center Service, said of these books: "We control the things from the very idea down to the final edited manuscript." Perhaps the books are accurate and valuable, perhaps they are self-serving or meretricious; what is certain is that they do not tell the reader what he surely wants to know: that they are works which the U.S.I.A. admits would never have been written without Government support and would not have been released by a commercial publishing house without subsidization—either because they were unworthy of publication or they were unmarketable.

Leonard Marks, director of U.S.I.A., and Ben Posner, assistant director, were questioned about the Book Development Program by Congressman Glenard Lipscomb (R.-Cal.). Portions of the exchange follow:

MR. LIPSCOMB: What were the books that were developed in the 1966 [sic] fiscal year Book Development Program?

MR. POSNER: In fiscal year 1965 there were four books that were developed: *The Ladder Dictionary* by John R. Shaw, *The Sword and the Plow* by Ralph Slater, *President Kennedy in Africa* by Robert Marshall, *The Truth About the Dominican Republic* by Jay Mallin . . . We will be pleased to make this information available to the committee. Because it has not been our policy to make our support known in connection with these items, the material that I have is not for the record, Mr. Chairman.

MR. LIPSCOMB: Do I understand that this list is considered as classified?

MR. POSNER: In the sense that we have not in the past divulged the Government's connection with it, yes sir.

MR. LIPSCOMB: Are any of these books on this classified list distributed and sold within the United States?

MR. POSNER: I believe that they are; yes.

MR. MARKS: In other words, we assist.

At this juncture, Mr. Marks agreed to put in the record the titles of the books and the cost, $90,258, of commissioning manuscripts and supporting the publication of books commissioned by private publishers. The taxpayer who buys one of these books pays for it three times: he pays to have it written, he pays to have it published, and he pays its retail price at the bookstore. He also pays to support a Government Printing Office which could publish and sell the book at a fraction of its cost as produced privately and secretly. But Mr. Marks, in later testimony, explained why books under Government *imprima-tur* are not useful to the purposes of U.S.I.A.

MR. LIPSCOMB: Why is it wrong to let the American people know when they buy and read the book that it was developed under Government sponsorship?

MR. MARKS: It minimizes their [sic] value.

MR. LIPSCOMB: Why is it not a good policy to maintain the same ground rules that you maintain with motion pictures, with newspaper stories, and do your work overseas and make it a policy that these books that are prepared with taxpayers' money are not for distribution within the United States?

MR. MARKS: . . . Where an audience overseas reads a book with the label of the United States Government they look upon it in a particular manner. Where they read a book that is published in the United States and we distribute it, they look upon it differently, as the expression of the author. It is the expression of the author, it is not our expression. We did not write that book. We merely bought copies and helped to distribute it. But if we say this is our book, then the author is a Government employee, in effect.

Of course, the author *is* a Government employee—in fact, not in effect. He does a chore at the order and to the requirements of the Government. Further, his work is then published under the copyright of a private publisher even though Section 8 of the Copyright Laws says that any book produced by a Government employee within the scope of his employment is not copyrightable, even though produced by a private publisher. Thus the taxpayer pays again: he pays royalties on each copy of a book that the U.S.I.A. buys for distribution—a book which is already their property. Mr. Lipscomb was very gentle with Mr. Marks on this point:

MR. LIPSCOMB: I am for the Book Development Program for distribution overseas. I believe you can do lots of good with it. But why not limit your activities for overseas? You are making a subsidy to the author and publisher. The taxpayer is not complaining about it, but there is a principle involved in my mind that when an American citizen who subsidizes a book reads it, he should know.

MR. MARKS: That is a point of view which I understand.

MR. LIPSCOMB: I assume you are distributing them overseas, for lack of a better word, for propaganda purposes.

MR. MARKS: Yes, definitely; to tell a story.

MR. LIPSCOMB: Is it being sold in the United States for propaganda purposes?

MR. MARKS: No.

In other words, what is meant to manipulate a foreign reader is believed by Mr. Marks to be a fair and objective account to an American reader. But the truth is that a student writing a paper about our intervention in the Dominican Republic has before him in Mallin's account of *The Truth About the Dominican Republic* a controlled package which is not truly labeled. If he is misled before he gets past the dust jacket and title page, what can he expect of the book itself? The C.I.A. also has had for years a great respect for the power of books to influence public opinion. The names of Frederick A. Praeger and the M.I.T. Press (The Center for International Studies at M.I.T. was set up with C.I.A. money fifteen years ago) are only two of many that crop up again and again in the company of the U.S.I.A. and the C.I.A. One welcomes the written views of men connected with such agencies as well as those of scholars working without such support, but the taxpayer has the right to know what he is paying for and the reader has the right to know the basic beliefs and qualifications and sources of the man whose book he buys.

And the evil is compounded by the fact that the reader is often guided to a book by the good reputation of its publisher. Praeger, who is one of the chief contractors of books purchased by U.S.I.A. and whose company was recently purchased by the Encyclopaedia Britannica (think of the potential *there!*), is no Government stooge. Praeger books on politics, foreign affairs, and history have an excellent reputation for accuracy and timeliness. But we have no way of knowing *which* Praeger books were supported by the Government. For example, Praeger is the publisher for Bernard Fall, whose books about Vietnam are indictments of Administration policy. Praeger also published Philip Geyelin's *Lyndon B. Johnson and the World,* an objective study of the President's foreign policy that was not purchased by U.S.I.A. for foreign distribution because it did not answer the Agency's propaganda needs. But Praeger is also named as the publisher of five of the sixteen titles the U.S.I.A. supported or generated in 1965. (*The Sword and the Plow* by Ralph P. Slater, *The Dragon's Embrace* by Joseph Hevi, *The Communist Front as a Weapon of Political Warfare* by J. E. Atkinson, *In Pursuit of World Order* by Richard N. Gardner, *From Colonialism to Communism* by Hoang Van Chi.)

The Agency also spends $6 million or so every year to buy books for distribution (in 1965 it purchased 175,032, representing 1,500 titles), and no one knows what effects the lure of this amount of money has on a publisher's agreement with an author concerning a book's tone and direction. Lipscomb and Marks touched on this question after it had been revealed that a substantial number of these books were ordered from Potomac Books, Inc., a Washington publishing company. The Agency agreed to pay $25,000 for six volumes on America, three of which had yet to be written and which would be distributed here and abroad without mention of the U.S.I.A. contract. Mr. Marks was asked about the agreement:

MR. MARKS: That is right, we bought a substantial number of books from that publisher but we did not write the books.

MR. LIPSCOMB: You hired the manuscripts done?

MR. MARKS: We worked with them. I would not say we hired them. We did not contract for them. We said, "If this book is written on this subject, we are a customer for you, and will buy X copies."

The case of William Manchester vs. The Kennedy Family brought to public view an arrangement whereby sources of information for the book attempted to exercise complete control over the book's content, tone, and publication date. Manchester has been accused of foolishness in entering into such a contract, and the Kennedy family has been accused of misunderstanding the ground rules by which history is written. On the contrary, what Manchester agreed to do has become common practice among historians and biographers and the Kennedys simply made the arrangement public.

A typical case of book control works this way: a Government agency keeps information essential to the writing of a given book under a security classification. The agency then contacts a writer and agrees to lift the classification in exchange for the right to edit the entire book—not just the portions that touch on the previously classified material. Whether such censorship is in the interest of national security is a moot question: the effect of such an agreement is to grant enormous leverage to the Establishment, whose editorial judgments are neither disclosed nor subject to review.

When one considers the tens of millions of dollars spent by the Government on books, the economic leverage that results must be enormous. Books by, about, and for the Government claim a massive share of the bookselling and writing business, and any publisher who flaunts the power structure does so at his peril. Recently, a freelance writer, Ralph Schoenstein, revealed that a book he wrote in 1965 about President Johnson and his three dogs, Blanco, Her, and the late Him, was submitted by his publisher, Doubleday, for review by Elizabeth Carpenter, Mrs. Johnson's press secretary. Mrs. Carpenter was furious: she fancied the sixty-five-page manuscript to be repellent to the dignity of the President's high office and made it clear that for Doubleday to print the book would be to sacrifice the cooperation of the White House with its future writers. It never appeared.

We should not lament the loss of the doggy book were it not that such *sub rosa* censorship sets extremely dangerous precedents. The writing of a book and the reading of one are private enterprises that constitute a crucial defense against the tyranny of the majority. The cornerstone of such a defense is the frank disclosure of the manner in which the book came to be written or controlled. John Milton, arguing in the seventeenth century against the Licensing Act, wrote in *Areopagitica:*

> I deny not but that it is of the greatest concernment in the Church and to the Commonwealth to have a vigilant eye how books demean themselves, as well as men, and thereafter to confine, imprison, and do sharpest justice on them as malefactors. . . . And yet, on the other hand, unless wariness be used, as good almost kill a man as kill a good book. Who kills a man kills a reasonable creature, God's image; but he who destroys a good book kills reason itself, kills the image of God, as it were, in the eye.

It is not Government money or Government interest itself that sullies books. All one wants is that Government acknowledge its involvement and keep its hands off the writer's work. To ask this is to ask for no more than the Government demands of charitable foundations. But now there is a double activity—the secret suppression and creation of history—which reinforces the fears of American writers that their Government cannot be trusted and that it is not mature or brave enough to subsidize the open dissemination of ideas.

CHAPTER SEVEN

When Government Controls (Abroad)

> *Why should freedom of speech and freedom of press be allowed? Why should a government which is doing what it believes to be right allow itself to be criticized? It would not allow opposition by lethal weapons. Ideas are much more fatal things than guns. Why should any man be allowed to buy a printing press and disseminate pernicious opinions calculated to embarrass the government?*
>
> —NIKOLAI LENIN

> *No* Spiegel, *no democracy.*
>
> —GERMAN SAYING

Whatever the encroachments of officialdom on the information system in the United States, many reporters who are sent abroad are likely to reflect at some point that home was a kind of heaven for reporters.

It is, of course, expected that an American journalist will find Communist countries less than hospitable. David Halberstam, who was reporting from Warsaw for the New York *Times* in 1965, has related what happened when he scratched around for evidences of anti-Semitism in Poland: "On the way to the Foreign Ministry that morning I looked in my rear-view mirror and saw a freshly washed Volkswagen. I stopped. It stopped. I turned left. It turned left. I knew I was going to be expelled."

Even in the foreign democracies, where the official declarations for free expression are quite as strong as those in the United States, the unofficial environment for the reporter is usually negative. He may be free to report what he learns, but getting the access to persons and events which alone enables him to develop significant stories is difficult. With a few notable exceptions, political journalists in the foreign democracies have not developed a climate that enables them to do much more than accept the news that is handed them. Few will ask challenging questions. At the risk of oversimplifying, the difference between English and American political journalists is that the English are better writers and worse reporters.

Some aspects of the United States system are being developed abroad by American correspondents. Acting on the American example, more and more foreign reporters are asking tough questions of high political figures. Slowly, some of the habits of Washington reportage are being adopted in foreign capitals. In Berlin, information officers of the United States Mission have distributed sets of rules which introduce foreign reporters to an elaborate system of interviewing and attribution developed by reporters and officials in Washington.

Nonetheless, the reporter in many foreign countries finds himself hedged about with stifling restrictions. Afghanistan is fairly typical of the great many small countries which have been edging toward democracy. Article 31 of its new Constitution declares: "Freedom of thought and expression is inviolable." But the letter and the spirit of this ringing declaration are sabotaged by thirteen provisions of the Press Law:

The Press on pain of punishment or suppression:

(1) *Must* safeguard the dignity of the State;

(2) *Must* preserve the fundamentals of Islam, the State religion;

(3) *Must* preserve the principles of the constitutional monarchy;

(4) *Must* be an effective means for the spread of culture and reflect public opinion honestly and usefully;

(5) *Must* obtain permission to print from the Ministry of Press and Information;

(6) *Must* deposit cash guarantees with the Ministry of Press and Information to guarantee this right;

(7) *Must* divulge amount and source of capital to Ministry of Press and Information;

(8) *Must* send one copy each of the publication to Minis-

try of Press and Information, the attorney general and to two public libraries immediately after it is printed;

(9) *Must not* incite disclosure of sacred government, parliamentary, or court proceedings, etc.;

(10) *Must not* publish false or distorted news that damages the interest or the dignity of the State or individual;

(11) *Must not* publish matter implying defamation of Islam or of the King;

(12) *Must not* publish comments that will divert courts from reaching correct decisions, and public prosecutors, police, witnesses or even public opinion from the correct path;

(13) *Must not* publish anything that causes direct and actual disruption of the country's social health or economic life or even deceives public opinion.

Leaders of the emerging nations maintain that such restrictions are essential to give the state an opportunity to establish its strength. When a viable democracy has been established, they argue, the restrictions can be removed. That would be persuasive if there were not dangers in controlling information. What they are is sketched by Don Dodson:*

> Ruled by a charismatic leader heading a mass party, Ghana was what David Apter calls a "mobilization" state. Shunning the pluralistic, competitive, and secular values of "reconciliation" states like Nigeria before its first coup, mobilization states use "political religion" to marshal their citizens and resources for the march toward modernization. "There is something magical or even sacred about the moral aspect of politics," Apter remarks in *The Politics of Modernization*. "Political ritual and ideological incantations, broadcast by means of the most up-to-date techniques in the mass media, dispense political grace not in the abstract but in terms of political development."
>
> State and regime in Ghana were infused with sacredness. They had an almost mythical past—that time of

* Don Dodson holds the Master's Degree in Journalism from Stanford. A former reporter, he is a candidate for the Ph.D. in the School of Journalism, University of Wisconsin.

darkness and despair called colonialism—and an agent of rebirth. Nkrumah was a messiah who, in poet Michael Dei-Anang's words, "drove a shaft of light through the gloom of our life." Named Osagyefo, meaning Redeemer or Savior, Nkrumah made the state a kind of church with saints and villains. Lashing imperialism, colonialism and neocolonialism as devils, he preached a theology of government called Nkrumaism or Consciencism in which the mass party was defender of the faith. Said Nkrumah: "The Convention People's Party is Ghana and Ghana is the Convention People's Party."

How did newspapers fit into the mobilization scheme? Any notion of an adversary role for the press would clearly have been taboo. The Ghanaian press "as a whole seems to live in absolute terror of offending the Government," K. A. B. Jones-Quartey, former assistant editor of an Accra daily, noted in 1960. "It seems, in short, to have nothing to offer except cagey neutrality or fulsome acquiescence." Only one major paper, *The Ashanti Pioneer*, opposed the Nkrumah regime—and it was suppressed in 1962 after warring with the censors for two years. Newspapers which endured were bridled.

Ghana's press was subject to general laws which tended to stifle dissent. More than a dozen journalists were expelled under the 1957 Deportation Act. The Avoidance of Discrimination Act in 1957 outlawed all organizations "using or engaging in tribal, regional, racial, or religious propaganda to the detriment of any other community." The Emergency Powers Act, as redrafted in 1961, gave Nkrumah the personal right to issue any fiat he thought was expedient to maintain public order. All political parties except the Convention People's Party were banned in 1964 when the Constitution was amended.

The most repressive measure of all was the Preventive Detention Act of 1958. As amended in 1963 and redrafted the next year, this act enabled Nkrumah to detain any Ghanaian without trial for up to ten years to prevent that person from "acting in a manner prejudicial" to the defense, foreign relations, or internal security of the state. Hundreds—perhaps thousands—of Nkrumah's opponents were jailed under this act.

Newspapers were also subject to specific laws which were designed to muzzle them. The False Reports Act of 1959 threatened a fifteen-year jail term for anyone spreading a "false statement or report which is likely to injure the credit or reputation of Ghana or the Government of Ghana, and which he knows or has reason to believe is false." The 1959 Sedition Act set a mandatory five-year prison term for anyone who had the temerity to "accuse any public officer of misconduct in the exercise of his official duties, knowing the accusation to be false or reckless whether it be true or false."

A 1960 Criminal Code Amendment allowed Nkrumah himself to ban or censor any newspaper, book, or document that he thought published "matter calculated to prejudice public order or safety, or the maintenance of the public services or economy of Ghana." It was this act which gagged *The Ashanti Pioneer*.

Another sweeping Criminal Code amendment the following year warned that anyone "who with intent to bring the President into hatred, ridicule or contempt publishes any defamatory or insulting matter" could be fined 500 pounds or jailed for three years. Neither truth nor fair comment was a permissible defense. Finally, in 1963, the government asserted complete control over the press with a Newspaper Licensing Act authorizing the Minister of Information to suspend or revoke the license (required for publication or circulation) of an uncooperative paper.

Government policy toward newspapers was not just negative. It established an Institute of Journalism at Accra Polytechnic in 1959. The school received a yearly government subsidy of $84,000 and most students held government scholarships. Taught in the two-year program were history, current affairs, economic geography, political science, and party ideology. Before graduating, each student had to take a three-month residential course at Kwame Nkrumah Ideological Institute.

The graduate could then take his place in the monolithic press establishment. He might work for the government's Ghana News Agency or the government's Ghana Radio and Television Corporation. Or the government's *Daily Graphic*. Or the party's *Evening News, The Ghanaian Times, The Spark* or *Weekly Spectator*. He might hope someday to become—like the managing director, editor-in-chief and editor of the *Times*—a CPP official and member of Parliament. Whatever his position, he would get his paycheck from the President's Office, either directly or through party conduits such as the Guinea Press.

The young journalist would not escape ideological guidelines when he graduated. *Osagyefo* did not want him to forget his lessons. Addressing the Second Conference of African Journalists at Accra in 1963, Nkrumah stated: "Just as in the capitalist countries the Press represents and carries out the purpose of capitalism, so in revolutionary Africa our revolutionary African Press must present and carry forward our revolutionary purpose. This is to establish a progressive political and economic system upon our continent that will free men from want and every form of injustice, and enable them to work out their social and cultural destinies in peace and at ease."

Elaborating on this theme when he dedicated the Ghana News Agency Building in 1965, Nkrumah remarked that "the journalist is one of the major architects of the New Ghana and of the new Africa." Since what is striking and timely in Africa is the revolutionary movement, he said, "our articles, our commentaries, our radio and television newscasts must be prepared and portrayed by *revolutionary* journalists."

Shouldn't the press, however, be neutral? "We do not believe that there are necessarily two sides to every question," Nkrumah explained. "We see right and wrong, just and unjust, progressive and reactionary, positive and negative, friend and foe. We are *partisan*." Asserting that the "capitalist" press is not neutral, he added: "What a journalist *sees* depends on what his education has been, what his intelligence is, what political sense he has, and what his general outlook on the world is—in other words, on his political consciousness and ideological background.

"The necessity for a clear ideology of the African Revolution must be to view problems in the right perspective so that they can write them with insight and understanding. The drumbeat of the African Revolution must throb in the pages of his newspapers and magazines, it must sound in the voices and feelings of our news readers. To this end, we need a new kind of journalist of the African Revolution."

African journalists, then, were expected to base their convictions on "the rock of a scientific understanding of the world" and to "hail those who advance and expose those who retard" the revolution. Among those who retarded the revolution were lesser officials who were improperly schooled in party ideology. Such men could endanger the fledgling state through ignorance, incompetence, or malevolence. As an Ashanti maxim puts it: "There is no such thing as a bad king, only bad counselors." Attacking petty bureaucrats tends to defuse criticism of those who really wield power.

What did practicing journalists think of Nkrumah's master plan for the press? Many applauded. "There can be no better definition of the role of the African journalist today," affirmed *The Spark*, a weekly ideological organ of the CPP. Commented Cecil Forde, head of the Ghana Radio and Television Corporation and chairman of the Association of Ghanaian Journalists and Writers: "With the right ideological orientation we should not go wrong. Indeed, we must not. No one has any excuse for lack of ideology. 'Consciencism' is with us, and it has come to stay. It is the philosophy that directs us."

If a journalist did "go wrong," extralegal constraints might be exerted to force him into line. Nkrumah used the "carrot and stick" method on *Times* editor T. D. Baffoe. A member of Nkrumah's inner circle of advisers, Baffoe apparently angered the President in 1961 with an editorial criticizing a cabinet reorganization. He was fired for his peccadillo. Later reinstated, Baffoe published another editorial which embarrassed Nkrumah. Since harassment had failed, Nkrumah took a tack that was only slightly more subtle but incalculably more effective. He gave Baffoe—and Eric Heyman of the *News* and Kofi Badu of the *Graphic*—a lavish estate house paid for out of public funds. Baffoe took the carrot.

How did newspaper content reflect the sticky web of relations between press and government in Ghana? Fairly typical content was displayed by Accra's *Weekly Spectator*, which was created out of the old *Sunday Spectator and Vanguard* on January 27, 1965—just four weeks before army troops converged on the capital in a pre-dawn coup. Each issue was laden with serial features: gossip (Dapper Dick's "It Happened"), advice ("Got a Problem? Auntie Akosua Will Help You Solve It"), maxims ("Words of Wisdom"), fables ("Children's Corner"), verses ("Sabbath Meditation"), news ("International Commentary"), Nkrumaism ("Flagstaff House Newsreel"), citizenship ("Ghana Rebuilds under Work and Happiness Program"), and grievances (Scrutator's "Things As I See Them"). Excluding sports stories, the four issues printed during Nkrumah's regime contained ninety-five items in English.

Trying to be an architect of the New Ghana, the *Weekly Spectator* ran thirty-one items that offered training in skills or morals needed in a modern state. The serial "Ghana Rebuilds under Work and Happiness Program," for example, outlined Ghana's mineral wealth, Ghana Young Pioneer Movement activities, structure and purposes of the National Investment Bank, and benefits of sound nutrition. Telling how science aids housewives, one story described the glories of silicone-coated saucepans: "The lining really does do all the things claimed for it."

To expose enemies of the state, another thirty-one items attacked the United States, Great Britain, NATO, capitalists, colonialists, neocolonialists, imperialists, profiteers, or divisionists. Since the *Weekly Spectator* resorted more to broad labels than to specific identities, villains were often shadowy—and perhaps, therefore, more ominous. A front-page article stated that "American sources," internal "propagandists for the British," and "colonialists" spreading "vile rumor" tried to wreck the Volta River Project.

Thirty items endowed Nkrumah or the CPP with sacred qualities. Calling the new dam a "dream come true," a reporter wrote that its site was picked "through the sheer enthusiasm and determination of Osagyefo the President, born of his wonder dream. He was the spirit and guiding light in all that happened." Suggesting that Nkrumah "does these things by inspiration," the writer opined: "The man's enthusiasm was so infectious that you can't resist its captivating fangs."

Ideology—Scientific Socialism, Nkrumaism, Consciencism, Pan-Africanism—appeared undisguised in twenty-one items. Sir Abubbakar Tafewa Balewa was overthrown by the Nigerian coup, asserted one editorial, because he "failed to realize the tempo of the neocolonialists and their wicked twists and turns, and never examined 'scientifically the basis of the society over which his Government governed.' " Concluded the editorial confidently: "There is something in Nkrumaism; one cannot fail to see this largely and brightly painted on the horizon."

Bureaucrats faced muted jibes from nineteen items in the *Weekly Spectator,* sometimes in letters complaining about such minor irritants as clogged toilets. Each *Scrutator* column contained four or five notes of advice to bureaucrats. Addressing one to Police Chief J. K. Harley, *Scrutator* asked: "Is it true that Ministers are having four policemen apiece when some parts of Accra are nightly under the cruel mercy of robbers? What! Can't they afford to engage watchmen? They should. THANKS." Flogging with a ribbon and salving the "injuries" afterward was a delicate art for Ghanaian journalists.

Only rarely was criticism unqualified, and when it was, the targets were always vague. Blasting profiteers in the Ghana National Trading Corporation, a front-page article urged the government to "be tough with rascally minded, big names or no big names, high positions or not." Somehow, critical darts missed Nkrumah: "These men constitute a vicious cycle whose aim is to bring Osagyefo's statesmanship, his foresight, and his directives, as well as the best planned distribution scheme of the Government of Ghana, into utter disrepute."

Ten *Weekly Spectator* items tried, in Apter's phrase, "to render massive change heroic and joyful, infectious and liberating." Advised one: "In everything we do we should be guided by the maxim: 'per ardua ad astra'—the way to the stars is not easy." Another warned, "Selfishness, bloodshed, and despair must be replaced with duty, nobility, patriotism, sacrifice, and generosity." And a third instructed that " 'Work and Happiness' is designed for all and not only a saintly few."

Hortatory appeals for the masses to back specific programs rang from nine items. "I have enrolled already in the Ghana National Militia," a columnist wrote. "Have you? If not, why not? Get cracking, pretty quickly." An editorial on literacy urged, "Let all people therefore get together in this attempt to erect a solid foundation for the young socialist State of Ghana. There is no doubt that great success will attend this literacy drive, if all the people will cooperate: the illiterate to learn and the literate to teach."

And, finally, memories of an almost mythical past echoed in five *Weekly Spectator* items. Commenting that Nkrumah's imprisonment under colonial rule "carried with it also joy and hope," one story noted: "For the past dubious circumstances gave birth to the Man of Destiny, who became the Founder of the Nation." Consciencism, said another, was "the type of society which prevailed in the great civilization of the ancestors of the African but the colonial powers sought to destroy this heritage."

Only seven items failed to show any of the characteristics treated here. Africa, in short, was the Holy Land and Ghana was the Jerusalem of Nkrumaism. Journalists were supposed to be true believers, crusaders against enemies of the political religion. Besides avoiding political sin, newsmen had to perform good works. They were agents of the state in rallying the people behind the revolutionary program of modernization through mobilization. Obedience to the dogmas of Nkrumaism brought political grace and personal salvation.

To question Osagyefo was as unthinkable for a reporter as it was for a crusader to slander the Pope. Ghanaian newsmen were affectionate watchdogs. Snarling only at enemies of the state, they whined softly and wagged their tails at officialdom. Why not bark louder? Nkrumah argued, justly, that the state could not survive without solidarity. His main tasks were to give ethnic loyalties wider scope and to maintain his own role as "king" for all tribes. Only then could the whole nation move toward modernization. Conflict, especially when voiced in ethnic terms, might shatter the fragile state.

"We are emerging from colonialism, and we are being stifled by imperialism and neocolonialism," said Nkrumah. "We face a long, hard life-and-death struggle in which all our people are engaged. How can the journalist be 'neutral' in circumstances as these?" Indeed, how could one be neutral? But partiality should not imply servility. Assuming that new nations may have to impose "measures of a totalitarian kind" to protect their very existence, as Nkrumah asserted in his autobiography, how much should they dam the flow of information?

Information, writes Apter, "is one functional requisite of government without which it cannot maintain itself." To be more than automatons in the churning process of modernization, citizens must understand the actions of their government. And officials, to rule wisely, must feel the public pulse. Apter notes that poor information results in "a completely chaotic and capricious pattern of political life" and "the setting of goals without reference to their political significance."

Politics and communication, everywhere, are intertwined. But nowhere can a regime—especially one identified with corruption and profligacy—persuade a balky public of its right to rule. Cohesion is not easy to impose on millions of ethnically diverse people. Consequently, popular acceptance of authority may continually elude those who govern. When coercion became the mortar that cemented Ghana and political religion became more a ritual than a faith, Nkrumah was in trouble.

He was the victim, in part, of his own philosophy of information. Misjudging his charisma, Nkrumah often seemed to base policy more on ideology than on political or economic reality. A less fettered press might have demonstrated that many programs lacked public approval. But Nkrumah himself made a dissenting press forbidden in theory, criminal in law, and nonexistent in practice. Like all rulers, he had to strike a balance between freedom and control, information and coercion. Nkrumah tipped the scales too much, and lost his own balance.

The issues are much more complex in South Africa, as this report by Trevor Brown* indicates:

In July 1969 a classic confrontation between press and government in the Republic of South Africa ended in a Johannesburg court. It will surprise no one that the press lost. The *Rand Daily Mail* was convicted of violating the Prisons Act, specifically, of failing to take "reasonable steps" to verify information in its exposé of prison conditions published in June 1965. The fines were negligible. The owners, South African Associated Newspapers, paid $420, editor Laurence Gandar $280, and senior reporter

---

* Trevor Brown is a candidate for the Public Affairs Ph.D. in the Department of Communication at Stanford. He has been a reporter and teacher in South Africa.

Benjamin Pogrund, the author of the articles, was given a six-month jail sentence suspended for three years. These details however, obscure the underlying struggle; the yawns of Gandar, apparently asleep in court for much of the eight-month trial, are apt comment on the *Mail's* actual violation of the law.

His real offense, and that of the entire English press in South Africa in its adversary relationship with government, emerged at different points in senior state counsel Liebenberg's address to the court. Cyril Dunn, reporting the trial for the London *Observer*, wrote:

> He had made it clear that in the opinion of the State there could be no such thing as a freedom which allowed the Press to be anything but subservient to the interests of the Government, with which Mr. Liebenberg plainly identified the interests of the country . . .
>
> Besides insisting that a newspaper must not attack Government officials, Mr. Liebenberg had also said that a newspaper must not cause "stirs or rumpuses," must not arrogate to itself rights it did not possess, and must serve the interest, not of small sections of extremists, but of the majority of its readers.

A few hours after his conviction Gandar responded in the *Mail* with a front-page editorial headed "A Free Press." He concluded:

> The obvious disadvantages of Press freedom —sensationalism, bias, invasion of privacy, and so on—are far outweighed by the incalculable advantages to society of the fullest possible disclosure of information, access to a variety of opinions, exposure of malpractices and the promotion of public discussion of matters of importance.
>
> Without this democracy would die. As Thomas Jefferson once said: "Were it left to me to decide whether we should have a government without

newspapers, or newspapers without government,
I should not hesitate for a moment to prefer the
latter."

The libertarian theory of the press is predicated on the
separation of the two institutions, press and government,
and approves an adversary relationship between them. In
defiance of the British Cape Colony government Thomas
Pringle introduced this Anglo-American journalistic ethic
to South Africa in 1824. The Republic's Nationalist
government is concerned not with the death of democracy,
however, but with the survival of white South Africa;
it tolerates no such separation and its authoritarian ideology concedes no conflict of interest when press and
government are one. The involvement of the Nationalist
Party leaders in the Afrikaans press is total.

Dr. D. F. Malan, victorious Nationalist Party leader in
the 1948 election, was editor of *Die Burger*, today the most
"independent" Afrikaans newspaper. He and his successor
as Nationalist prime minister, Johannes Strydom, formed
the Voortrekkerpers company to publish *Die Transvaler*
as official organ for the Nationalist Party in the Transvaal. First editor of this Afrikaans daily was Dr. Hendrik
Verwoerd, prime minister after Strydom's death in 1958.
Publication of Verwoerd's estate after his assassination in
1966 revealed his substantial shareholdings in the Voortrekkerpers, and in the Afrikaansepers (publishers of *Die
Vaderland* and *Dagbreek*). The then Minister of Justice,
Johannes Vorster, was chairman of the boards of both the
Voortrekkerpers and Afrikaansepers, posts he resigned
when he became premier. Minister of Bantu Administration and Development, M. C. Botha, took over the chair-
manships from him.

The unity of ideology, purpose, and function in Afrikaans press and government pervades the administrative
structure of much governed South Africa. Attack on any
institution of government is attack on all. The *Mail*'s
exposé on prisons, therefore, did not merely embarrass

the government but struck at Afrikanerdom, that is, at South Africa. The *Mail* was guilty of a form of treason, and such unpatriotic, if not indeed communistic, individuals as Gandar and Pogrund had to be stopped. Before the prison series was complete the *Mail*'s offices were raided by the security police; Gandar's and Pogrund's passports were seized. For various reasons leading journalists on other papers such as Anthony Delius of the *Cape Times*, Ronnie Gill, editor of the *Pretoria News*, and John Sutherland, editor of the Port Elizabeth *Evening Post* have suffered similar harassment. But the Nationalist government has ample legislation at its disposal to silence individuals; the corporate institution of the English press is less manageable, and its resilience is well illustrated by the career of one newspaper.

The left-wing *Guardian*, begun in 1937, was banned in 1952. It reappeared as the *Clarion*, the *People's World*, and *Advance*, and was banned again in 1954. It appeared as *New Age*, claiming a circulation of 20,000, 90 per cent of it nonwhite. In 1962 that was banned; within a week *Spark* was on the streets. This time the government banned its staff members and in March 1963 *Spark* announced it could appear no longer.

The Nationalist government matches resilience with relentlessness. Two years after coming to power, it had appointed a Commission on the Press. The Commission sat for thirteen years and its voluminous report on the activities of stringers and foreign correspondents was essentially an indictment of the English press, whose "crimes" are suggested by the title of a pamphlet compiled from cables quoted in the 1964 report: "How They Hate Us: South Africa, and in particular the Afrikaners, their church, culture, and leaders, under fire in the world press" (published by the Voortrekkerpers).

The attacks of the Nationalist government on the English press are echoed by the South African Broadcasting Corporation, a state monopoly. As a public corporation maintained by public funds, it should, theoretically, be above political partisanship. Yet Dr. Dennis Worrall, a

political scientist at the University of South Africa, in an analysis of a program called "Current Affairs," counted six attacks on the *Mail*, four on the *Star*, three on the *Cape Times*, and three on the English press as a whole between June 1966 and July 1967. Accused in Parliament of using the SABC as a propaganda machine for the Nationalist Party, former Minister of Posts and Telegraphs, Dr. Albert Hertzog, himself an owner of Afrikaans newspapers and an immovable obstacle to the introduction of television to South Africa, replied that the English press had over the years published "slanted news." The "Current Affairs" program, he said, could "bring home to the English-speaking South Africans the true facts in regard to the news."

But the "true facts" are difficult to obtain because of legislation indirectly inhibiting the press. Horace Flather, former editor of the *Star*, has said that this legislation makes editing a newspaper in South Africa "like walking blindfolded through a minefield." Most formidable is Section 6 (d) of the Suppression of Communism Act:

> If the President is satisfied that any periodical or other publication serves *inter alia* as a means for expressing views or conveying information, the publication of which is calculated to further the achievement of any of the objects of communism, he may, without notice to any person concerned, by proclamation in the *Gazette* prohibit the printing, publication or dissemination of such periodical publication or the dissemination of such other publication . . .

The section can be widely interpreted—virtually all reform advocated in South Africa by critics of the government can be equated with *some* of the aims of communism. Characteristically, power is vested in one man. Gandar and Pogrund, for example, were convicted for their failure to take "reasonable steps," which apparently means clearing information with the Commissioner

are ignored by readers. Since 1948 Nationalist electoral majorities have steadily increased.

Editorial criticism of the Nationalist Government and its policy of *apartheid* creates a misleading impression of South Africa, exaggerating the division among whites. Depiction of the liberal, democratic Englishman struggling against the racist, authoritarian Afrikaner for civil liberty and the rights of the black man distorts reality. Many English-speaking South Africans, and Afrikaners, have battled against the *apartheid* ideology embodied in legislation since 1948, but, except briefly in the seventeenth century, the majority of all whites has always practiced a form of *apartheid*. English press denunciation of *apartheid* invests English-speaking South Africans with a moral glow. It is their press and they profit by association, but its editorial influence over them is negligible. The quarrel among English and Afrikaners is not about the substance of *apartheid*, only about its form, and even those differences are subsiding. The English-speaking South African's view of himself as a liberal, egalitarian democrat was false even before 1948. The myth should have been killed in 1936 when a Fusion ministry representative of both language groups, with a majority of 169 to eleven, passed the Natives Representation Act, removing Africans to a separate roll and fixing their number.

Friction between English press and Afrikaans government obscures the growing unity among whites. The idealism inherent in the adversary relationship has been contaminated by commercial and partisan concerns absent when that journalistic ethic was introduced to South Africa. London printer George Greig, publisher in 1824 of the country's first independent newspaper, the weekly *South African Commercial Advertiser*, was banished and his paper suppressed for constantly criticizing the Governor. His editor, Thomas Pringle, nevertheless, persisted with publication of his own monthly, the *South African Journal*, until Governor Lord Charles Somerset accused him of insulting and opposing the government. "He wished the magazine to continue," writes Pringle,

"... if I would conduct myself 'discreetly'. . . . I resolutely declined . . . his repeated invitations to recommence the magazine unless *legal protection* were granted to the press." Pringle stopped publishing the *Journal.*

In the recent trial state counsel Liebenberg asked Gandar, "Have you sometimes used strong language against the Government?" "That may be," replied Gandar, "I do not think journalists were brought into the world to be discreet and obsequious." The similarity in editorial stance and language conceals, however, the differences in the two men's situations. Pringle was his own master and Governor Somerset was uncomfortable about his actions.

> Though great public inconvenience might arise from the adoption of the measure, it is one of those subjects which a person in office finds it difficult to word a refusal that can meet the public eye. The Radical Party would perhaps like nothing better than to bring the letter of a Colonial Governor into Parliament positively refusing the existence of a free Press in a British Colony . . .

Secretary of Colonies Earl Bathurst overruled Somerset and sanctioned Greig's return to South Africa with liberty to publish the *Commercial Advertiser*. Somerset resigned in 1827 and legal protection of the press was secured the next year with only the laws of libel inhibiting press freedom.

The Nationalist Government shares none of Somerset's discomfort, and though Gandar and other editors are uncompromising in their defiance, English press management is less principled. Gandar's editorial states the ideal; in practice management has diluted it. Morris Broughton, after two decades of editorial experience in South Africa, is adamant: "Freedom became secondary to the necessity of commercial and financial stability . . . The outcome has been that the balance of power rests to this day with the owners, through their instruments, the business managers and directorates. . . . There is no genuine editorial power of decision, only and fundamentally of conformity." But editors are less conformist than management. To a greater extent than in any western democracy, big business, notably the mining companies, controls the English press and its sensibilities are commercial not moral. Government dictates *apartheid* and the people by and large approve it. Gandar's editorial reads less as a statement of English press philosophy than as an expression of personal conviction; he voices the disquieting conscience of his readers, but his stand doesn't sell newspapers.

The *Rand Daily Mail* trial cost South African Associated Newspapers an estimated $280,000 in legal fees. Soon after the trial began, a consortium of shareholders in SAAN announced that it wished to sell its controlling interest. Key figure in the consortium was Cape Town businessman Clive Corder, who has long disapproved of the *Mail's* stand, which he considers bad for business. Gandar had already been "promoted" from editor to editor-in-chief, rumor being that he'd been "kicked upstairs." Corder's failure to muffle the voice of the *Mail* and the paper's declining circulation may explain his anxiety to sell.

In 1962 the response of the corporate structure of the English press to the Press Commission had been a predictable blend of libertarian responsibility and commercial expediency. Anticipating the criticisms of the report, the South African Press Union, the association of newspaper owners, drew up its own code of conduct. A Board of Reference, composed of two managerial nominees under the chairmanship of a retired judge, was to try to ensure that newspaper reports were accurate and not offensive to decency. The Board may reprimand any editor or journalist who is adjudged to have been guilty of an infringement of the code; and such reprimand will be published in other newspapers. The ambiguity of the code's final clause reveals the subtle modification of the libertarian tradition Pringle brought from Britain: "Comment (by newspapers) should take due cognisance of the complex racial problems of South Africa and should also take into account the general good and the safety of the country and its peoples." Implicit in the clause is the potential for the owners' suppression of criticism of government. The Gandar trial suggests why they might want to do so.

This is harsh criticism of management whose commercial priorities, after all, are merely sensitive to the mood of the white population. The editorial stance of the English press by contrast is increasingly distant from its readers and imperfectly reflects the source of division among them.

For much of South Africa's history two white cultures have competed for dominance. At the end of the eighteenth century the Dutch had the advantage of a 150-year start on the English, of having created an indigenous culture sensitive to a new way of life and environment. During that period of comparative isolation from Europe, a new race was formed. The Dutchman became an Afrikaner. If he suffered because the ideas of the American and French Revolutions virtually passed him by, he was unaware of the loss. But the arrival of the English at the beginning of the nineteenth century was a dangerous threat. Evasion, migration, and defiance characterized his struggle. Finally, from 1899 to 1902, the Afrikaner fought his War of Independence and Civil War. The quality of his resistance, his courage and endurance, and his commitment to South Africa made defeat in the Anglo-Boer War merely temporary. Since 1652 his power and influence had ebbed and flowed; after that war they grew remorselessly. Today the Afrikaner's position seems impregnable and he guards it with religious fervor and vigilance.

English-speaking South Africans, most of them commercial townsmen contemptuous of rural Afrikaners, enjoyed supremacy for the half century ending in 1948. Defeat was shattering to the Englishman's psychology. The date Afrikaners' political reconquest of South Africa profoundly disturbed his notions of his own effortless superiority, his conviction that part of the white man's burden was leadership of the backward Afrikaner to civilization.

To the outside world the crux and pivot of South African politics, and the only source of division among whites, is the black man. Race is at the heart of party politics, but it isn't everything; if it were, South African politics would be greatly simplified. For the distortion the English press must take considerable responsibility. It has perpetuated, within and without South Africa, one of the country's most potent myths. The orthodoxy runs: 1948 marks a violent break and reversal in the development of race relations in South Africa.

English-speaking South Africans born during World War II will recall the stunned disbelief of their parents' generation when Dr. Malan led the Afrikaner people and his National Party to electoral victory in 1948. Their feelings were similar to those of H. F. Rose, former editor of the *Natal Witness,* who said in 1926, "The place is ruined. I heard Afrikaans being spoken in the main street today, in public." Optimism and confidence soon returned. The Nationalists, after all, had won by only five seats, with a minority (40 per cent) of the popular vote.

In February 1950 the defeated prime minister, General J. C. Smuts, leader of the United Party which English-speaking South Africans supported, congratulated Winston Churchill on his comeback in the British elections. "Here the Nationalist Government are continuing to lose ground all round," he wrote, "and I look forward to my victory following yours in Britain in due course." Six months later, on September 11, 1950, the eighty-year-old general died of a heart attack, and a generation of English-speaking South Africans never recovered. Disbelief gave way to a sense of betrayal, to charges of Nationalist trickery and gerrymandering. In 1953 the Nationalists increased their representation from 79 to 94 seats and won 45.5 per cent of the popular vote; in 1958 they won 103 seats and 49 per cent of the vote; in 1961, 105 and 53.5 per cent; in 1966, 126 and 58.6 per cent.

If Smuts had left the liberal Cape to become State Attorney in Paul Kruger's independent South African Republic (now the Transvaal), had written *A Century of*

Wrong (an attack on the British more bitter than any Boer leader had delivered), had been a distinguished Boer general in the Anglo-Boer War, since then he had nonetheless demonstrated his greatness to English-speaking South Africans by defending the British Empire. Member of the Imperial War Cabinet in the first World War and admirer of Campbell-Bannerman, successful advocate against fierce Nationalist opposition of South Africa's entry at Britain's side in the second and friend of Churchill, Smuts epitomized the triumph of his own policy—conciliation of Boer and Briton, which English-speaking South Africans apparently understood to mean the anglicization of the Afrikaner. They approved his British acculturation, in fitting tribute to which he was elected in 1948 as Rector of Cambridge University.

Most of all they approved his priorities—conciliation before the "native question." Under English-speaking guidance the latter would take care of itself, and their attitude to the racial issue has always followed their party's current slogan, "White Leadership with Justice." Smuts, the international statesman, was never anything else than a South African. The shock of victorious Afrikaner nationalism in 1948 exposed the slogan's real meaning. English-speaking South Africans may have contemplated the ideal of equality for the far distant future, but they rarely doubted that leadership to the ideal would be English. In the years of continuing political defeat they have faced the knowledge that, like Smuts, they too are South Africans. For all the complexity and contradictions of South African politics, for all the sectional antagonism, white South Africans want essentially the same thing—segregation of black and white.

There is a difference in philosophy, tradition and life style between the two white sections and it continues to divide them, but their shared experiences and fears predominate, and increasingly so. In 1961 the Union of South Africa became a Republic and left the British Commonwealth. The last symbolic link was cut, yet the pain of separation was brief. In the 1966 election Smuts' policy of conciliation was working not by anglicization but in reverse. English-speaking South Africans were voting for the Nationalist Party in defense of an essentially shared way of life.

Principled and courageous as its fight for the voteless has been, the English press has not always transcended this struggle between Boer and Briton. Morris Broughton may overstate his criticism, but his point is well taken:

> Instead of being an arbiter it [the South African press] has become, through varied historical, political and economic causes, the vehicle of one section. It stands for non-partisanship but is, in fact, politically partisan. What it pronounces good, is immediately branded by the opposing section as bad. There is thus, even in the small White minority, no moral judge of public affairs, but only instruments of endlessly contending parties.

Confined largely to a negative role, to reaction to government act and declaration, denied meaningful interaction with government, and isolated from the power and influence it had previously enjoyed, the English press often responds shrilly and with a partisanship at variance with its stated ideals. It performs no better then than the Afrikaans press. While frustration is understandable in situations where the news is second hand and propagandist, reporting in the same tone of events to which access is free is inexcusable.

Die Transvaler and *Rand Daily Mail* reports, for example, of Senator Robert Kennedy's talk at Afrikaans Stellenbosch University (from which every Nationalist prime minister since 1948 has graduated) during his visit to South Africa in June 1966, reveal how nonpartisan, interpretive reporting has been perverted in South Africa.

Transvaler	*Mail*
STELLENBOSCH THROWS COLD WATER ON KENNEDY	HE CAME UP TOPS IN MATIELAND

The welcome which Stellenbosch students at Simonsberg residence gave Kennedy was a sharp contrast to the violent welcome he received last night from Cape Town students. About 300 Simonsbergers waited calmly for him along with a group of 200 others and naturally the crowd of newsmen which accompanies Senator Kennedy. The calmness of the welcome in contrast to the virtual hysteria in Cape Town put Senator Kennedy in his right perspective—a young enterprising politician who through skillful use of publicity media and personal charm has been built up to a five-day wonder.	Senator Kennedy yesterday tackled the intellectual and spiritual home of Afrikanerdom, Stellenbosch—and came up tops. At Stellenbosch University students gave him and Mrs. Kennedy an unexpectedly warm welcome. He was enthusiastically applauded after an impromptu speech on the steps of Simonsberg residence.

In view of the adherence to the traditions of Anglo-American journalism professed in Gandar's editorial, the *Mail* cannot be complacent that its report is only less slanted than *Die Transvaler*'s. What is the South African reader to make of these two reports? Regrettably his response is usually sectional. If he's English-speaking, the truth is the *Mail*'s account; if Afrikaans, the *Transvaler*'s. The only medium shared by everyone is radio, and that is as partisan. South Africans are helpless when seeking accurate political information; they must choose between sectional versions of the truth and they seldom go beyond the limitations of their own prejudices. And *the* truth? To secure it, Anglo-American journalism relies heavily on the adversary system. That system barely operates in South Africa. It cannot.

Broughton may exaggerate the sectionalism and partisanship of the English press, but his harshness is a valuable corrective to what is sometimes perceived by Americans as a press no different from their own. Gandar's clash with government and his admirable defense of a free press dramatize the conflicting conceptions of press function between the English press and government. Outstanding editor and journalist though he is, and there are others like him, his paper is nevertheless tainted by the sectional and commercial realities of South Africa. Besides Gandar's editorials, the *Mail* best upholds the philosophy it professes when it takes on government with the kind of investigative reporting which produced the exposé of prison conditions. That was responsible, courageous, and independent journalism of a high order in the context of South African society. A South African journalist, "who has to remain anonymous," ended his report on the trial for the *Guardian* in England: "Fear has and will shut out much but it will not silence South Africa's opposition press. They will speak out, they will still expose the iniquities where they find them anew, but they will do it less often and more mutedly."

They will, however, do so less often not only because of government power and managerial control, but also because they lack reader support. In 1942 General Smuts arrested a young general of the Ossewa Brandwag, an extremist Afrikaner organization determined to establish a Christian-National Republic and to sabotage South Africa's war effort against Hitler. Implacably hostile to Britain and to conciliation, and dedicated to Afrikanerdom, Johannes Vorster was interned until January 1944 at Koffiefontein. There in August 1967, Vorster—now prime minister of the Republic whose white electorate had recently given his party the biggest majority in its history—told his supporters that he was dissatisfied with the laws of libel, that he would introduce legislation "making untruths in fact punishable." He responded to the English newspapers' outcry against such government curtailment of press freedom with the complacency of a leader whose call for white unity, a new form of conciliation, was triumphing over sectionalism: "I know one thing. If I go to the public and ask if they are in favor of legislation against factual lies, there will be only one answer—and it will be yes."

South Africans have tolerated and approved extraordinary restrictions of civil liberty and the English press has little reason to doubt the truth of that taunt.

It would be misleading to leave the impression that foreign reporters bow to authority routinely. Although it is true that American journalists, by and large, are far more likely to strike an adversary stance than are political journalists in almost any other country, it is not true that they are alone in challenging governmental authority. One of the best examples of adversary journalism is the German magazine *Der Spiegel*, which is the subject of this sketch by Barbara Packer:*

"Wie steht ein Demokrat seiner Demokratie?" How does a democrat stand to his democracy? This, according to Hans Tiede, Berlin editor for *Der Spiegel*, was the central question in West Germany's celebrated "*Spiegel* Affair" of late 1962. In the *Spiegel* affair, Herr Tiede might have been more accurate in asking, "How does a democrat stand *up* to his democracy?" For the *Spiegel* incident has become, to many Germans, the symbol of the necessity to guard vigilantly against any violation of the democratic process by an overly secretive government. In a country as self-conscious about democracy as the Federal Republic—whose citizens' only prior experience with a nonauthoritarian form of government had been the ill-fated Weimar Republic—the importance of such an event can hardly be overstated.

The history of the "*Spiegel* Affair" reads like a mixture of TV-spy-thriller and Keystone Cops script, with enough espionage to fill an entire cloak-and-dagger room. But the comic confusion of plot details was overshadowed by the ugly, Gestapo-like overtones produced by the actions of the Bonn government.

The affair began with *Spiegel*'s main article in the October 6, 1962, issue. Called "Fallex 62," after the code

* Barbara Packer holds the B.A. in English from Stanford. A Phi Beta Kappa, she has published in *Mademoiselle* and is now a graduate student in English at Yale.

name of the NATO exercises it described, the article was an attack on General Friedrich Foertsch, the reviewing general for Germany's forces during the exercises. Foertsch had reported "chaotic neglect" and "dismal preparation" in Germany's ground forces. Although the article directed its criticism at the General, the real target was the head of the Defense Ministry, Franz-Josef Strauss.

The "Fallex 62" article was, in fact, the culmination of a long-standing feud between *Spiegel* and Strauss. Since 1956, when Strauss assumed the job of Defense Minister, *Spiegel* had delighted in pointing out inconsistencies in his policies, evidences of corruption in distribution of defense and military housing contracts, and inadequacies in the state of the German police force. In particular, *Spiegel* felt that Strauss had built up the Bundeswehr much too quickly, sacrificing more careful organization to his own economic interests.

But the feud had political roots that reached much deeper than contract scandals. *Spiegel*, or more specifically publisher Rudolph Augstein (whom *Time* magazine once described as "militantly pacifistic"), was violently opposed to Strauss' pro-nuclear, pro-European-community policy. Reunification of Germany had always occupied top place on *Spiegel*'s agenda, and Augstein feared that Strauss' insistence on nuclear weapons for the Federal Republic could not help but alienate the East Germans and injure future efforts toward reunification. (The fear was justifiable: an East Berlin cabaret had recently featured a spoof of Strauss' policy which derided, "Bavarian *gemütlichkeit*/ A Hofbräu mug in one hand, and an H-bomb in the other.")

New ammunition had been given *Spiegel* only a few months before the October 6 issue. *Spiegel* gleefully reported that Strauss had attempted to obtain the removal of a police officer who ticketed him for driving the wrong way down a one-way street. But "Fallex 62" provided the devastating final blow; *Spiegel* blamed the sorry state of Germany's ground forces not only on Strauss' contract favoritism, but also on his concentration on nuclear weapons at the expense of conventional forces.

There was, however, a catch in the *Spiegel* article. Nearly all the material in the Foertsch report was classified "top secret" by NATO headquarters in Paris. Upon receiving confirmation of this fact from NATO, a Dr. Gerhard Wesgram of the Ministry of Justice, apparently acting on suggestions from Strauss, drafted arrest warrants charging Augstein and four other *Spiegel* editors with suspicion of treason, treasonable falsification, and bribery.

The arrests were made with an astounding lack of political *savoir faire*. A special delegation of security police arrived at *Spiegel*'s Bonn bureau at ten o'clock at night. They evacuated and then ransacked the office, discovering copies of the "Fallex 62" report in Augstein's safe— reports that were clearly marked "top secret." Most of the editors were at home, and the arrests were conducted in a manner that could not help but remind Germans of the old Gestapo knock-in-the-middle-of-the-night tactics.

One of the editors, Conrad Ahlers, was vacationing in Spain at the time. Since the security police denied having any power of extradition, Wesgram called in the Defense Ministry. Strauss then arranged for the military attaché in Madrid, named Oster, to request that the Spanish police arrest Ahlers. Strauss himself spoke to Oster at one time during the night, after Oster had refused to believe the order he received was legitimate. The Spanish police duly carried out the request, and Ahlers was arrested and held for twenty-eight hours before he was sent to Germany with an escort.

The complications soon attained farcial proportions. Strauss first denied any connection with the arrests, then admitted telephoning Oster. The Minister of Justice, Wolfgang Stammberger, who had not even been informed that his underlings were making a series of political arrests, angrily tendered his resignation to Adenauer. Four other cabinet members of Stammberger's FDP (Free Democratic Party)—necessary for Adenauer to maintain his coalition cabinet—also resigned in protest against Strauss' action. Meanwhile, the opposition party, the SPD (Social-Democratic Party of Germany), found the political climate most conducive to haymaking. SPD Bundestag members charged Adenauer with incipient neofascism. Adenauer replied that Augstein was a vulgar and treacherous opportunist. Adenauer had pledged to stand by Strauss, but public outcry as well as political pressure forced him to ask for Strauss' resignation. On December 11, a new coalition cabinet was formed—without Strauss.

In the meantime, new and incredibly complicated facets of the affair were coming to light. Several new characters were revealed. One was General Reinhard Gehlen, chief of the German intelligence service. Another was henchman-of-all-trades Colonel Adolf Wicht, who seemed to have a finger in nearly everybody's pie: nominally a member of Strauss' staff, he was actually Gehlen's agent, as well as a worker in an unofficial capacity for *Spiegel* during the "Fallex 62" story. It was Wicht who was charged with leaking the top-secret material to *Spiegel,* but it soon became obvious that Gehlen himself was really behind the affair. Gehlen, an appropriately shadowy character (the only known photograph of him dated from 1944), had his own reasons for wanting the story to be published. Like Augstein, he had been bitterly opposed to Strauss' attempt to secure nuclear weapons for Germany, although his opposition stemmed less from political grounds than from purely military ones—he felt strengthening the ground forces was more important than the vague promise of nuclear weapons. Gehlen used *Spiegel* to get at Strauss, by making available secret documents concerning Fallex 62. Unfortunately, he picked a singularly inopportune time; Strauss had recently received severe reprimands from NATO about leaks in the German security system.

The immediate outcome of the affair was, for *Spiegel,* triumphant. By the beginning of 1963 most of *Spiegel's* editors had been released and the charges against them dropped. *Spiegel*'s circulation had risen mercurially—from 500,000 to 850,000. Most important, Strauss was out of the cabinet.

Repercussions of the affair, however, are still echoing in law chambers of the Federal Republic, and in the Bundestag itself. Suits filed by *Spiegel* are still pending, and there is a bill being debated in the German Parliament which would grant special political immunity to journalists—a bill which the *Spiegel* affair avowedly initiated. Perhaps most important was the *Spiegel* affair's role in pointing up Adenauer's unfitness for office. Many political analysts credit the *Spiegel* affair with bringing about Der Alte's decision to step down.

It is essential that one understand, however, that the event's importance to the German people would probably not be diminished even if it had had none of these country-shaking consequences. The word that the observer soon discovers is ubiquitous in all conversations with Germans about the *Spiegel* affair is "democracy"—not merely democracy as it concerns the freedom of the press, but democracy as it concerns Germany and its citizens in general. To understand *Spiegel*'s importance as an exemplar of democracy, as well as the overall importance of the affair, it is necessary to probe deeper into the peculiar German attitude toward *Der Spiegel,* and the German hypersensitivity about democracy.

"Undemocratic procedure" or "lack of appreciation for democracy" are typical catch-all phrases which are likely to be used in every accusation-hurling bout in the Federal Republic. The memory of the Hitler years is no doubt responsible for the preoccupation with questions of democracy, but it certainly seems to be true that each element of German society is continually suspicious that others are trying to nibble away at the foundations of a democratic Germany.

The people accuse the government of wanting to assume dictatorial powers. The government, on the other hand, often accuses the people of political apathy bred by lack of democratic tradition. The government accuses the press of neglecting to censor itself, or of profiteering on matters of national interest. Kurt Mattick, Berlin chairman of the Social-Democratic Party, and member of the Bundestag, voiced a common government sentiment when he remarked, "The German press is young and lacks a tradition of self-censorship. Too many young reporters think only of the money they can earn through a sensational exposé, rather than considering the effects which might be detrimental to the country."

The press, for its part, has no lack of complaints about the government. Herr Tiede protested, "If you criticize the government in Germany, you are immediately accused of 'dirtying your nest,' of being a Communist, a Fascist, or what have you. The government does not seem to be able to distinguish between criticism and sedition." The German people also come in for a share of press criticism. Herr W. E. Süskind, one of the editors of the *Suddeutsche Zeitung*, said in regard to the *Spiegel* affair, "The people are still far from recognizing that it is their freedom that the liberty of the press guarantees."

Herr Süskind may have been a bit too hasty in applying that last generalization to the *Spiegel* affair, however. Kurt Mattick allowed that "it was really the people who protested the government action" during the affair. And, despite an overall attitude of ambivalence toward *Spiegel*, there is a common sentiment among Germans that, as one man put it, "If there were no *Spiegel*, our freedom would be in danger."

What is, and what causes, this ambivalence? On the one hand, *Spiegel* is criticized for its blatant distortion of news. "*Spiegel* is very much like *Time* magazine in format," explained a professor in a beginning German course, "but it is even worse." On the other hand, it is praised for persistently hanging political dirty laundry in the public view. The only publication of its kind in postwar Germany, *Spiegel* has acquired, since its founding in 1947, such a formidable reputation for damaging inquisitiveness that many political figures refuse to grant interviews to *Spiegel* reporters. In general, *Spiegel* remains true to its conviction that, as Tiede put it, "*Spiegel* has a democratic duty to bring out that which is embarrassing to the other papers."

Tiede also replied to accusations leveled against the German press in such statements as Mattick's. *Spiegel* is above economic opportunism, Tiede declared. *Spiegel* journalists are all experienced men, established and respected, and they are paid a flat salary, removing the incentive to produce scandal merely for economic reasons.

As for the charge that the press lacks a tradition of self-censorship, Tiede replied with a countercharge. *Spiegel* believes that the press has a responsibility to suppress material which could be truly detrimental to the safety of the nation. He gave the example of a *Bild-Zeitung* reporter who had been punished—rightly so, believed Tiede—for publishing secret information let slip by a drunken Bürgermeister concerning the location of a new NATO base. But Tiede did not agree that a reporter should suppress material merely because it was *labeled* "top secret." "Too much material in Germany is immediately labeled 'classified,'" he said. "If we avoided all so-called 'top secret' material, investigation of any problem would be impossible."

Tiede continued that the journalist has the right—and the duty—to publish material labeled "top secret" purely for political reasons. As long as the government attempts to hide embarrassing material by "classifying" it, the journalist "can decide for himself whether the matter is a real state secret or merely a subterfuge to cover mistakes."

Spiegel, then, is a news magazine continuing the long and honorable tradition of the adversary press. By exposing material which the government is attempting to conceal, and which other papers are too reticent to discuss, *Spiegel* intends to remain the Republic's political watchdog—and a very effective one, since *Spiegel's* bark is impossible to silence or ignore. It is fitting, then, that it was an affair concerning *Spiegel* which brought the attention of the German people to latent authoritarian tendencies in the Bonn regime, which provided the impetus for a bill guaranteeing the safety of the inquiring reporter, and which, as Mr. Süskind put it, taught the German people, no less than the government, a "lesson in democracy."

CHAPTER EIGHT

The Abrasive Adversaries

Liberty means responsibility. That is why most men dread it.

—GEORGE BERNARD SHAW

"There are more muckmakers than there are muckrakers."

—DREW PEARSON

Let us imagine an American journalism which faces up to its clear responsibility to stand as an adversary to government. Let us imagine that at each point of contact with officialdom—in the cities, in the special governmental districts, in the county halls of government, in the state capitals, and in Washington—reporters are respectful but persistent in demanding that the public business be made public.

It is comfortable to think that because the American system allows such reportage—indeed, is based upon it—we can at least hope for it. A good many journalists say that something like the adversary system described above now exists, and they cite example after example to prove the case. Examining their examples supports their arguments here and there. *Life* magazine brought down Supreme Court Justice Abe Fortas almost single-handedly. Drew Pearson and Jack Anderson revealed so much about Senator Thomas Dodd of Connecticut that the United States Senate was forced to perform the act that pains it most: censuring one of its own members. The examples are easily multiplied. Far more often, however, examination shows that most adversary reporting results from reactions to events. One official contradicts another, or attacks him, and the press responds by investigating—perhaps *both* men. A minor suit is brought, as in the Bobby Baker case, and the press begins to sniff out much larger game. Senator Ted Kennedy drives off a narrow bridge at midnight, the girl accompanying him drowns, and the press investigates so persistently that authorities who have closed the case are forced to open it again. These are high marks, perhaps, but they are *re*actions. Independent investigation and action by the press are needed—and often missing.

But the really sobering question is whether a true adversary relationship with government alone is enough today. President Eisenhower, of all unlikely people, popularized the concept of the dangerous military-industrial complex. As the shape of that complex began to emerge from investigations by scholars and journalists, it became clear that it is actually a military-industrial-labor-education complex. Big labor and the research components of higher education are deeply involved, and they try powerfully to lure the mass media into equal and tranquil partnership.

Moreover, the emergence of this intricate complex at the federal level enables us to see more clearly that government at all levels is entangled with industry, with labor, with education—with every institution of the American society. Because city, county, and state governments do not construct their own offices, build their own roads, manufacture their own equipment, write and print books for public schools—because they do not perform for themselves the myriad activities which are essential in modern governance, the interlocking of government and other institutions follows as surely as the dawn.

When one adds the fact that governmental action and inaction at every level affect *all* the institutions of society ... Consider the churches, which are too often thought to be separate from government. In fact, of course, the nation's churches benefit by millions of dollars because they operate commercial businesses which are not taxed.

The question, then, is: Should the press be an adversary to government alone? Must not those elements of the press which have accepted their role as adversary to government take the next step and range themselves in an adversary position with respect to all the institutions of society? Not belligerently—but questioning, probing, requiring that society's institutions provide the society with the information which alone can enable us to organize our lives.

It must be axiomatic that hardly any of the publications which are deemed "successful" by commercial standards strike anything like an adversary stance toward business, toward higher education (except when students are revolting), toward big labor, toward the church, and all the other pivotal institutions. (Perhaps most of all, the commercial press does not print critiques of itself. Let one of its members be attacked—even the sleaziest—and the others gather around protectively like so many doctors reacting to a malpractice suit.) Like the Communists, who will not question the basic structures of their society, American journalists approach every institution gingerly, and with notable deference. On the left, *Harper's, The Progressive, The New Republic, The Atlantic,* and a few others run occasional articles questioning untaxed church businesses and the like. On the right, *National Review* and similar publications offer occasional challenges from their special perspective, although not to business and industry. But it is notable that those publications which are most likely to pursue such touchy subjects consistently are the least likely to be "successful" in the commercial sense. It is oversimplifying to say that advertisers and advertising agencies blacklist those who question the system, but it is not much more complex than that. Let a *Consumer Reports* rate and grade products without fear or favor, and it must do so without advertising as well.

There is no hope that commercial broadcasting will ever serve as a proper adversary to society's institutions. On the few occasions when bold men have attempted to make broadcasting an adversary, they have felt a little pressure and have collapsed obligingly—or their superiors have collapsed for them. CBS's Edward R. Murrow broadcast on radio a program exposing the use of prostitutes by businessmen. Big business howled; CBS radio apologized . . . During a short but distinguished period, Murrow's *See It Now* series explored several flaws in the American society. But it could not last, even with Murrow's great prestige to protect it. As the series was being killed by CBS, Murrow asked board chairman William Paley, "Don't you want an instrument like the

See It Now organization, which you have poured so much into for
so long, to continue?" Paley replied, "Yes, but I don't want this
constant stomach ache every time you do a controversial program." Broadcasting is too susceptible to stomach aches ever to
become a real adversary.

There is some hope for a wide-ranging adversary journalism, however. It is evident in the birth of the many little weeklies,
biweeklies, and monthlies which have sprung up in several states,
especially on the West Coast. These are *not* underground papers
like the Berkeley *Barb,* which at first attract us with an amalgam
of valuable muckraking and hymns to the sex-and-drug culture,
then, because so few undergrounders have any real interest in
journalism, lose us when the muckraking is all but submerged in a
sea of four-letter words, stark pictures, and protests in the plati-
tudes of the New Left.

No, the underground press is quite different from the real
adversary press, which questions and challenges pivotal institutions. One of the best is the San Francisco *Bay Guardian.* It has
published solid exposés of giant powers like the Pacific Gas & Electric Company, the Southern Pacific Railroad, Pacific Telephone,
and the influential communications empire which is made up of
the San Francisco *Chronicle* and *Examiner,* KRON-TV, and
related enterprises.

What the *Bay Guardian* and similar papers are has been
well expressed by *Guardian* Editor Bruce Brugmann:

> I aim my derringer at every reporter and tell him, by
> God, that I don't want to see an objective piece of report-
> ing. . . . But this is not dishonest journalism; it is "point of
> view" journalism. Our facts are as straight as we can make
> them; we don't run a story until we feel we can prove it or
> make it stick; we always talk with the adversary and try to
> print his side as part of the story; he always gets the chance
> of reply in the next issue (rarely do they, even when I offer
> in letter or by phone). We run almost all the critical reac-
> tion we get to stories; but the point is we don't run a story
> until we think it is in the public interest to do so.
>
> How do you talk about our major stories, environmen-
> tal pollution, Vietnam, the Manhattanization of San

Francisco, saving the Bay, unless you do some "point of view" reporting? We're not just covering meetings. We're not just checking in with the official sources. We're going after stories, hopefully before they become certifiable facts (as did the Embarcadero Freeway in San Francisco—the *cause célèbre* of objective journalism—as did Candlestick Park, as will the Rockefeller Building and the TransAmerica Building and a whole host of things that don't become news until the Planning Commission or the City Council is ready to decide). Along with this come different forms of the new journalism: letting participants write their own stuff, using experts with special knowledge, more literary writing, the use of irony, poetry, impressionistic writing—everything, really, that has relevance, and merit, and readability—and goes for the jugular. "Nothing is too good to print in a daily newspaper," Franklin Pierce Adams once said, and it ought to be graven in 64-point Poster Bodoni—hell, 96-point Garamond Bold—on every city editor's desk in the Bay Area. And, most important in the new journalism: looking at a news story with another slant that is never, ever, printed in the big press: how *the media* covered, why, who, what, where, etc. If an event *isn't* covered in San Francisco, as Marshall McLuhan and Howard Gossage showed us, it hasn't happened.

The chief of many dangers inherent in such an approach is obvious: if the editor is a conspiracy theorist, the appearance of evil is the same as evil. But for all his free-swinging stance, Brugmann has never had to answer a libel suit. How he runs his valuable paper is explored here by Linda Moulton Howe:*

> *"It is a newspaper's duty to print*
> *the news and raise hell."*

(Wilbur F. Storey: Statement of the aims of the *Chicago Times*, 1861, and adopted as a theme by *The Bay Guardian*)

* Linda Moulton Howe holds the Master's Degree in Broadcasting and Film from Stanford. She is now a television news writer in Los Angeles.

Taped on the front door of an old pink warehouse at 1040 Bryant Street, not far from San Francisco's Seventh Street turnoff, is a cardboard advertising sign for "*The Bay Guardian*—a fortnightly newspaper." Inside, newspapers, old and new, are stacked in piles on the floor, and copy is piled in an S & W Apricot Nectar box. Several brooms scattered throughout the two or three office rooms suggest that some day the makeshift box-and-paper chaos will be put into some permanent order.

Tall, thirty-four-year-old Bruce B. Brugmann, whom *Chronicle* columnist Herb Caen describes as "hotly talented," is publisher and editor of *The Bay Guardian*. One might also call Brugmann a natural adversary.

He was at the University of Nebraska editing the college newspaper in the last years of the McCarthy era. "At that time," he says, "the American Legion and the Farm Bureau were trying to oust the liberal 'Communist professors' from the University and our paper got hold of this and created a stir for several months. I was up for expulsion eight or nine times."

Brugmann went on to the Columbia University School of Journalism for a Master's Degree and then into the army. Still writing, he became bureau chief of the ten-man *Stars and Stripes* paper in Seoul, Korea.

When he returned to the United States, he got a job as city reporter for the *Milwaukee Journal* in Wisconsin. "Usually on a big paper," Brugmann says, "you are pretty much directed by the City Desk." After three and a half years, he got tired of being directed and moved to Redwood City, California, in 1964 to report for the Redwood City *Tribune* and plan his own newspaper.

"It seems to me," he says, "that the whole point of a newspaper is to set itself independent of all groups and movements so that on the one hand it isn't part of the usually recognized team effort where the paper is working with the city hall and chamber of commerce, . . . or on the other hand, doesn't represent only a particular movement like the New Left or a particular political action group."

San Francisco, he felt, would be the best place to

establish his paper. "First," he explains, "the local papers are so uniformly bad. Second, there is a concentration of educated people here—the universities, ratio of industry, etc. Third, it is one of the few areas that is truly becoming a 'region' in the sense of regional government, transportation, and commuters. BART (Bay Area Rapid Transit) could have a very good effect, especially for a tabloid newspaper, because you would have a captive audience for thirty or forty-five minutes each day traveling between San Francisco and peninsula cities—an audience not only interested in the local neighborhood newspaper, but what goes on in San Francisco and the entire Bay region."

While Brugmann was thinking about his future paper, he began writing in May 1964 a series of articles for the Redwood City *Tribune* entitled "Points of No Return," critical reviews of proposed development projects on Bay tidelands. Among these is a vast land development plan called Redwood Shores. The pertinence of Redwood Shores to Bruce Brugmann's career and to Bay history to this date is vital, and it is important that some background be outlined.

A private land developer, the Leslie Salt Co., acquired 53,000 acres of South Bay land in 1850–1909, when California statutes permitted the state to grant tidelands by patent to private parties, even though the state constitution specifies that all navigable waterways are held in perpetual trust for the right of the people to fish, navigate, and have commerce over those waterways. The state policy, until 1964 when the McAteer bill was passed prohibiting Bay fill, was to grant patents to anybody willing to make them productive and taxable. With its patents, Leslie Salt built dikes into the Bay as far as possible, to make shallow ponds for salt evaporation. The old patents were made by linear or perimeter description, and the fluctuating tides caused changes in the land, clouding the accuracy of title descriptions.

Around 1959 the Bay area population began to rise and Redwood City firmed up its city government with a new city manager and a council that agreed it would be to the city's advantage to have large, privately owned land tracts like that of Leslie Salt developed as integrated wholes under municipal planning and jurisdiction, rather than see the Bay front deteriorate into hodgepodge, piecemeal, independent developments. Leslie, who no doubt realized its salt profit was small compared to the potential economic value in developing its 53,000 acres for housing, industry, and recreation, decided to go along with the city's long-range perspective.

The company's first step was to get the legislature to pass a law which would authorize clarification of all land titles south of the thirty-seven-degree, forty-minute parallel (roughly the San Mateo Bridge); e.g., that definition be made of what the state owned and what it didn't. Leslie could not safely begin acreage development until titles could be guaranteed. In 1959 the right to exchange and clarify titles with the state was granted (Chapter 1885 of the California Statutes of 1959), but the exchange had yet to be approved by the State Lands Commission.

A major problem was that throughout Leslie's patents were navigable waterways ("navigable" defined as two feet of water at mean low tide). The California Constitution states that (1) the state cannot give away state property without a fair exchange, and that (2) all navigable waterways are held in perpetual trust for the right of the people to fish, navigate, and have commerce over those waterways.

Leslie initiated action to convey to the state 1,551 acres of navigable sloughs received in patents, and to have the state, in exchange, grant to Leslie clear title to everything else in its patents, a total of more than 50,000 acres. In acreage comparison, the exchange would be vastly out of proportion in Leslie's favor. So, no doubt to make the deal look better, Leslie defined its share of the land exchange as nonnavigable sloughs totaling 458 acres. More simply, Leslie Salt proposed that the state exchange 458 acres of nonnavigable sloughs for 1,551 acres of navigable sloughs.

However, in 1951 a decision had been made which clearly defined the state's attitude on slough ownership. In the earlier case (a suit filed by San Jose against Leslie Salt, concerning Coyote Slough at the south end of the Bay), the state took the following position filed in Action #78426 in the Supreme Court of Santa Clara County on March 15, 1951, signed by Edmund G. Brown, Attorney General, and Miriam E. Wolff, Deputy Attorney General:

> Prior to September 9, 1850, a portion of the lands were tide and submerged lands covered by the water of the Bay of San Francisco. On that date, California became a member of the Union and by that fact acquired title to all such tide and submerged lands and to all lands lying in the beds of title waterways. That is to such lands so described as now owned by defendant (Leslie Salt) neither the whole nor any portion thereof has ever been conveyed by (the State of California).

Thus, in 1951, California claimed, by sovereign right, ownership not only of all waterways but also of their underlying beds. Leslie would have, at the most, only nominal title by early patents.

Nevertheless, Leslie and the Redwood City government proceeded to lay the groundwork for future development of Leslie land. On March 9, 1964, Redwood City passed an enabling ordinance (#1128) to allow the city to create a special district, and on April 13, the council passed Resolution 4255, creating a special improvement district to be known as Redwood Shores, totaling 4,300 acres of Leslie Salt Co. land, including thirty-nine acres of slough land still not clear in title. Redwood Shores was annexed to Redwood City, the City Council became its Board of Directors, and a bond proposal to finance future development was discussed. In matters concerning special improvement districts, those authorized to vote are the landowners. In the case of Redwood Shores, the voters were Leslie Salt Co. and Leslie Properties, Inc.—two votes if you count by companies, one if you count by owner. In June, Leslie voted for a $176 million bond authorization.

Bruce Brugmann began writing articles in his column, "Point of No Return," questioning the wisdom of building plans for homes and schools on potential earthquake tideland, and the public began to express concern. People wanted to know what the city planned to do with the special district and how it would affect them as taxpayers. Mrs. Mary Henderson, a recently elected councilwoman, recalled that at the time the 1964 resolution was passed to create Redwood Shores:

> It was one of those things that went through without public information or discussion. The enabling ordinance . . . was printed in the local newspaper in the back pages in the legal notices in columns that filled two pages. It was printed on a Thursday night to be heard by the council on the following Monday. The citizenry had to look there to read the small print and still you didn't know what the implications were or what it all meant. And we were there, those of us who were concerned, asking for time to understand it all, but we didn't get any information. We were just told that the council had to stick to the timetable.

She believes the pressure to quickly pass the resolution was caused by the pending McAteer bill in Sacramento, which would ban any future filling in of the Bay and would thus confine any tideland development behind the dikes.

At the beginning of 1965, Bruce Brugmann became the *Tribune*'s City Hall reporter and his articles criticizing the City Council–Leslie Salt Co. marriage and its plans for Redwood Shores were, according to Mary Henderson, "keeping people awake to the situation and giving Brug-

mann a name." Many were happy to see Brugmann's critical appraisals of the city's actions, but there were also
heavy pressures on the other side. "Some council member
would come to see me after each article I wrote," Brugmann said, "wanting to know why I was against the city."

One group deeply impressed by Brugmann's efforts was
the Redwood City Civic Association. The members' chief
complaint was that more housing development on the
Redwood Shores peninsula with a weak tax base was not
the best use for the land. They wanted to see more
thought given to industry, recreational centers, and parks.
When the City Council voted on May 19, 1966, to sell $5.6
million in bonds of the $176 authorized, the Civic Associa-
tion approached Palo Alto attorney Paul N. McCloskey,
requesting that he study the legality of the city-Leslie marriage in Redwood Shores.

"I looked at it very carefully, spent hours on it," said
McCloskey, "and reached the conclusion that the legislature had acted within its powers. If it is wrong, the legislature was wrong in permitting it to be done. But there is a
valid question about slough ownership."

One of the proposed Redwood Shores developments is
an eighty-acre "Marine World" to be financed by the
American Broadcasting Company. It is important that
the Marine World land have water circulation. On September 2, 1966, the Redwood City Council appeared in
San Francisco before the Bay Conservation and Development Commission with an application requesting
approval to dredge the Belmont Slough to provide the
necessary flushing action for Marine World and to provide drainage for the planned residential subdivisions on
the Redwood Shores Peninsula. Brugmann covered the
meeting and reported that there was great opposition
from the Redwood City Civic Association, State Fish and
Game Department, Brisbane Citizens for Civic Progress
and the Council for Governmental Responsibility, largely
on grounds of conservation and questionable public

advantages. The Commission delayed decision. In the same article, Brugmann reported that the Redwood City Council had approved a $176 million bond issue "with the consent of the sole landowner, Leslie Salt—to construct Redwood Shores under a special improvement district. Bonds totaling $5.6 million have already been sold."

On October 6, 1966, despite continuing opposition from the previously mentioned groups, the Bay Commission approved the application. Brugmann reported that Joseph Bodovitz, the Commission's Executive Director, admitted "that the dredging would damage the slough's wildlife balance, that it would adversely affect the Commission's bayfront planning, and that it wasn't of regional necessity. However, the dredging project involves no bay fill, and even if the dredging weren't allowed, Redwood Shores could be built on Leslie property behind existing dikes; the city had threatened to do it at one point." Commissioner Hans A. Feibusch stated, "This is a prime example of the piecemeal planning we're trying to avoid. We're allowed a small piece of a gigantic project and we're asked to approve it."

In an editorial on October 10, 1966, the Redwood City *Tribune* supported the Commission's approval and revealed a difference of opinion with its City Hall reporter.

Thanks to a cautious city council, Redwood Shores promises to be a model of excellent community planning. The city already has required special seismic, financial, and education need studies at the developer's expense. There is evidence of a sincere wish by Leslie to do a good job.

To those whose efforts brought about the affirmative action by BCDC we offer congratulations. . . . Despite some misgivings by members of BCDC, we cannot help but feel that the entire Bay Area will be the big gainer from the proposed development.

Brugmann said recently:

> The management of the *Tribune* is in sympathy with Redwood Shores interests. They see the potential 60,000 subscribers in the new town and so the paper that was once critical becomes a booster of the local Chamber of Commerce. . . . I tried to go to the negotiations meetings (on the application before the BCDC), but they wouldn't let me in. I was kicked out and the newspaper wouldn't give me any support, so I didn't try to go back.

In the second week of October, 1966, Bruce Brugmann left the *Tribune*.

Mary Henderson says:

> There was a very strong effort on the part of the city council and the city family to get rid of him as a reporter on the *Tribune*. There were many who felt they were successful in this. They went to the editorial department on more than a few occasions to complain about his reporting covering City Hall, particularly concerning Redwood Shores. . . . They seem to feel that if you get rid of the guy who's writing it, it won't be there anymore.

Brugmann had planned to leave the *Tribune* anyway at the beginning of November to devote full-time to publishing and editing his newspaper. He had, by then, received financial backing, and he went directly to work. He had talked with attorney McCloskey several times about Redwood Shores and knew the facts the lawyer was assembling for a case against Leslie Salt and the state, including signed affidavits from long-time residents of San Mateo County who had sailed up the sloughs Leslie claimed to be nonnavigable. Brugmann also knew that McCloskey,

cisco Bay Area will be ruined beyond redemption in our life times." He specified Redwood Shores, Bay Farm Island, San Bruno Mountain as fill land, and Coyote Point as major problems, then continued:

> It will be a purpose of *The Bay Guardian,* in its news columns and its editorials, to show that these environmental problems exist, that something can be done about them. . . . This is neither a scientific nor a technological problem, but a political problem. The first priority is to bring the pressure of conservation, planning and good sense to bear on the political process. This the *Guardian* will seek to do.

On December 8, 1966, the State Lands Commission held a public hearing on the proposed Leslie-State land swap. The meeting was held in the large San Mateo City Council Chambers, and the room was filled. Brugmann wrote of the hearing in his December 20 issue:

> The most damaging evidence to Leslie's case was presented by Paul N. McCloskey, Palo Alto attorney representing the RCCA, Redwood City's fiery conservation group.
> Leslie's slough filling, (McCloskey) said, constitutes "an intrusion" on public rights and he requested Keith Sorenson, San Mateo County District Attorney, to remove Leslie as "an intruder." He based his request on Public Resources Code Section 7992, which reads: "If any person under any claim inconsistent with the sovereignty and jurisdiction of the State intrudes upon any of the waste or ungranted lands of the State, the district attorney of the county shall thereupon report the intrusion to the governor, who shall, by a written order, direct the sheriff of the county to remove the intruder."

In an effort to learn the state's position, this writer called the State Lands Commission in Los Angeles and was referred to Mrs. Lorraine Tooker, the Commission's attorney handling Redwood Shores. Mrs. Tooker's only comment was: "The Leslie-State land swap proceedings are being reviewed by the Attorney General's office and nothing more has been decided. If litigation is brought against the State, then the State will have to define its position, but not until then." McCloskey contends that the state has traditionally held that it owns not only the waterways but the underlying beds, as cited previously.

Arthur Balsamo, an engineer with Daniel, Mann, Johnson and Mendenhall—a Los Angeles firm hired by Leslie to build Redwood Shores and liaison between the City Council and Leslie—says of the pending litigation: "It won't affect the Shores project. It's just a nuisance deal. How can the tail wag the dog?" he says, referring to the thirty-nine acres of Smith Slough. "We expect to issue more bonds in a while."

Not only is there a question in many people's minds about going ahead with bond sales before the title question has been settled, but there is also the matter of public subsidy of private land development. In his March 9, 1967, issue, Brugmann writes:

> The use of a public agency (in Redwood City, seven council members sit as district directors for Redwood Shores) to perform an essentially private and proprietary function provides no guarantee that any lasting public interest is served.
>
> From a community point of view, this method has a twin-edged danger: it encourages marginal and speculative projects (which, admittedly, developers find too risky to finance on their own) and accelerates urban sprawl at bayside. Higher priced land, more immediately in the path of urban growth, is leap-frogged for marginal slough and baylands which can be developed with less capital because of the public subsidy. To use

municipal bonds to finance risky ventures also endangers the state's municipal bond market and low interest rates for capital for public necessities.

In sum: it is one thing to fill the baylands, but it is another to do it as a matter of public finance and municipal policy.

While Bruce Brugmann continues his investigative efforts into Bay development projects, he is also trying to cope with the business details that must support his newspaper's life.

I need a business manager, but I can't afford one. Money is always a problem—there is never enough. It would not be very difficult at all to have great editorial successes in just a few months if we had enough capital to hire some help, put together a very professional direct mail campaign, and spend a little money for advertising and have a few more people here in the office. Most of our people are just volunteers. Very few people want to work for nothing.

Like all papers, he must compete in the marketplace, and in San Francisco, the *Chronicle* and *Examiner* have a monopoly over wire service and feature inputs because they have the money to invest in such services. Much of Brugmann's information comes from frustrated reporters on those papers who have stories they can't print. Brugmann says: "You don't want to establish yourself as anti-Establishment, . . . but the point is to be independent of the Establishment so you are free to criticize and free to applaud without being identified as a spokesman for the Chamber of Commerce or big industry or some political group." He considers his main problem advertising. The combination of the *Chronicle* and the *Examiner*, he says, "gobble it up."

Two men who apparently like what Brugmann is trying to do and would like to see his paper survive are television's Steve Allen and San Francisco's Bill Roth, a University of California Regent and member of the Matson steamline family. Roth and Brugmann's family put up the largest backing sums. Brugmann is now trying to increase circulation and subscription sales. The paper began with twelve pages and very little advertising, and now has $1,200 to $1,400 worth of advertising in twenty-page issues. The present circulation is around 31,000 and two promotional mailings were sent to 30,000 people.

"I am convinced it would work," says Brugmann, "if there were enough money available to keep the paper going over a long period of time. I think it's the new frontier."

Bruce Brugmann is not the first nor will he be the last journalist who believes in free discussion of public issues and wants the freedom to print the facts he finds. But unlike many who only dream, Bruce Brugmann has begun a newspaper he believes in—one that is printing facts and stating frank opinions that caused one Redwood City official to say: "It can exert a lot of pressure—there's no doubt about it."

John Durham's* report on the *Texas Observer* indicates that it has similar aims and problems:

Texas politics is in its adolescence—growing from a one- to a two-party system and experiencing all the doubts and confusions that accompany any major change in a life style. The process is still in its early stages. It began in 1960 when Texas sent Republican John Tower to the United States Senate to fill the seat Lyndon Johnson vacated to become Vice President. It has continued with the occasional election of a Republican to the House of Representatives or the state legislature. It has been marked by an emotional turbulence within the majority party as liberal and conservative Democrats practice political fratricide.

* John Durham holds the Master's Degree in Journalism from Stanford. He worked for VISTA and in public relations at Rice University. He is now in the Army.

Conservative Democrats, under the leadership of former Governor John Connally, were reasonably well united during the early and middle sixties. Connally chose not to stand for reelection in 1968 and his successor, Preston Smith, has watched his party splinter even more since he took office in January 1969. Almost all of Connally's legislative proposals sailed through both chambers in Austin with no more than an occasional whimper or muffled cry of rage from liberal forces. This year Smith has had to call two special sessions of the legislature to approve a taxation and spending program for the new biennium. The legislature had, during the regular session, substituted their own program for the Governor's, and he subsequently vetoed it.

Leadership of conservatives in the majority party in Texas is currently divided among three elected officials—Smith, Lieutenant-Governor Ben Barnes, and Speaker of the House Gus Mutscher. Barnes, barely a member of the over-thirty crowd, received a larger number of popular votes in the 1968 general election than any other candidate. Mutscher, by controlling committee assignments in the House, wields much the same power as any speaker. Smith, as governor, is at least the nominal head of the party. At the moment, however, none of them commands the necessary prestige or loyalty to qualify as the head of Texas conservative Democrats.

Still, conservative Democrats are the political establishment in Texas. And they receive enthusiastic support, financial and otherwise, from the commercial half of the establishment—a group of wealthy men who have made their money in oil, insurance, shell dredging, ranching, and farming.

One legislative assistant in Austin recently commented rather bitterly, "Anyone who thinks that the legislature has representatives from Houston, Dallas, Midland, El Paso, Brownsville, or any other city or town in the state is kidding himself. What we do have is representatives from Humble Oil Company, the Texas Manufacturers' Association, the Texas Medical Association, the shell dredgers, the cattlemen, and other special interest groups."

The product of government by conservative Democrats (a term which many liberals insist should be pronounced "Re-pub-li-can") has naturally not been very progressive. There is no state income tax, only a sales tax. Antipollution laws are laxly enforced. In spite of the University of Texas' having the second largest endowment of any school in the country, the salaries of Texas public school teachers from the first grade through graduate school are low in any national ranking. To change this situation, liberal Democrats have been using a divide-and-conquer technique—throwing their support to Republicans in many cases when a GOP candidate is running against a conservative member of their own party. The latest example of such tactics was the Governor's race in November 1969. The liberals' candidate, Don Yarborough, lost to Smith in the primary. Many liberals voted in the general election for Republican Paul Eggers. The attempt to elect Eggers over Smith failed, but the philosophy behind such endeavors is to force conservative Democrats to join ranks with conservatives in the Republican Party to get their candidates elected, thus leaving the Democratic Party in control of the liberals.

The activities of Texas government are reported to the people by a press that has received scathing criticism in national magazines in recent years. Houston, the largest city in the state and the home of many prominent oilmen, has been hit especially hard. In August 1966, the *Atlantic Monthly* published a critique entitled "The Shame of Houston's Press." More recently *Newsweek* commented that neither of Houston's two dailies is much better than mediocre and it ill behooves anyone to try to change that situation. The other large Texas dailies are not much better. Nearly all of them are under conservative ownership and few of them speak out against the governor or report more than the surface activities of the legislature. The chief difficulty, according to a former editorial writer for one of the state's largest papers, is that the press merely reports what public officials say: "It doesn't matter if the man is lying, we just tell the public what he tells us. There is no investigation, no checking with the opposition, no independent spirit, much less crusading zeal."

Another measure of the general failure of the Texas press to oppose government action is found in the admiration which the administration holds for the newspapers. Bill Carter, former press secretary to Governor Connally, said that while Connally was in office there was "a mutual respect between the Governor and the press. The papers in Texas represent the Governor well." He contrasted the state newspapers with those from the East and the North, which he says are "not as far to the right of center as this administration."

No daily newspaper in Texas, according to the administrative assistant to one liberal state representative, consistently treats the governor or the legislature badly, or even honestly. The only journalistic opposition to the state government comes from two sources.

First there are a few weeklies, including H. M. Baggarly's Tulia *Herald,* which criticize conservative Democratic programs. But the weeklies generally have no direct contact with either the legislature or the governor in Austin, and their opposition is reflected more in editorial columns than in-depth reporting.

The second source of opposition is the *Texas Observer,* a liberal biweekly journal published in Austin. It is an adversary of the Texas Establishment by any definition, and its relationship with the governor and the legislature offers a unique example of how an adversary paper functions under less than ideal conditions.

The *Observer* calls itself an "Independent Fortnightly" on its letterhead and "A Journal of Free Voices" and "A Window to the South" on its flag. Its editorial philosophy is best expressed in its masthead: "We will serve no group or party but will hew hard to the truth as we find it and the right as we see it. We are dedicated to the whole truth, to human values above all interests . . . and never will we overlook or misrepresent the truth to serve the interests of the powerful or cater to the ignoble in the human spirit."

There are two full-time editorial staff members—editor Greg Olds and associate editor Kaye Northcott. Former editor Ronnie Dugger has taken the position of editor-at-large. The *Observer* offices are in a rather rundown two-story white frame building three blocks away from the University of Texas campus and five minutes by car from the state capitol. The writing is done on old Royal typewriters; bricks and boards serve as bookcases; and large stacks of yellowing copies of the New York *Times* provide dividers between the two editorial cubicles.

The *Observer* concerns itself chiefly with politics at a statewide level. When the legislature is in session, it devotes at least half of each issue to the workings of that body, giving the machinations of the successes and failures of various bills. During election seasons, it reports on the progress of statewide campaigns and local races of special interest. It also features a "Political Intelligence" column—a series of short items reporting spot news from around the state and from Texans in Washington. Almost all of the reports on the legislature are done by either Olds or Miss Northcott, but for activities in other parts of the state and nation, the *Observer* frequently relies on articles from a large staff of contributing editors, including Willie Morris, editor of *Harper's,* and Larry L. King, a *Harper's* associate editor. Both King and Morris once served as staffers for the *Observer*.

But the *Observer* does not deal exclusively with politics. It publishes reviews of books that are important to Texans—novels by native authors or books about President Johnson or the assassination of President Kennedy. An occasional special issue features a notable individual such as the University of Texas' J. Frank Dobie, or a pressing problem such as a proposed constitutional amendment which would have allowed the state to commit $5 billion to transport water from east to west Texas. Its pages frequently contain whimsical and light pieces by

Dugger and several contributing editors. And finally, the back page of each issue is filled with letters from readers who have both high praise and frequent damnation for the journal.

Sacred cows are as nonexistent for the *Observer* as they are prevalent for the rest of Texas' newspapers. It has criticized, among others, insurance companies for their rate-setting practices, oil companies both for their air- and water-pollution and depletion allowances, Hemisfair, San Antonio's 1968 World's Fair, and Presidents for their conduct of the war in Vietnam. It even takes an occasional poke at Texas' liberal Democratic Senator Ralph Yarborough, chiding him for such things as paying his son a higher salary than any other relative of a Congressman working on Capitol Hill.

The *Observer*'s most recent coup was an investigation of Dr. James McClendon, former president of Southwest Texas State College in San Marcos (Lyndon Johnson's alma mater). Thorough research revealed marked similarities between McClendon's Ph.D. dissertation and his wife's master's thesis. There were also strong resemblances between the two papers and a Marine Corps report prepared on the same subject (Marine Corps intervention in Haiti during the early twentieth century).

The *Observer* broke the story, but no other Texas paper picked it up until after the national press had given it prominent display. McClendon subsequently resigned from Southwest Texas and the University of Texas regents are currently considering whether to revoke his degree.

The *Observer* has about 10,000 subscribers, including a former United States President, several congressmen, and many of the Texas legislators. Olds says that about one-fifth of the subscribers are from out of state. There are few advertisements, so most of the yearly budget must come from subscriptions. The *Observer* is now close to being self-sustaining, a goal that has been brought within reach by extensive subscription campaigns. In past years, the operating deficit was made up by Mrs. R. D. (Frankie)

Randolph, a Houston liberal, but the *Observer* must now make it on its own.

On the surface, the *Observer* appears to have few attributes that would enable it to serve effectively as an adversary to the state government. First of all, it is an avowed opponent of the most powerful politicians, industrialists, and businessmen in the state, a condition which might easily lead to disappearing news sources. Second, it has a small staff, precluding the possibility of different reporters developing different contacts. And third, its low circulation and small amount of advertising revenue make its very existence precarious at best.

Arrayed against these disadvantages are several factors which allow the *Observer* to continue to be a liberal and independent critic in what is still an inherently conservative state governed by conservative politicians. Probably the most important asset strengthening the *Observer's* position is its tradition of accuracy and fairness. "If we hadn't been fair from the beginning," says Dugger, "we would have had a hard time with news sources. If you are fair, it gives you an electric ability to get information. Controversiality opens doors, and the people know you are trying to get the truth. Even a man like (State Representative Bill) Heatly will talk to you even though he is bitterly opposed to your views."

Olds agrees with the need to be fair. Although he says the *Observer* doesn't make a "concerted effort" to represent the other side, its pages are more balanced than those of any other paper in Texas. Even though the *Observer* urged its readers editorially to write in or abstain in the 1968 Presidential elections, it gave an abundance of space to Humphrey supporters. When it ran a critical issue on insurance companies several years ago, there was column after column giving the companies' side of the problem. This fairness has gained for the *Observer* a healthy respect from most people in Texas government. The liberals, of course, are more than glad to have a publication supporting their efforts. State Representative Joe Allen, a liberal legislator from Baytown, says that the *Observer* is easily the most accurate publication in the state. Another liberal representative, Ed Harris from Galveston, notes that the *Observer* is not only accurate and fair, but it is "too intelligent for most people in this state."

The praise is not so warm from those whom the journal opposes, but there is a grudging admiration. Carter, while he was Connally's press secretary, claimed that "the *Observer* to us is kind of like water to a duck's back." A conservative state representative from central Texas says that the *Observer* is not any more or less fair than any other newspaper around. "You can't really expect papers to be fair," he charges, "because they all have special interests."

"The biggest problem with sources in the beginning," Dugger reports, "was the fact that no one knew who we were. You're handicapped when people don't know what your publication is. It helped at that time to be a stringer for *Time-Life*. That opened a few doors."

Fairness and accuracy have paid off in accessibility to most sources for *Observer* staffers. "I haven't been thrown out of any offices," Olds notes. "People talk to us because they have the feeling that we will get the information we want somewhere else if they don't cooperate. We do have a core of really good sources— mostly the liberal legislators. But a conservative who has an ax to grind will occasionally come to us with some information because no one else will print it."

Another important factor in getting access to information for the *Observer* in its early years was the sheer investigative and reportorial skill of Ronnie Dugger. Now editor-at-large, Dugger served as editor from 1954, when the *Observer* was established (incorporating several other publications over a period of years), until 1967, when he relinquished the editorship to Olds. A Master's thesis at the University of Texas details Dugger's early and persistent efforts to uncover and report the activities of some of the most powerful groups in the state, including insurance companies, oil companies, and lobbyists in Austin. Dugger relinquished the number-one position at the *Observer* to devote more time to his own writing. But Olds, a thirty-four-year-old Texan-by-choice, has shown little inclination to change the effort or emphasis of the journal.

Finally, the early financial support of Mrs. Randolph cannot be ignored. Publications similar to the *Observer* have been tried in other areas, but they have died because of lack of funds. Subscription drives have increased the *Observer*'s readership to the break-even point. But until it developed a core of loyal readers, the subsidy from Mrs. Randolph was essential.

It would be encouraging to liberal journalists to think that the increase in the political strength of liberals in Texas has been a result of the activities of the *Observer*. But while it undoubtedly did play some part, it cannot be credited solely with this growth. What is more important is the existence of the *Observer* as an adversary to the government in a state where there is little other healthy tension between the press and officialdom. A tradition of honesty, accuracy, fairness, and tireless investigation has enabled the *Texas Observer* to occupy a unique place in Texas journalism.

When Peter Sandman began to analyze the *Midpeninsula Observer* (now known as the *Peninsula Observer*), he had a limited notion of the adversary relationship between the mass media and government, as he admits. Two years later, in the summer of 1969, he wrote a more cogent analysis of the relationship than appears in his sketch of the *Observer*. His later thoughts ran:

"The adversary relationship between the mass media and government may be defined as a relationship in which each institution perceives its own role and the role of the other to be such that they must, and should, come into conflict some appreciable percentage of the time.

"If we accept this sociological definition, the following criteria for the adversary relationship are obvious: (1) There is a mass media system; (2) There is a government; (3) The mass media are aware of a role or set of roles for themselves, and another role or set of roles for the government, and there is substantial internal agreement as to the nature of these roles; (4) The government is aware of a role or set of roles for itself, and another role or set of roles for the mass media, and there is substantial internal agreement as to the nature of these roles; (5) There is substantial agreement between the mass media and government as to the appropriate roles of each; (6) These roles are such that to a significant extent each can be adequately performed only at the expense of the other; and (7) There is substantial agreement between the mass media and government that both institutions, to a greater or lesser extent, have valid claims to the legitimacy and desirability of their respective roles.

"Ideally, the theory says, one of the primary roles of the newspaper is to provide the public with the information about "public affairs" that it needs to make correct decisions. The assumption behind this role is that the more information available to the public, the better its decisions are likely to be and the more favorable to its interests the conduct of public affairs is likely to be. The primary role of government, meanwhile, is to carry out the day-to-day business of public affairs and to plan for long-range policies. This also is in the public interest, and the greater the freedom of government officials to act as they think best, the better decisions *they* are likely to make and the more favorable to the public interest their decisions are likely to be. Here, then, is the conflict: the public interest is served by free flow of information, but it is also served by freedom of action for government officials—yet the two collide, since public knowledge of the actions or intended actions of public officials is likely to impede their freedom."

Here is Peter Sandman's* 1968 article on an adversary publication:

It is a rare thing for a local leftist newspaper to survive long enough to be studied. That *The Midpeninsula Observer* has done so raises several questions of interest.

* Peter Sandman is a candidate for the Public Affairs Ph.D. in Communication at Stanford. He is the author of several books and has written for *Playboy*, *The Reader's Digest*, *Look*, and other magazines.

Why is the *Observer* succeeding while so many similar ventures have failed? What effect, if any, is the *Observer* having on the Midpeninsula? What sort of relationship does the *Observer* have with its local news sources? The answers to these three questions are interrelated. Together they have some interesting implications for minority community newspapers in general.

A newspaper appeals to its readers; this is a fundamental truism of journalism. Any individual to whom the newspaper does not appeal—whether for its news or its comics, its sports or its A&P ads—will not be a reader for long. The two crucial editorial decisions, what to write and whom to write for, must therefore be made together.

The editor with a minority ax to grind may aim his newspaper at any of three groups. If he wants to appeal to the general public, he smuggles in his special interest amidst the usual run of news and features. If he hopes to attract converts from among those in partial sympathy with his position, he tones down his opinions or surrounds them with related material of a more moderate cast. If he wishes to gather around him only those who share his basic attitudes, he publishes an underground newspaper.

The Midpeninsula Observer is committed to the third strategy. Editor Barry Greenberg admits that "there is something to be said for a newspaper that tries to radicalize moderates and liberals," but that is not his goal. "The radical community has to build up its own norms and customs and sense of community until it is strong enough to withstand assimilation with the Establishment," he says. "Until we do that, it is too dangerous to try to appeal to peripheral Establishment types." Greenberg feels that at this point in history a leftist paper which proselytizes beyond its own community is "inherently unstable." He points to the (New York) *Village Voice* as an example of a newspaper that "tried to convert the Scarsdale commuters and wound up being converted itself, assimilated right back into the Establishment."

But Greenberg is also aware of the dangers of too restricted an appeal. "We want to help build the radical community on the Peninsula," he states. "That means uniting a lot of different kinds of people, informing them, and providing them with a forum for serious debate. We don't want to fill our pages with doctrinaire hot air that just reaffirms the prejudices of our readers without educating them or directing them or sharpening them."

In particular, Greenberg shies away from the hippy emphasis of most student radical newspapers. "Most hippies may be radical," he comments, "but not all radicals are hip." He believes that a hippy newspaper "is destined to fold when the hippy fad folds," while a politically oriented paper "will never fold until its goals are realized." Greenberg doesn't care about the life style of his readers; he's interested in their politics. Uniforms in the *Observer* "city room" range from tweeds to beads, from overalls to the alltogether. Political orientations range from labor-union socialism to black nationalism. "We want to serve an informing function for as many radical viewpoints as we can," says Greenberg, "in the hope of knitting them together into an effective community for political action."

The middle course between liberal assimilationism and radical introversion is reflected on the pages of the *Observer*. Potential issues for liberal muckraking—urban planning in San Jose, bayshore development in Redwood City, Mormon control in Palo Alto—are ignored. So are national objects of liberal preoccupation, such as the candidacy of Eugene McCarthy and the current civil rights bill. Equally conspicuous by their absence are the cluttered montages, self-conscious obscenities, psychedelic cartoons and lysergic poetry so typical of the underground press. The tone of the newspaper is opinionated and interpretive, but lucid and straight as well. Hard, objective news stories are rare, but so are winging jive metaphors. And for titillating classified ads à la Berkeley *Barb*, you'd best get the Berkeley *Barb*.

In the spectrum of *Observer* coverage, the right edge is represented by stories on counterinsurgency study at Stanford Research Institute or the composition of Peninsula draft boards. Greenberg refers to these as "our wide interest articles." The SRI piece was quoted extensively in the Stanford *Daily,* while the *Observer* itself is distributing thousands of tear sheets of the draft board article to interested Stanford students. The left edge of the spectrum is shown in stories like "Does double standard exist in The Movement?" and "America's radicals: time for violence?" These are Greenberg's concessions to "the need for philosophical debate within the radical community." Between the two extremes are the bulk of the *Observer*'s articles—coverage of Stokely Carmichael speeches, draft resistance trials, high school racial conflicts, Dow Chemical demonstrations, South Vietnamese scandals, and the like.

The Greenberg formula has produced a newspaper reminiscent of the socialist dailies of the 1930s. The *Observer* has something for everybody—so long as you're radical enough. The Peninsula has a fairly large but very heterogeneous leftist population. It also has a very large and still more heterogeneous liberal Establishment-fringe population. The task of *The Midpeninsula Observer* has been to capture the interest and loyalty of the former without diffusing itself by trying to appeal to the latter. It has succeeded.

The *Observer* has outlasted most underground newspapers because it has successfully steered the middle course. The majority of its predecessors foundered on the rock of hippy navel contemplation or lost their way in the whirlpool of liberal moderation. The *Observer* is designed for lots of different kinds of radicals, but for radicals only. For the rest of the Peninsula the newspaper is a cipher or an anathema. But for the growing leftist community, it is an indispensable spokesman, forum, and newspaper. That is why it survives.

The success of the *Observer* as an anti-Establishment

newspaper has implications for its probable relations with Establishment news sources. Any small-circulation special-interest newspaper has reason to expect something less than wholehearted cooperation from a government official; its readership is too small and too compact to deserve the Full Treatment accorded the Establishment press. The more potential for conflict there is between the views of the particular newspaper and the position of the particular official, the less cooperation there is likely to be between them. How much cooperation can a newspaper expect, then, if its consistent position is anti-Establishment? The likeliest answer: not much.

Editor Greenberg says there's no problem. "Maybe it's because they don't know what we are yet, but we get perfect cooperation from every government official we contact," he claims. "As far as I know no one has refused us an interview or refused to answer our questions."

In a literal sense Greenberg may be almost right. The *Observer* is rarely refused an interview—because the *Observer* rarely requests one. In fact, the last eight issues of the newspaper contain only one article in which a government official made a statement directly to an *Observer* reporter. Every other story falls into one of five categories.

(1) Syndicated material from the Liberation News Service or similar organizations.

(2) Participant analysis, in which a local or visiting leftist writes about his own activities.

(3) Summaries of national or international news, with appropriate comment thereon appended or intermixed.

(4) Quotations from printed documents, including everything from the Palo Alto *Times* to the Congressional Record to *Pravda*.

(5) Reports of events open to the public, such as speeches and trials.

All five categories include articles with plentiful quotations from government officials. But only one article could be found in which a representative of the Establishment said something directly to the *Observer*. Reporters for the *Midpeninsula Observer* do a lot of library research, but not much interviewing.

The sole exception was John McChesney's recent article on local draft boards. The story filled five entire columns of the *Observer*, and included quotations from an even dozen Selective Service officials. Among the most quoted was Judge Stanley Evans of the Santa Clara Superior Court, the man responsible for recommending local board appointees.

Evans described the interview as follows: "He called me at my home on a Saturday afternoon. He told me he was from the *Midpeninsula Observer*, which is a newspaper I have never heard of. Then he started asking me questions about who I recommended and what procedure was followed for draft board recommendations. I answered his questions, but pretty soon he started debating the draft system with me. I got a pretty good idea what his viewpoint was, but he was asking mostly factual, procedural questions so I answered him anyway. When he was finished I asked him what kind of paper it was. He said 'Oh, it's a little left-wing paper over in East Palo Alto.'* If I'd known that when he'd started, I would probably have insisted that he make an appointment for business hours and send me his questions in writing. That is certainly what I will do next time if that paper calls me again."

More typical of the *Observer*'s local coverage is its story on Stanford Research Institute, an on-going exposé which has filled more than ten columns in four different issues to date. The *Observer*'s only source at SRI is Homer Medders, head of the Institute public information department. On several occasions reporters for the *Observer* have gotten in touch with Medders. Each time they asked him for copies of public documents and press releases,

---

* The *Observer*'s offices are on University Avenue in Palo Alto. It is difficult to guess whether the East Palo Alto designation was McChesney's slip of the tongue or Evans' misperception. Palo Alto is upper middle class; East Palo Alto is black.

which he gave them. They have never asked him for an interview, nor have they requested that he help arrange interviews with other SRI officials. Ernest Arbuckle, dean of the Stanford Business School and chairman of the SRI Board of Trustees, has been quoted and excoriated in several articles; he was never contacted by the *Observer*. H. E. Robison, vice president of SRI-International, was credited with most of the responsibility for the Institute's counterinsurgency research; he was never contacted by the *Observer*.

Asked about the research habits of his reporters, Greenberg was somewhat surprised. After a little thought, he attributed the scarcity of interviews to the staff's lack of experience. "Most of them have no training in journalism," he explained. "I guess they're a little afraid of the interview situation." Greenberg himself was editor of the Stanford *Daily* (the student newspaper) when David Harris was Stanford's militant student body president. He hopes to start teaching his staff the rudiments of journalism, and expects that "they will eventually get so they do more reporting and interviewing on their own."

Should they ever get to that point, they may find that no Establishment news source is willing to talk to them. "I'm not sure whether I'd give the *Observer* an interview or not," stated Robison. "I would certainly be very careful of what I said. It's not as though they were an objective newspaper interested in getting the facts, the whole story." Evans seconded the motion. "A newspaper like that," he said, "has its own preconceived idea of the truth. They're looking for ammunition, not information, and I for one would give them as little as possible."

Comments like these raise serious questions about the "adversary" model of press-government relations. It has been argued that a reporter and a news source ought to be adversaries. An adversary is an opponent; the ideal adversary, then, is the complete opponent. Few newspapers are directly and enthusiastically opposed to everything their news sources favor. Such 180-degree ideological confrontation is rare, but it can happen. If the *Midpeninsula Observer* ever starts interviewing representatives of government and the Establishment, it will happen. The result will almost certainly be withdrawal of access, total or partial cessation of communication. No government official is going to spend a great deal of time talking with an avowed enemy, particularly an avowed enemy with a low circulation.

A certain tension between government and press may be desirable, but direct adversarity apparently is not. Nor is this simply a matter of degree. If the *Observer* were less extreme, less blatant, less offensive in its anti-Establishment posture, it would only be a weaker adversary. So long as it remained dedicated to the proposition that its governmental news sources were by definition in the wrong, it would continue to have trouble approaching them for news. Total adversarity is inimical to satisfactory press-government relations.

The paradigmatic *news*paper has no ax to grind at all on its news pages. It therefore cannot possibly have an ideological disagreement with a news source. Yet there is still potential for conflict—stemming not from differences in viewpoint, but from a dispute as to what constitutes news. The newspaper wants to discover and print what it thinks will interest its readers; the source wants to disseminate and see printed what he thinks will benefit himself and his organization. Conflict results when the paper goes after a story the source would prefer to hide, or when the source plumps for a story the paper would prefer to ignore. There is tension here, but no adversarity. Most of the time the newspaper and the news source will agree in their assignment of news value to a given piece of information. Occasionally they will find themselves working at cross-purposes, when the paper's goal (to interest its readers) happens to conflict with the source's goal (to benefit his organization). Never will their aims be in direct opposition.

A special-interest newspaper with a viewpoint to propound is in a somewhat different position. To one extent or another its readership appeal is founded on its ax-grinding. The goal of interesting its readers becomes identified with the goal of illustrating and demonstrating a point of view. It therefore may happen that the newspaper and its news source will be ideological opponents. But still not true adversaries. The prototypic special-interest newspaper is not likely ever to become a full-time 180-degree opponent of any single source. A California conservation newspaper, for example, would frequently find itself in opposition to Governor Reagan's activities. But as long as it remained a proconservation newspaper and not an anti-Reagan newspaper, there would always be a possibility that next week it might wind up on Reagan's side. The wider its interests, the smaller the likelihood of its always being on the opposite side of the fence from any single source. Our conservation paper might oppose Reagan on the redwoods controversy, but support him on Central Valley irrigation. The potential for conflict between a special-interest newspaper and a news source may be very high, even disastrously high. But it can never reach adversarity. At worst, the newspaper is an advocate. It may find itself working at cross-purposes to some sources nearly always. But "cross-purposes" is not direct opposition, and "nearly always" is not always.

The *Midpeninsula Observer* transcends advocacy. The newspaper is not so much antiwar, antidraft, or antidiscrimination as it is anti-Establishment. Its position on any specific issue is determined by its fundamental position that anything the Establishment does is wrong. It is dead set against every government official, regardless of what that official may be for or against. It is a true adversary. As such, it can expect very little cooperation from its ideological opponents in the Establishment.

The distinction is important. The typical newspaper may come into conflict with a news source only in that the two may disagree as to whether X is important or not. The conflict is between two different "degrees" of X. With a special-interest newspaper, the conflict may be between X and Y, two viewpoints in partial contradiction to each other. Only a true adversary like the *Observer* can find itself enmeshed in a conflict between X and Not-X.

Up to now the *Observer* has not been forced to come to grips with the problem of adversarity. Until it starts trying to collect its own news, it will not have to do so. According to editor Greenberg, this is already beginning to happen. The recent article on local draft boards represents a first step in the direction of independent coverage. Last week the newspaper submitted its application for police press cards for its staff members. Greenberg says he plans to use them. "The radical movement is trying to localize. We are going to start looking around for more local issues to report. We are going to try to generate more political action right in this area. We are going to deemphasize some of the national issues and cultivate our own garden a little." For the *Observer,* cultivating its own garden will mean cultivating news sources within the local Establishment. That may turn out to be impossible.

The *Midpeninsula Observer* must make a choice. If it perseveres as a total adversary, a rallying point for the growing radical community on the Peninsula, then it will have to settle for second-hand news. If it elects to do more of its own news collection and interviewing, then it will have to blunt and broaden its political posture and cease to be a total adversary. Every special-interest publication faces the same dilemma to an extent, but none faces it so starkly as the anti-Establishment press, the radical left. On the one hand a newspaper, on the other a house organ; the *Midpeninsula Observer* can never be both.

CHAPTER NINE

Prescription for the Press

> *The American reporter of my generation was brought up to believe in the cocky frontier tradition of "publish and be damned," but the American diplomat of the same age quickly came to believe that if he helped you to publish the facts, he was likely to be damned, and this was only one of the conflicts that soon developed between the government and the press.*
>
> —JAMES RESTON

> *I wonder where Christianity would be today if some of these reporters had been Matthew, Mark, Luke, and John.*
>
> —SENATOR BARRY GOLDWATER

> *A democratic society is inconceivable without tension, and the objective reporting that democracy requires will always produce tension.*
>
> —GEORGE REEDY

> *First get your facts, then you can distort 'em as much as you like.*
>
> —MARK TWAIN

Where among all these cases is a consistent guide to adversary journalism?

We cannot look for guidelines in broadcasting, for surely John Jennings is right in concluding that networks and stations are unlikely to assert any consistent force when they are themselves so entangled in government. Even the educational stations are not notably eager to act as adversaries. The few examples of an adversary stance that exist in broadcasting are misleading. Broadcasters are not brave. They can teach us little.

237

Jennings' essay, Geoffrey Wolff's report on government book publishing, and especially the reports on the public information practices of the Presidents and the United States military indicate that, in sometimes subtle ways, government is heavily and directly involved in mass communication.

All this is complicated by the attitude of the journalist. No doubt James McCartney is right in suggesting that any reporter is likely to be lured by the vested interests of his work. The Bobby Baker case is the most pertinent of many examples. Sadly, it seems obvious that most developing countries adopt mass communication policies like the Ghana of Nkrumah's time. And Cincinnati journalism is probably all too representative of the sweetheart press in most American cities. The doughty little *Chicago Journalism Review,* which was recently launched by young reporters who were disgusted by news policies, offers evidence in every issue that even the proud Chicago papers cozy up to the local powers.

Does this mean that we must look to the abrasive adversaries—to newspapers like the *Bay Guardian* and the *Texas Observer*—as the only genuine check upon government and the other major institutions which are entangled with government? It might seem so. Certainly, the major media are not eager to probe into business. After all, it was not one of the large corps of Detroit reporters who challenged the automakers, but Ralph Nader, a lawyer. It was not a journalist who exposed the American way of death, but Jessica Mitford. It was not a journalist who awakened us to the destruction of the environment with *Silent Spring,* but Rachel Carson—and journalism has lagged far behind citizens' groups like the Sierra Club in demanding a change.

How timid the major media actually are is revealed in a comment by Arnold B. Elkind, chairman of the National Commission on Product Safety: "The news media to whom our records and hearings are available have generally not availed themselves of the opportunity to alert the public to product hazards. With few exceptions, they have deleted brand names and identifying information from reports about product hazards."

Unfortunately, the fearless little newspapers which will

report such matters are often too weak to be fearsome. Like the little national magazines which bow to few taboos—*The Progressive, The New Republic, The Washington Monthly, The Nation,* and the like—they are chronically undercapitalized, forever scratching up the money to continue publication. The economics of journalism seem to argue that only specialized publications of challenge and protest, like *Consumer Reports* and the conservation magazines and newspapers, can command the resources essential to adversary journalism.

That may be too dismal. There certainly are in modern journalism—working for many conventional newspapers and magazines—many young reporters and editors who are dedicated to the idea of a professionalism which transcends taboos. Whether they will defeat the taboos or be defeated by them is the unknown.

It is certain, though, that developing an adversary system which stands up to all the major institutions must begin with developing one which stands up to government itself. This book is a catalogue of the successes and the failures of the press as an adversary. The record is confusing; here I must define the limits of adversarity.

Let us begin by showing what an adversary stance is *not*.

The proper adversary relationship is not expressed by an article in the *Quill*, a magazine published by the journalism fraternity Sigma Delta Chi, titled "Our Enemy, the Government." Written by Eugene Pulliam, a stentorian old publisher of Arizona and Indiana newspapers, the article was aptly titled. It simply called for know-nothing belligerence toward government.

Nor is the proper adversary relationship expressed by publication incidents of the John Kennedy assassination period. Early on the morning of November 22, 1963, the issue of *Editor & Publisher* dated November 23 came off the press carrying a curious article. Headlined "THE S.S. RUFFIANS," it was a reporter's protest that the Secret Service is overprotective in guarding the President—and the writer's acidity creates the suspicion that the use of "s.s." was not so much designed to save space as to suggest an unpleasant analogy with Hitler's crack troops. The reporter, Thomas Del Vecchio, wrote as a veteran of twenty-four years of interviewing dignitaries who arrive at airports. His complaint was that reporters were often excluded from the groups that greeted President Kennedy at Idlewild:

> "How come? What's happened here?
>
> "It's all in the name of security.
>
> "Now where does the problem of security end and the problem of a controlled press, kept from access to the news, begin?
>
> "There is no question that the press and the Secret Service have reached that point and beyond.
>
> "On top of all this is the rudeness and ruffian manner a good many of these agents assume toward the press under the guise of security.
>
> "They often act as though newsmen were not Americans and did not have a record almost as impressive as theirs for respect for their President and his security.
>
> "Just where do the rights under the First Amendment end and the assumed and overriding rights of the Secret Service take complete charge?"

There was much more in the same outraged tone. Predictably, the article provoked a strong reaction. One reader's reproving letter to the editor of the magazine pointed out that even aside from the assassination Del Vecchio's article was bitter, petty, subjective, and poor journalism. Editor Robert U. Brown responded with a column entitled "Hindsight Criticism," holding, "If such articles have to be written with some intuition as to whether the President might not be alive tomorrow because of an assassin's bullet, there would be very little criticism." It was a predictable rejoinder, and perhaps a persuasive one, but it dealt not at all with the central question: Was Del Vecchio right? Brown might have decided this easily by pondering a related question: Would he have published the article after the assassination?

It would have been a curious article had there been no assassination. Despite charges that the Kennedy Administration "managed the news," the President's own relations with the press were open to the point of porosity. Never in history had so many reporters been so free to talk with the President and explore the

Presidency. In sharp contrast to his predecessor, Eisenhower (who preferred the company of businessmen to journalists and preferred reading Luke Short to Walter Lippmann), Mr. Kennedy fostered such warm relations with many Washington correspondents that his press secretary once complained amiably that the comings and goings of reporters were creating a traffic problem in White House corridors.

Reporters like Del Vecchio want too much. Not content with continuing dialogues with the President in Washington and during frequent confrontations elsewhere, they demand unlimited access wherever the President touches ground, world without end. The President is not to be a public servant, but public property. That Del Vecchio's opinion is something more than one peeved reporter's view is suggested by the fact that *Editor & Publisher,* which echoes the opinions and yearnings of a good many newspapers, chose to make "THE S.S. RUFFIANS" its lead article. Copies of the issue were flown to Miami for distribution at a meeting of the Inter-American Press Association on the morning of November 22. Presumably, some editors and publishers were reading the article when they learned of the assassination.

The two issues of the Dallas *Morning News* that appeared immediately before the assassination are similarly revealing. Much has been made of the full-page advertisement purchased by the "American Fact-Finding Committee" that informed the issue of November 22. It was certainly noteworthy. Headed "WELCOME MR. KENNEDY," the advertisement posed questions like, "*Why* have you scrapped the Monroe Doctrine in favor of the Spirit of Moscow?" and "*Why* have you ordered or permitted your brother Bobby, the Attorney General, to go soft on Communists ... ?" (Incredibly, dauntless Robert U. Brown of *Editor & Publisher* undertook, in a column entitled "More Hindsight," to defend the *News.* "In the first place, he wrote, "it was not a 'hate' ad. It was a political advertisement. ..." Then, in a defense for which few editors and publishers will thank him, Brown held that not one of the questions in the advertisement "hasn't been asked in one form or another on the editorial page of some American newspaper.")

The editors of the *News* have answered critics by pointing to the sweetly phrased editorial with which they greeted the President. One editorial could hardly change the image of a paper whose publisher, E. M. "Ted" Dealey, had become a national figure of a sort in 1961 by charging at a White House luncheon that Kennedy and his administration were "weak sisters." Dealey had interrupted the President to say that the nation needs a man on horseback, but "you are riding Caroline's tricycle." Nonetheless, the most provocative aspect of Dealey's paper during Kennedy's tour of Texas was neither the advertisement nor the editorial but the news columns. The day before the President arrived, the top of the front page was covered, almost five inches deep across seven columns, with a story epitomized by the headline "JFK VISIT IRES SAN ANTONIO LIBERALS." Three columns at the bottom were given over to "RAIN SEEN IN DALLAS DURING JFK VISIT"—a "weather story" in the conventional sense only until it reached the third paragraph, where the reporter slid smoothly into the real subject with "political skies should remain dark" and went predictably on from there.

The *News* of the following morning, the day Kennedy was to arrive, was a strange celebration of a Presidential visit. The lead story on the front page ran across two columns that extended from the top almost to the bottom of the page. Headed in huge type across seven columns "STORM OF POLITICAL CONTROVERSY SWIRLS AROUND KENNEDY VISIT," it was built largely on Senator Ralph Yarborough's complaint that Governor John Connally had not invited Yarborough to a reception at the Governor's Mansion. Nearly four columns at the bottom of the page were covered with a story headed "YARBOROUGH SNUBS LBJ." All eight columns at the top of page 12 were four inches deep with "PRESIDENT'S VISIT SEEN WIDENING DEMOCRATIC SPLIT."

One cannot know the extent to which the *News*, always passionate, excites the passions of Dallas. But surely Walter Lippmann is correct in contending that Dallas is the very atmosphere of violence and that it is only incidental that Lee Oswald turned left while those Dallas-ites who assaulted Lyndon Johnson and his wife in 1960 and those who hit and spat upon Adlai Stevenson a month before the assassination turned right. "The common characteristic of all of them," Lippmann wrote, "was their alienation, the loss of their ties, the rupture of the community."

On the morning that this analysis was published, Jack Ruby killed Lee Oswald. One could hardly ask for stronger confirmation.

But one can commend these issues of the *News* to those who study conflict as it is promoted in the press. And one can venture that the *News* and similar papers, so notably devoted to seeking out political conflict, should consider the possibility that they are manufacturing it as well.

Manufacturing conflict as the Dallas *News* does is, of course, adversarity with a vengeance, but only a sadist can admire it. Such cases suggest that one cannot blindly approve any and all challenges to authority.

Perhaps the best focus on adversarity springs from looking at a theory developed by one of my former students, Dr. William Blankenburg* of the University of Wisconsin. He begins with the observation that government is naturally sensitive to news and events that are potentially damaging to itself or the community it governs. In the face of threat, government exerts certain controls. Blankenburg classifies them as *facilitation* (producing releases, providing interviews, and giving access to data and sources), *regulation* (setting release dates, favoring certain journalists, and requiring pooling and accreditation), and *suppression* (lying, barring access, and censoring). Further, he holds that the press, too, attempts to control news and events, first through *facilitation* (taking the news as it comes), then through *initiation* (exposing, crusading, or otherwise promoting news and events), and *suppression* (withholding news when it is very dull or very dangerous).

Blankenburg illustrates his points with:

● A state attorney general has compiled an annual summary of reported crimes. He is happy to release it because it brings publicity to his office, and the reporter is happy to receive the makings of an interesting story. Ostensibly, press and government are cooperative here, but a closer look shows latent adversarity. The reporter

*William B. Blankenburg holds the Ph.D. in Public Affairs Communication from Stanford. He is the author of several articles and now teaches in the School of Journalism at the University of Wisconsin.

may wonder if the crime categories hide important trends, and the attorney general is worried that the reporter may sensationalize the increase in some types of crime.

● To visualize a case of government regulation, imagine that another attorney general has just prepared an opinion as to whether the state can lease certain of its oil lands. Thousands of dollars are involved, and he fears the effect of a premature announcement. He regulates disclosure by setting a weekend release date and by informing only a few reliable reporters.

● A delicate area is illustrated by an attorney general's plans for a raid on a gambling syndicate. He forbids his investigators to talk with reporters while he plans the elaborate raid. Expecting such an event, reporters begin to speculate in print. Adversarity is quite high, and the attorney general must decide whether to ride it out or to end adversarity by inviting the press to censor itself after hearing the plans. This area of adversarity dissolves rather abruptly if the reporters agree to suppression—which they will if they perceive a strong enough threat to the community. Such examples at the national level are frequent in wartime.

● The press exhibits anxiety over "slow" events by using controls of initiation, either digging deeper into, or sometimes dressing up what it has. The reporter's temptation to make something extraordinary out of the attorney general's crime summary is considerable, especially in competitive news situations.

● If an event is hopelessly dull the press simply omits it. Imagine that an attorney general wants publicity about an award he has received from the River City Chamber of Commerce and the reporter ignores the story. For all its pettiness, adversarity can be quite extreme here. The press is ignoring news government officials consider worthwhile.

● For a variety of reasons, government is the adversary which usually occupies the villain's role. First, the other party to the adversary relationship describes the contest to the public. Government's views on the relationship must filter through the press if they are to become widely known. Second, government has several agonizing conflicts that must produce struggles with the news ethic. These include needs for military secrecy and Constitutional guarantees of due process. Third, members of government have a need for image-building that transcends mere vanity; their official survival and operating effectiveness depend on prestige. Public officials are naturally tempted to bias news and events in their own favor.

● The press lives cheerfully with the news ethic, seizing upon government deviations as good stories; and, of course, the press is inclined to forgive its own trespasses. Whatever self-righteousness derives from this situation is justified by the press in terms of defense of liberty, and at the polemic level the press is always right.

● Adversarity is good because it promotes a skeptical surveillance of government—the watchdog activity—rather than blind acceptance. If democracy is virtuous, then surveillance is a necessity, not just as a check on government but as a way to keep the valuable currency of information in circulation. The other great advantage is that adversarity requires frequent reference to the ideals of liberty—to the news ethic and to the national philosophy.

● While the virtues are strategic, the defects are tactical. The adversaries are tempted either to reduce or increase the strain of their relationship. Government may try to hide, modify, or misrepresent threatening events; the press, tiring of its strict stance, may reduce adversarity by reducing surveillance. (A need for friendship, which reduces adversarity, is perhaps felt most by the small-town editor.) On the other hand, a rambunctious press may try to provoke government for the sake of the stories that result. Adversarity contains the seeds of escalation. But if the two institutions are driven to polar positions, heat exceeds light.

● How much adversarity is enough? Valuing a libertarian press and a responsive government, we become equally alarmed if adversarity disappears altogether or if it remains constantly high. Either extreme is dangerous, and the government source or the reporter who says he "always had trouble" or "never has trouble" is worthy of suspicion. Perhaps the indicator of either extreme is a certain self-consciousness about adversarity; a relationship that is adversary as a norm should be treated with respect and attention but not obsession. When we hear talk of a "honeymoon with the press" or of a "growing credibility gap" we should fret about the health of the relationship.

● What should the adversaries do about it? Like the puberty-stricken youngster, they should realize that their condition can be lived with in good health and conscience. They must remember, in the turbulence of adversarity, that their goals are not inimical, and that there can be a valuable equilibrium in the tension.

To focus sharply on the adversary role: It seems quite clear that there should be a necessary level of tension between a reporter and an official. It may vary slightly with different reporters, and different officials, but it never allows one to be entirely relaxed in the presence of the other. At the other extreme, the political reporter is probably wrong when he assumes that he is a successful adversary merely because he gets bitter complaints from both Republicans and Democrats. As David Broder, one of the best of the breed, points out, such a reporter is apt to say to himself, "Good, I'm catching hell from both sides, so I must be writing it right down the middle," but there is another possibility: that his reporting is so bad that it outrages anyone in either party who knows what is really happening.

Above all, the political journalist must remember that he and the official may serve the same constituency, but their obligations to it are quite different.

Curiously, one of the best expressions of the relationship was made by a politician, former California Governor Pat Brown. He wrote a letter to his successor, Ronald Reagan on a wild range of subjects—taxes, education, lobbyists, learning to live with the legislature, and the logic of taking a speedreading course to get through all the paperwork. Significantly, however, the letter both began with and gave chief attention to the problems of coping with the press:

> There's a passage in *War and Peace* that every new Governor with a big majority should tack on his office wall. In it young Count Rostov, after weeks as the toast of elegant farewell parties, gallops off on his first cavalry charge and then finds real bullets snapping at his ears.
>
> "Why, they're shooting at me," he says. "Me, whom everybody loves."
>
> Nothing worse will happen to you in the next four years. Learn to live with that. The rest is easy.
>
> As you have noticed by now, the press fires the first real bullets at new governors. And the hardest lesson to learn is that it is futile to fire back. Never get into an argument with a newspaper unless you own it. A newspaper fails to get in the last word only if it goes broke in mid-debate.
>
> Publishers in California generally will be more tolerant of a new governor before he raises taxes, much as a young man will take more nonsense from a fiancée whose father is rich. But you will be amazed at how easily even a friendly publisher's tolerance is strained by trivial matters—a freeway route through his backyard; a rollback in government construction in his city; failure to follow his advice on the appointment of a judge.
>
> . . . There is also not much that I can tell you about the weekly news conference that you haven't already learned. You will find that while both surgeons and reporters operate with professional detachment there is only one real difference between them. Surgeons make more money for cutting you up.
>
> But their motives are the same—to make sure everything is running properly. And in the case of the press, they operate with a proxy from the voters. For the voters, news

conferences are as close to a first-hand accounting of what happened to their money as they ever get. . . .

Invest as much time preparing for these inquisitions as you can spare, but don't feel bad if you are caught off guard. I can still hear a voice from the back of the room asking: "Governor, do you think lobbyists should be required to wear little green buttons on their lapels?" Maybe you would have a ready answer for that. I didn't.

Harrowing as they are, news conferences do provide a chance for correspondents to bore in, a practice that philosophers find a healthy thing for the democratic process. Few governors take any comfort in that.

One last word about dealing with reporters. If you don't want it in the papers, don't do it.

If all this seems to suggest that officialdom is only corrupt and the press is only pure, it is misleading. One must sympathize with those officials who are faced day after day with brilliant reporters, with good reporters, with mediocre reporters, and with reporters who are often in error but seldom in doubt. One must sympathize with an official whose program has been distorted because a journalist has examined only a superficial aspect, then stumbled to a conclusion. Even the high-placed official is powerless when the wire services distribute erroneous reports to thousands of newspapers and broadcast stations which serve millions of readers, listeners, and viewers. What of the fact that some newsmen seem more concerned with getting it now then getting it right?

Accuracy? Some reporters will admit that it is often sacrificed at the altar of speed. "I phone in the stuff from my beat," a wire service reporter complains, "and it gets botched." A newspaperman: "My editor doesn't realize how complicated politics can be. He just wants copy." One of the leading columnists confesses, "I have to keep in mind always that if I don't get my column in, the money won't come in either."

Depth reporting? At least one Washington correspondent customarily accosts his news sources with the cub reporter's query: "Have you got any news for me today?" It is interesting, too, that when the correspondents are asked to name the Washington reporters whose work is characterized by hard-digging investigation, the list is never very long.

It is not even certain that the press is pure in all its demands that the public business be conducted in public. Several thoughtful journalists who served one year as the Freedom of Information Committee of Sigma Delta Chi asked these questions about the secret executive sessions of government bodies which so inflame the press:

1. Is the star chamber session actually one in which public officials are discussing things which belong in the public prints? For example: Premature publicity on a city council's plan to condemn private property for a street or parks project might artificially inflate the price of property under consideration. The council members feel an obligation to the taxpayers and hope to arrange a good deal for them. If the proposition they are considering is actually on the up-and-up, they would not hesitate to tell the newspaper about it for background purposes. But do they have the assurance that the newspaper is as interested in acting with patience and restraint in the public interest as it is in obtaining a story and printing it—regardless of its implications?

2. Are public officials given enough protection against inaccurate, adolescent, or outright malicious treatment of "sensitive" information? Do competitive pressures by two or more newspapers force reporters to betray confidence after they have been admitted to executive sessions of public officials? Are the stories the reporter writes published as written? Or are they jazzed up to his embarrassment and to the humiliation of his news sources?

3. When news and information are withheld or suppressed, does the newspaper enter its complaint on sound ground and with clean hands?

> (a) Does the paper have a consistent and generally unimpeachable record of having tried to cover the area of news in contention with intelligent, knowledgeable, and trustworthy reporters? Or is it asserting its traditional rights to information through personnel who are demonstrably unfit to treat it with perspective, balance, and comprehension?

(b) Does the paper burden the source of information by spasmodic attention which demands time-consuming explanations of the obvious, the only alternative being a distorted and possibly damaging report?

(c) Is the information sought and published in an objective manner, or is it treated as an instrument of editorial policy preconceived by the front office?

4. Are objections to the suppression and withholding of information asserted and argued personally by responsible people in a manner that is considerate, logical, and convincing? Or do the objections take the form of personal recrimination, arbitrary criticism, or reckless insinuation?

5. Are newspapers alert enough and consistent enough in their insistence upon "all the news that's fit to print"? Or do some of them invite indifference to release of news through neglect of offices upon which they are supposed to keep a sharp eye? Are not some newspapers guilty of encouraging news suppression that they may promote a certain candidacy, a pet project, or protect a special set of friends?

It is not necessary, though, to consider only the plight of the official who is covered by bad reporters. Journalism is so demanding that even the good ones distort the truth, usually unwittingly. Consider the wild array of impressions generated by the first-rank writers who covered the Israelis' trial of Adolf Eichmann for World War II crimes:

"I would never have noticed Eichmann in a crowd."

—New York *Daily News*

"Impressive or at least sitting impressively in his bullet-proof dock."

—Associated Press

"Eichmann is a dead ringer for a window cleaner who used to operate along 49th Street in New York in the thirties."

—New York *Post*

"He looked respectable but not likeable, like an aging footman who will never make butler."

—New York *Herald Tribune*

"He looked like a lawyer himself perhaps, or perhaps a recently retired brigadier, or perhaps a textile manufacturer of vaguely intellectual pursuits."

—Manchester *Guardian*

"He looks like a clerk but if he is a clerk he is a clerk with a past, a clerk in the grip of perversion."

—New York *Journal American*

Did he look like a window cleaner, a footman, a lawyer, a brigadier, a clerk? Surely not all of them. And yet many of the writers of these wildly varying impressions interpret government policies and programs. The officials seem to deserve sympathy.

If all this suggests that acting as an adversary to officialdom is complex, it has barely hinted at the full dimension.

It sometimes seems to those who are impatient with conventional journalism that only "The Washington Merry-Go-Round" column is fearless enough to slay the real dragons. And the ambivalence about *it* is aptly revealed by James Reston's comment on the case of Senator Thomas Dodd. The late Drew Pearson had exposed Dodd's easy morality with documents taken from the Senator's office. Reston pointed out that it was difficult to judge whether Pearson should be awarded the Pulitzer Prize or thrown in jail.

And what, for example, is the political reporter to do when he discovers that his government is flying U-2 planes over Russia? That question confronted James Reston of the New York *Times* a year before a U-2 was brought down in Russia in 1960. Rather than following the "publish and be damned" tradition of the old thunderers of journalism, Reston placed above it what he considered the national interest. He did not disclose what he had discovered, and we learned of the U-2 flights only when Francis Gary Powers confessed to his Russian captors.

In another case, the *Times* elected not to disclose everything it had learned about the Bay of Pigs invasion of 1961. Well before the scheduled invasion by Cuban refugees, the *Times* knew enough to publish a detailed story. The editors decided to publish a much less revealing account because the United States goven-ment was sponsoring the invasion. Again, a presumed national interest was placed above the public's interest in full disclosure. (Later, President Kennedy confessed to *Times* editors that they would have saved the United States from the embarrassment of a fiasco had they published everything their reporters had learned.)

These cases, which can be multiplied by hundreds of others, suggest first that the real power of the press is an *informational* power; the press often has the option of vetoing a decision of government by making full disclosures. A government cannot, for example, stage an invasion if the day, the hour, and the point of attack of invading forces are front-page items. (The power of the press is too often thought of as a simplistic force growing out of the thunder of an editorial campaign. Such a power is a pale thing in comparison to the power of information.)

Moreover, these cases indicate that standing as an adversary poses questions which honest journalists will answer differently. It is all very well to say that the press must print the news and raise hell. But it is another matter to print news so revealing or so damning that journalists are, because of the veto power of the information they publish, placing themselves far above the President and the Congress.

Having made that point, it is necessary at once to balance it off. The power of political journalism is dangerous, but it is also necessary. What happens when journalism fails is indicated by the mess in Vietnam. In 1961, well before the United States became deeply committed, only a few hundred "advisers" were in Viet-nam. Then, quite secretly, President Kennedy and his lieutenants decided to increase the United States presence to 15,000. But they said publicly that only a "modest" increase was contemplated, and the press dutifully reported the statement. Had reporters discov-ered and publicized the details of the secret meeting at which the decision was made, the disaster that Vietnam has become might never have occurred. For the principals in this meeting openly dis-cussed the possibility that their decision might eventually call for the commitment to battle of 300,000 soldiers—and had *that* reached the headlines in 1961. . . .

Certainly, if the reporting of government affairs were left to government officials, we could expect an endless series of secret decisions on controversial issues—and reports in the form of peaceful pictures, unceasing optimism, and heartening statistics. The impulses of political self-preservation are always strong.

It is not true, as cynical old journalists used to maintain, that "The only way for a reporter to look at an official is down."

The only way for a reporter to look at an official is skeptically.

Epilogue

As the preceding chapters were being set into type, Vice President Spiro Agnew inadvertently demonstrated exactly how fierce the adversary system has become. In two speeches during November 1969, he lashed out at the news media—first at television, then at newspapers.

In all the furor over these speeches, the most interesting items were the speculations of commentators and reporters as to whether President Nixon had set Agnew on his course. Only a few men will ever know until the memoirs of this Administration are written. The likelihood is very slender that the President will decide some day to chortle the truth during a news conference: "I finally got back at you bastards through Spiro."

The only reasonable speculation about Nixon's role in Agnew's attacks begins with Nixon's own role in the Eisenhower Administration. He was the Republican hatchet man. While Eisenhower posed as the national leader, well above the battle, Nixon implied that the Democrats were traitors. (He called Adlai Stevenson "a Ph.D. from the Acheson College of Cowardly Communist Containment"; termed the Truman Administration "the four-headed monster that was Korea, Communism, corruption, and controls"; and said that "The Eisenhower Administration has kicked out the Communists and fellow travelers and security risks not by the hundreds but by the thousands.") It worked. Eisenhower was so far above the political struggle for the eight years of his Presidency that he was not even considered a politician by most Americans. Nixon, the embattled partisan, is not stupid; the lesson was not lost on him.

Moreover, anyone who argues that Agnew is speaking on his own must take into account that when he spoke too wildly during the 1968 campaign, Nixon shut him up. After Agnew embarrassed the Republican ticket with "fat Jap," "Polack," and other unfortunate references, the Nixon entourage sent a man over to keep watch on the Vice Presidential candidate. The reminiscences about the campaign that have filtered out since the election suggest that the emissary was to do anything short of cupping a hand over Agnew's mouth.

Can Nixon silence Agnew? The question answers itself.

Did Nixon instruct Agnew to attack the news media? The fact that one of Nixon's speech-writers worked on Agnew's speeches suggests the answer.

All this is important, even if it must remain speculation, because it suggests that Nixon may have found a new way to tilt the balance in the adversary relationship. Presidents have, of course, used Vice Presidents and other subordinates for political purposes before. But a consistent and detailed series of attacks on *reporters and commentators* (not, and the distinction is important, on the *press* or the *broadcasting industry*) is almost unknown. It is significant that the only notable precedent was Mr. Nixon's "last press conference" in 1962, when he lost the race for California governor. He, too, hit the reporters, not their employers.

The importance of the distinction—and the fact that it has been obscured—is emphasized by an incident of 1963. I took a class of Stanford students to Sacramento to interview Nixon's successful rival, Governor Pat Brown. I told him that I thought Nixon's attack was the first of its kind. "Oh, no," Brown responded, "we Democrats have been hitting the press for years." Of course, this was true. But it ignored the subtle distinction between attacking the press and attacking reporters. Politicians of both parties have been attacking the press since the beginning of the American system. Some have even attacked individual reporters. But to attack all liberal reporters (which Nixon did in 1962 and Agnew in 1969) is something new in American politics. It is also shrewd politics; in cataclysmic times, the bringers of the bad news cannot be popular—or so we can assume from the flood of congratulatory letters, telegrams, and telephone calls which warmed the

Vice President, and from Gallup Poll soundings indicating over-whelming support.*

The value to Nixon is made clear by a Republican Sena-tor: "If Nixon were to say the things that Agnew does, he would disaffect tremendously powerful elements in America—organized labor, the communications media, the blacks. He would create a great confrontation. Heartland America feels that Nixon is the same as Agnew, though he cannot, as President, be saying these things. So Nixon has it both ways. Through Spiro Agnew, the word gets out to this segment of America that it has not been betrayed."

There remains the substance of Agnew's attacks. Even if we grant the political potency of his speeches on news reporting, we have yet to assess their quality.

The first speech was delivered little more than a week after President Nixon attempted to explain his Vietnam policy on national television. Agnew's basic complaint was that liberal TV commentators muted the effect of his address during their own half-hour discussions conducted immediately after the President concluded. Agnew's speech was vintage Nixon, emphasizing James Reston's point that Nixon believes the news media should act as an inanimate transmission belt, carrying anything he chooses to dump on it. In this case, the networks had acted as a transmission belt carrying what Nixon had to say, and in a live broadcast. But the television reporters were hardly inanimate. It was this that aroused Agnew's (and Nixon's) ire.

There is rich irony in all this. For the "instant analysis" by the network reporters that seemed to Agnew so reprehensible was

*When a courier brought Cleopatra the news that her lover, Antony, had married Caesar's sister, Cleopatra knocked the courier to the floor and de-clared, "The most infectious pestilence upon thee!" Then she shouted at the poor courier, "Hence, horrible villain! or I'll spurn thine eyes like balls before me; I'll unhair thy head: Thou shalt be whipped with wire, and stew'd in brine, smarting in a lingering pickle."

When the courier protested, "Gracious madam, I that do bring the news made not the match," Cleopatra drew a dagger, and the courier had to scramble to save his life.

born, in part, because of complaints from Richard Nixon and his friends. This can be traced back to June 1957, when CBS broadcast an interview with Nikita Khrushchev, who was then the Soviet premier. So outraged were Eisenhower Administration officials that Khrushchev had been allowed to speak directly and at length to the American people that broadcasting, ever mindful of its precarious relationship to the federal government, took the advice of the most influential television critic, Jack Gould of the New York *Times.* He suggested that CBS had "many able and thoughtful commentators" and that "they should have been used immediately to analyze Khrushchev's words." Thus began the system of instant analysis which would cause Mr. Agnew such anguish.

There were other, equally rich, ironies growing from the Vice President's speeches on news reporting. Not the least of them was the site of his speech on the danger of a monopoly press. For he chose to criticize the Washington *Post* and the New York *Times*—both of which compete with two other newspapers in their home cities—in *Montgomery, Alabama.* That is the home of the Montgomery *Advertiser* and the *Alabama Journal,* both of which are published by the Advertiser Company, both of which tread a single line of thought, neither of which is notable for jarring Alabama readers out of the comfortable immoralities by which they live.

Mr. Agnew slashed at the *Times* for failing to report a story that reflected favorably on the Nixon Administration, apparently not realizing that every edition of the *Times* except the one he read had carried the story. Mr. Agnew slashed at the Washington Post Company because it owns not only the *Post,* but *Newsweek,* WTOP-TV, and an all-news radio station as well. This, he held, is dangerous because all four are "grinding out the same editorial line." Had Mr. Agnew bothered to check on the "editorial line," he would have discovered that the Washington *Post* editorially supported the confirmation of Mr. Nixon's Supreme Court appointee, Judge Clement Haynsworth, while the *Post's* editorial cartoonist, Herblock, was acidly opposing Haynsworth, as was WTOP-TV. The *Post* advised Justice Fortas to resign from the

Supreme Court; WTOP left that decision to him without advice. The *Post* supports the building in Washington of the Three Sisters Bridge. WTOP opposes it. The *Post* and WTOP express different views on the kind of representation the District of Columbia should have in Congress. The *Post* does not oppose the Vietnam War. *Newsweek* does.

But the richest irony springs from Agnew's attack on the television commentators and analysts for what he called their "hostility" to President Nixon. Anyone who cares about the way the American people are informed may be equally critical of television, but for quite another reason. Because they are aware that they are "guests in the nation's living rooms," because they are fearful of government regulation, and because cottage cheese blandness is the epitome of all broadcasting, television journalists are almost never hostile. In fact, anyone who is advised to look in on this television journalist or that one because "he's really aggressive" may be certain without looking that the man only seems aggressive because he appears on a news program immediately after Lucille Ball or a similar show. As it is presently constituted, commercial television is not capable of producing the aggressive or challenging journalism the nation needs, much less anything properly described as "hostility."

And having said all this to show that Mr. Agnew was wrong in nearly every particular he chose to outline, I must say instantly that he was right in general. That is, the Vice President was right in holding that the news media need criticism. (He was right also in saying that most journalists are liberals, but that must be balanced by the fact that most of their employers are conservative.) This is an era in which we cannot escape the power of mass communication. It is also the era of the monumental merger, and there is a growing danger that the most important voices of the mass media will soon be emitted from conglomerates.

But if criticism is to be useful, it should not come from officials whose words may be fearsome. The fact that the Nixon Administration can strike fear into television is suggested by events following the very next Presidential appearance. While Mr. Agnew's words were still reverberating, President Nixon appeared on national television for one of his infrequent press conferences. Immediately after it, the commentators and analysts for commercial television appeared, talked at length, and said nothing. Instead of supplying the background information on Mr. Nixon's words and the closely reasoned analysis of those words that were so desperately needed, the commentators simply cited what he had said, almost as though they were not aware that *he* had been doing exactly that for thirty minutes. It was a pathetic performance. Mr. Agnew may still be chuckling.

What the television men should have been doing was demonstrated strikingly the next day by Tom Wicker of the New York *Times*. He said in response to criticism of reporters: "What of the responsibility of Presidents to inform the American people accurately and fully?"

Then Wicker pointed out that the President had said that the Marines had built this year "over 250,000 churches, pagodas and temples" for the people of Vietnam. Actually, the Marines have built 117 churches and 251 schools, Wicker reported.

Further, the President had declared that if a $5,400 minimum income were established for every family of four in America, the cost to the goverment would be $70 billion to $80 billion a year. "Actually," Wicker pointed out, "the government could guarantee every family of four the difference in what its breadwinner now earns and $5,400 for perhaps $20 billion. It could, that is, if they all kept on working and earning as much as they do now. If, on the other hand, they all quit earning anything, and started taking the full $5,400 from the government, the cost would zoom up to at least $40 or $50 billion, and probably more."

The President misled the people again, Wicker said, when he answered a question about Laos by saying that there are no American "combat troops" there. In fact, as Wicker made clear, this is true only if one considers "combat troops" to be those who fight on the ground. "There are Air Force pilots who drop bombs, and plenty of CIA agents and Army personnel who organize, train, accompany and support native armies."

Wicker's catalog of President Nixon's false and misleading statements went on, but that is enough to demonstrate the point. By lashing out at the television newsmen, Agnew cowed them, and the American people were seriously misled.

No, what is needed is not criticisms from officials, although the adversary relationship assures that they will be heard. The explicit need is for a citizenry that understands mass communication and how it works, and is prepared to criticize it, challenge it, and require that it live up to its best possibilities.

Index